How Would You Rule?

How Would You Rule?

LEGAL PUZZLES, BRAINTEASERS, AND
DILEMMAS FROM THE LAW'S STRANGEST
CASES

Daniel W. Park

UNIVERSITY OF CALIFORNIA PRESS

University of California Press, one of the most distinguished university presses in the United States, enriches lives around the world by advancing scholarship in the humanities, social sciences, and natural sciences. Its activities are supported by the UC Press Foundation and by philanthropic contributions from individuals and institutions. For more information, visit www.ucpress.edu.

University of California Press
Oakland, California

Library of Congress Cataloging-in-Publication Data

Names: Park, Daniel W., 1971- author.
Title: How would you rule? : legal puzzles, brainteasers, and dilemmas
    from the law's strangest cases / Daniel W. Park.
Description: Oakland, California : University of California Press, [2016]
    | Includes bibliographical references and index.
Identifiers: LCCN 2016017734 (print) | LCCN 2016018318 (ebook) |
    ISBN 9780520290570 (cloth : alk. paper) | ISBN 9780520290587
    (pbk. : alk. paper) | ISBN 9780520964709 (e-edition)
Subjects: LCSH: Law—Cases—Popular works. | Law—United States—
    Cases—Popular works. | Judgments—United States—Case studies—
    Popular works.
Classification: LCC KF385.A4 P36 2016 (print) | LCC KF385.A4 (ebook)
    | DDC 349.73—dc23
LC record available at https://lccn.loc.gov/2016017734

Manufactured in the United States of America

25 24 23 22 21 20 19 18 17 16

10 9 8 7 6 5 4 3 2 1

For Andrew and Eric. You asked for a book about law
that was fun and interesting. Here you go.

Contents

Introduction

Here's a legal puzzle: at great expense, you build an addition to your house, and by accident the addition extends six inches over the property line onto your neighbor's land. Obviously, you had no right to occupy your neighbor's land without permission, but the addition is already built, and it can't be moved. The neighbor complains. He wants you to tear the addition down. Tearing down the addition would cost you tens of thousands of dollars, far more than the fair market value of the six inches of land. You offer to pay a reasonable amount for the six inches, but the neighbor refuses and instead demands a prince's ransom. To you, this feels like extortion. To your neighbor, it feels like you stole part of his land. The dispute goes to court. What should a judge do to make things right?

Accidental encroachment is just one example of the puzzles, problems, and dilemmas that courts must wrestle with every day. It's not an easy job. What if you had the chance to be the judge in some of the toughest, strangest, and most puzzling cases that have ever arisen in courts of law? Would you rule with wisdom and grace, or would you be left scratching your head? Every judge who has taken the bench to hear a case has had to answer that question. The only way to find out if you have the right stuff is to try a few cases for yourself. Consider this book a dress rehearsal to see how you would do if you were ever tapped to take the bench and called upon to answer the toughest questions.

Everyone loves a good story, and in these pages you'll find thirty-one of the best the legal system has to offer. You will meet a man who complains that he bought a haunted house. Another man collides with a woman in a church and claims that Jesus made him do it. A teenager wants to buy a fighter jet with bottle tops. Police make up fantastic lies to get a confession. A mother goes to court to break up her daughter's friendship with another girl.

Each chapter tells a story based on a real legal dispute. The cases range from the quirky (can you sue your lover for injuring you during intercourse?) to the profound (does a person with a terminal illness have the right to end her own life?). The facts are simplified and the legal arguments summarized, so only the essence of the dilemma remains for you to decide. After that, it's up to you. Justice, fairness, and precedents are your guide; but in the end, you must use your judgment and intuition, pick a winner and a loser, and make a decision.

The best way to learn the law is by practicing it. This book gives you that chance. By working your way through the stories in this book, you will get a chance, just as real judges do, to try your hand at teasing out the strands of justice from tangles of competing claims and contentions.

There are three benefits to learning the law by puzzling out legal dilemmas on your own. First, learning is easiest when it's also fun, and these cases are entertaining and thought-provoking puzzles that will engage your imagination and test your wits. Dry and stodgy legalese has been stripped out, leaving only the essence of the legal question and the pathos of people dealing with difficult situations.

Second, the most lasting learning is learning by doing. It is one thing to hear someone else's explanation of how to do something. It is quite another to do it yourself. Watching a master pianist play a Chopin étude is no substitute for sitting at the piano and banging away at the keys. The same is true with legal thinking. You can read the reasoning of lawyers and judges, but the only way to sharpen your own acumen is by actively thinking about what's right and what's wrong and why.

Finally, learning leads to mastery only when you test yourself. It is all too easy to get caught in the echo chamber of your own mind, confirming and corroborating your own thoughts without testing them against the thoughts of others. After you have read the facts and decided for yourself the legal questions presented, you can compare your analysis to the logic and reasoning of the judges who had to rule on these cases. You will see where the courts picked up on certain details and ignored others, and how competing rules and equities were balanced in the search for justice. To move from novice to ninja, you will have one final challenge after reading the court's reasoning: deciding for yourself whether the court got the answer right.

The dirty secret of the legal system is that the law's requirements are often less than crystal clear. Consider again the encroachment example offered at the outset of this introduction. Property was occupied unjustly and without permission, but correction comes only at extraordinary expense out of all proportion to the harm done. What would you do if you were the judge? What rule would be just in cases such as this? What effect might that rule have on people's future behavior? How should that rule be applied in these particular circumstances? Should a court order the new addition torn down, or should the court order the encroacher to pay a reasonable sum to the encroached-upon and otherwise leave things where they stand? These are the questions that judges must answer. For a taste of what this book is all about, take a moment and decide how you would rule.

It will come as no surprise that the presumption in encroachment cases is that property owners should not have to accept annexation of their property by careless neighbors who build across property lines; and therefore, courts generally order the encroacher to remove the offending structure. If the costs of removal are exorbitant, encroachers have no one to blame but themselves. The high costs serve as an incentive to future builders to mind the boundaries of property. Generally, that's the rule—but not always.

Against this general rule, courts will make exceptions if the encroachment is innocent and the cost of removal is greatly disproportionate to the injury to the plaintiff.[1] Does the six-inch encroachment of the home addition in our example fall under the general rule or the exception? The occupation is relatively small (six inches) and the cost of removal relatively high (the entire structure must be demolished), and we have posited that the encroachment was innocent and accidental. So it's likely a court would find that this case falls into the exception; but then again, maybe not. The law could be applied to support either result. Making this kind of judgment call is what judging is all about.

The other secret about judging is that judges, like everyone else, make mistakes. They reach conclusions based on faulty logic or shaky assumptions or misguided values. Their sense of justice in a particular case might be off. By putting yourself in the judge's shoes, you will see how mistakes happen and how they might be avoided.

This book is a workout for your legal mind. The lawyers' task is to come up with the best arguments and reasons to support their positions. The cases and controversies within these pages challenge you to do the same. By going through the cases presented in this book, you will sharpen your thinking and deepen your understanding of the law.

So put on your black robe and grab a gavel. In these pages, you are the judge. Prepare to test your legal knowledge, intuition, insight, and acumen by deciding for yourself these challenging legal cases and comparing your decisions with those of the judges who had to pick the winners and losers when these disputes came to court.

It's time for you to take the bench. All rise. Court is now in session. How will you rule?

A NOTE ABOUT THE CASES

The stories in this book are derived from real cases as recorded in law reports. Each chapter includes a citation to the official judicial opinion that the chapter is based on. To take your understanding of the law to the next level, you can—and should—read the judges' opinions as recorded by the judges themselves.

This book is meant to be a learning tool, and the goal is to help you think through legal problems on your own so you can develop your own intuitions about how the law works and how it ought to work. To make the book most effective as an aid to learning, the case descriptions are simplified and occasionally dramatized to bring into focus the questions that are most likely to make you think. You should also know that, depending on the procedural posture of a case, courts sometimes assume certain facts to be true, even though those facts have not been proven with evidence. We won't let nuances of procedure slow us down, but this means that you should think of each case description as "based on a true story" rather than as a historically precise account.

Just as not every fact is described exactly, not every legal argument is presented. In the cases discussed in this book, the focus is on the most interesting, accessible, and illustrative points. The idea here is to learn broad themes that will sharpen your legal intuition while not getting bogged down in arcane rules.

Summaries, by definition, condense, omit, and elide, sacrificing punctilious accuracy for clarity of main ideas. If you want to see the evidence and arguments considered by the courts in their original, exact, and most accurate form, there is no substitute for reading the original judicial opinions, an exercise that is highly recommended.

The purpose of this book is for you to discover how *you* would rule. As you read each case, pause before turning to see how the court answered the questions presented. The best way to find out what you think is to stop and reflect. Give your mind space to process your own ideas.

If you have the inclination, write your thoughts down. What are the critical facts? What are the rules and principles that ought to govern? What does justice mean in this particular case? What changes in the facts might lead you to change your mind? You may be surprised how writing sharpens, shapes, and sometimes changes your thoughts. It is a powerful tool, and I encourage you to use it.

When you read the resolutions reached by the courts, you may find yourself disagreeing with the courts' decisions. Or maybe you agree with parts of the courts' decisions and disagree with other parts. If that happens, congratulations; you're well on your way to thinking for yourself.

Courts have been wrong in the past, and they may be wrong in the cases here. On the toughest questions, reasonable minds can, and do, disagree. Values change from generation to generation, so a decision that made sense to judges of the past might seem like lunacy to modern minds. No person or age has a monopoly on insight.

Many of these cases generated sharp disagreements—dissents—among the judges who heard them. The positions of the dissenters are not set out in these pages, but just knowing that they are out there should encourage you to feel free to disagree with the judges whose opinions happened to prevail. Underneath their black robes, judges are just ordinary people, no different and no better than you. Your ideas have an equal claim on justice—if supported by compelling reasons.

If you think the court got the answer wrong, your challenge is to articulate where the court's reasoning went astray. In some cases, your disagreement might be simply a gut feeling or intuition. That's a good start, but don't let yourself off the hook too easily. Put into words exactly where the court went wrong. Did the court weigh the facts improperly? Did the court misapply or misunderstand the legal rules? Are the legal rules themselves unjust or unfair? Disagreement is healthy, but a good judge makes decisions based on reasons, and so you should hold yourself to the same standard you apply to others and insist that your judgments have clear, logical, defensible rationales.

As you go along, you might think up arguments that the parties to the lawsuit did not raise. That's another excellent sign. Your creative juices are working. It is not uncommon in the heat of litigation to miss the strongest argument. If you spot weaknesses in the parties' positions, ask yourself how they might have sharpened their points to make them more persuasive. The ability to come up with the best arguments and present them in their strongest form is what distinguishes great lawyers and judges from the run of the mill.

Each chapter ends with a few questions. Don't skip them. The questions are there to prompt more thinking. Don't just skim them either. Try to answer them, even if only briefly in your own mind; or better yet, discuss and debate them with a friend.

It is a very good thing to resolve a particular case with reasoned justice. But that is just the beginning. To take your legal thinking to the next level, you should consider how rules that may seem to make sense for a particular case might apply in other contexts. What are the limits of a rule? Should there be exceptions? When should a new rule take its place? If after reading and answering the questions set out at the end of each chapter, you come up with more questions of your own, this book will have succeeded.

The title of this book is *How Would You Rule?* My hope is that you would rule with wisdom tempered by humility, justice tempered by empathy, and reason tempered by compassion. But there is only one way to find out. Turn the page and match your wits against those of judges from across the centuries on some of the most interesting cases ever considered in court. Only by deciding the cases for yourself will you ever learn how you would rule.

1 A Duty to Die

The job was dangerous, no doubt about it. John Henry Want, an Australian lawyer, had purchased the *Mignonette*, a fifty-two-foot pleasure yacht, and needed a crew to sail it from England, down the coast of Africa, around the Cape of Good Hope, and across the Southern Pacific to Australia. The vessel was small for the open ocean, and much could happen in the fifteen thousand miles between England and Australia. The task was not for the faint of heart, but weighing against the risks was the handsome price to be paid to the person with the courage to claim it. Captain Thomas Dudley took the job and assembled a crew for the voyage.

Captain Dudley chose Edwin Stephens to be his first mate, and Edmund Brooks as the only other member of the crew. For a cabin boy, Captain Dudley took on Richard Parker, an orphan of seventeen. Young Richard had never before left the shores of England; but without a family to support him, he needed to learn a trade to make a living, and so he signed on with Captain Dudley for a chance at a better life and a bit of adventure on the high seas.

As the intrepid crew boarded the *Mignonette* on May 19, 1884, and cast off from the shores of Southampton, scarcely could they have imagined in their most tormented nightmares the unspeakable horrors that awaited them at their journey's end.

The trip proceeded without notable event as the tiny crew guided their vessel into the Atlantic, down the coast of France, across the equator, and around the West Coast of Africa. They made good time, with fair winds and sunny skies. All signs pointed toward a successful and uneventful voyage. Then the weather turned.

On July 5, forty-seven days into the journey, a gale gathered behind the *Mignonette*. Thus far, the weather had been a friend, and Captain Dudley was determined to stay out of the clutches of foul winds. He ordered the crew to press forward at full speed to stay ahead of the gale that whipped the waters behind them. By evening, by all appearances, the Captain's efforts succeeded. The waters were calm and the wind settled. Captain Dudley could breathe easy. Fortune had smiled on them again. They had outrun the storm.

Captain Dudley and his crew were about sixteen hundred miles off of the Cape of Good Hope, the southernmost point of Africa. Soon, they would round the Cape, and then it would be a straight shot to Australia, where payment awaited them for their services. Everyone had worked hard to escape the gale, so Captain Dudley decided that his crew had earned a rest. He directed the crew to stop the ship for the night. The crew heaved to, arresting the ship's forward motion by setting the sails in opposition to each other so that the force from one sail counteracted the force from the other. Everyone looked forward to a peaceful night's sleep under starry, southern skies. They didn't get it.

While the crew slept, a massive wave reared up and towered over the small sloop. For someone watching from afar, it might have looked like a giant fist hovering over a table, ready to pound. And pound it did. The water crashed down on ship and crew with crushing force. The lash of the sea punched a hole in the side of the ship. The *Mignonette* lurched violently to one side. Water rushed in. The *Mignonette* sagged under the weight of the waves that lapped hungrily over its bow. The sea had come to claim it.

Captain Dudley immediately recognized that the *Mignonette* was lost. He gave the order to abandon ship. There was no time to gather supplies. The *Mignonette* took on water ever more quickly and settled deeper and deeper into the waves around them. The crew scrambled onto a tiny lifeboat only thirteen feet long. The lifeboat had no mast and no sail and only two oars to propel it. It offered no shelter from the sun, the wind, or the rains. The flimsy boards that held it together were thin and weak. The small skiff was not the ideal place to fly to for safety, but it had one thing possessed by nothing else in the world of the terrified crew: it was not sinking, and at that panic-filled moment, that was all that mattered.

The lifeboat pushed away from the larger vessel just in time. The stunned sailors could only watch in horror as the sea, whipped by the wind, rose up and swallowed the *Mignonette,* dragging it toward the bottom of the ocean. The time from when the wave struck the *Mignonette* to the time it disappeared below the surface never again to see the light of day must have felt like a lifetime, yet only five minutes had passed.

Through the night, the stunned crew clung to their skiff for dear life. As dawn spread over the sky, the four men took stock of their situation. It wasn't pretty. In the rush to abandon the *Mignonette,* the crew had saved themselves but little else. They had no water. They had no food, with the exception of two one-pound tins of turnips. The sun beat down upon them mercilessly, and the lifeboat offered no shade in which to take refuge from the relentless rays. The lifeboat kept the men above water but provided little else.

For three days, the four men rationed the turnips until their provisions were exhausted. The meager meals did little to blunt the hunger gnawing on their stomachs and did nothing to quench the thirst that tore at their throats. All the while, they searched the horizon for any sign of a passing ship, their only hope of rescue.

On the fourth day, their spirits rose as they encountered a bit of luck. A small turtle had made the mistake of swimming too close to the skiff. The turtle's mistake was the men's great fortune. They captured the turtle and nibbled away at it for a few more days, hoping that this little bit of nourishment would preserve them until help arrived or at least until they could find more food.

But help did not arrive. Nor did any more food. By the twelfth day of the ordeal, every scrap of the turtle had been licked clean. Every day, hunger, heat, and exhaustion threatened to overwhelm the men and drive them to collapse. Thirst was the worst. The only freshwater they had was made up of the drops of rain they could catch in their oilskin capes. Lack of water wreaks havoc on the senses. Hallucinations are not uncommon, and judgment is clouded. The days dragged on; and despite the crew's best resolve, their situation became more desperate and more hopeless.

A week wore on without food. Five days passed without water. On the eighteenth day adrift at sea, Captain Dudley came to a grim conclusion. They were not all going to make it. Already, the four men were on the brink of death by dehydration. Even if the rains fell, starvation loomed not far behind. Nothing short of immediate rescue could save them from this dark reality, but two and a half weeks had passed without sign of ship or sail anywhere on the horizon. With no supplies to sustain them, the hapless crew was eyeball-to-eyeball with death, and death wasn't blinking.

On the eighteenth day of the ordeal, Captain Dudley and First Mate Stephens approached Brooks, the third member of the crew, with a startling suggestion. Not everyone had to die. If one of their number were sacrificed, the rest could be saved—at least for a while, maybe long enough for a ship to cross paths with their lifeboat. Brooks caught their meaning. "One of their number" meant the boy.

At a callow seventeen, Richard Parker was by far the youngest member of the crew. He had no experience with the sea. This had been his first voyage. He was a cabin boy, not a sailor. He had no father and no mother. No wife waited for him in England; no child depended on him for support. What's more, his health was fading fastest among the group. In his inexperience and desperation, Parker had made the mistake of drinking water from the sea to slake the thirst that was driving him to madness. As the sailors could have told him, the salt from the seawater only hastened his dehydration and brought him that much closer to the brink. Death would take them all, of that there was no doubt, but it would start with the boy; on this, all three men agreed. What difference would a few days of semiconscious, delirious life mean to the boy? For the rest of the crew, those days could be the difference between life and death.

Brooks recoiled with horror at the radical suggestion and refused to listen to Dudley and Stephens. No more was said among them, and the topic was dropped. No one said anything to Richard Parker. The hunger and thirst continued.

On the nineteenth day, Captain Dudley could endure no more. He corralled Stephens and Brooks and, in whispers, proposed that they should cast lots. The loser would save the others with his own death. It was the only way. How often in life is one man called upon to sacrifice himself for his fellows? In war it is an everyday occurrence, a noble duty. Necessity had driven the men into a fight for their lives as desperate as any faced by the most beleaguered soldier. The hour for sacrifice had come. One had to die, lest all perish.

Stephens concurred with Dudley's grim assessment of their circumstances and saw no course other than the one the captain proposed. Brooks demurred. Dudley and Stephens sympathized with Brooks's reluctance and tried to win him over. No one had wanted things to come to this, but here they were, on the precipice of death, with only this slim reed upon which to hang all hope. Brooks remained firm in his dissent.

Frustrated by Brooks's refusal, Dudley and Stephens dropped the idea of casting lots and turned their arguments to the boy, whose sleeping body could be their salvation. Think of their families, argued Dudley and Stephens. The sailors had wives and children. What would those innocents do when their husbands and fathers who supported them were swallowed by the sea? The boy was an orphan. Who would miss him if he failed to return? Every death is a tragedy, but if someone had to die, whose death would matter least? Again, no one spoke a word of this to Richard Parker.

The three men came to no agreement that day, but Dudley warned that if no vessel were seen by the next day, the deed would have to be done. The men returned to their watches and waited.

The next day dawned. It was July 25, the twentieth day since the *Mignonette* sank, the tenth day the men had gone without food. No ship could be seen anywhere in the wide expanse of ocean that was their watery prison. The time had come, Dudley decided, to act.

Once again, Dudley approached Stephens and Brooks. The plan was outside the bounds of all morality, but their dire situation was outside the bounds of all endurance. Survival was at stake. Should one die or should all? Dudley needed to know where the other men stood. Stephens agreed to the killing. Brooks did not. Dudley told Brooks that he might want to take a nap on the far side of the lifeboat. Brooks moved aside and did not interfere.

Dudley made his way to where Richard Parker lay semiconscious, near the back of the boat. Dudley towered over the boy. Parker's body was thin, his skin almost translucent. The boy did not move, probably because he could not. He was utterly helpless.

Dudley said a short prayer. He prayed for forgiveness and asked that all their souls might be saved. He withdrew his knife. He spoke to Richard Parker. "Your time has come," he whispered, and found he had nothing more to say. Words were meaningless. All that mattered was the knife. Captain Dudley slit Richard Parker's throat, killing him.

The three men fed upon Richard Parker, the boy's body and blood nourishing and reviving the fading frames of his former shipmates. Four days later, a passing vessel found the lifeboat. The three men were alive, but just barely. The ordeal at sea was over.

But the ordeal for Dudley and Stephens was not quite done. Dudley had killed a boy, and Stephens had concurred in the act. The two were charged with murder. In their defense, they claimed that they were driven to the deed by the most extreme necessity imaginable. It is beyond dispute, they argued, that a person may lawfully kill another in self-defense to preserve his or her own life; and in that lifeboat, in those circumstances, their lives were in as much mortal danger as any person had ever faced. If they had not taken the action they took, they would all be dead, including Brooks, who took no part in the killing, and Parker, who was their sacrificial lamb. Had they stayed their hands and let Parker die on nature's schedule as he was bound to do, the boy would be just as dead, the only difference being that the three other members of the crew would have been his companions in death. While the killing was deeply sad and regrettable, the two men argued, the extreme necessity of the situation had justified it.

Dudley and Stephens rested their case. To the charge of murder, they claimed the defense of justifiable homicide. The question is now put to you. How would you rule?

HOW THE COURT RULED

No one could argue that the ordeal on the lifeboat had not pushed Dudley and Stephens to the furthest extremes of human suffering. For nearly three weeks they were baked by the sun by day and chilled to the bone by night. They had no food and little water. Every day their hopes of rescue faded further. These circumstances were, as the reviewing court put it, "appalling, loathsome, harrowing," more than enough to break even the strongest among us.

And yet Dudley and Stephens took the life of an innocent boy. Richard Parker had done nothing to them. He had not threatened them with a weapon of any kind. He had not put their lives in danger. He was a cabin boy with no authority or command. He did not bring on the storm or conjure the wave that sank the *Mignonette*. He did not take more than his share of the meager supplies aboard the lifeboat. He did just what the other men did: he hoped for rescue and waited to die.

Richard Parker's death did not guarantee the survival of the other members of the crew. For twenty days there had been no sign of any other vessel on the sea. The crew might have been picked up the very day they did the deed, in which case Parker's death would have been wholly unnecessary. The crew might never have been picked up, in which case Parker's death would have saved no lives.

The court rejected war as an appropriate analogy for Dudley and Stephen's situation. War is a service imposed upon people by the nation. This was a private homicide to achieve a private end, the saving of their own skins. Dudley and Stephens urged the court to accept that they had a duty to preserve their own lives, but the court rejected this as well. True, without the killing of Richard Parker, the other men might have died, but turning the sailors' war analogy against them, the court stated, "To preserve one's life is generally speaking a duty, but it may be the plainest and the highest duty to sacrifice it. War is full of instances in which it is a man's duty not to live, but to die."

Dudley and Stephen's killing of Richard Parker was not, in the court's words, "devilish." They were honest men, who, when driven to an extreme, gave in to a temptation that, if we are honest with ourselves, we would be hard pressed to say for certain that we would be able to resist. But if the law were to allow people to kill for their private benefit when they feel that extreme necessity compels it, the door would swing wide open to the dangers of "unbridled passion and atrocious crime."

Dudley and Stephens commanded the sympathies of the court, but nevertheless, the court felt the facts were clear enough. Dudley and Stephens had taken the life of a person who was not threatening them at the time. That was not self-defense, but murder, no matter how extreme the circumstances they faced when they made their fatal choice. The verdict was guilty. The men would have to pay for their crime.

Did the court get it right or wrong? You decide.

REFLECTIONS

A case like *Dudley and Stephens* challenges us to put ourselves on that same raft, trapped in the open ocean, with no rescue in sight and hunger and thirst gnawing away at our lives, and to ask ourselves the terrible question: what would we have done if it had been us on that boat? Without experiencing what those men experienced, we can only speculate how we would have acted if confronted with the same horrible choices.

The judges who sat in judgment over Dudley and Stephens had the inestimable luxury of full bellies and comfortable beds and were free from the dread that their strength would give out and that their last breath could be taken at any moment, far from family and friends, in a cruel sea that would indifferently swallow them whole with no remnant or marker, as if they had never existed at all. What could the judges know of the rightness or wrongness of an act in a situation that they could at best but dimly imagine, never mind fully comprehend?

Fortunately for would-be adventurers, the tragic end of poor Richard Parker is far from the norm; but at the same time it is hardly the only case where men and women trapped in impossible circumstances turned to the unspeakable, but apparently not-so-unthinkable, choice of feeding on their fellows. The Donner party waylaid by a snowstorm on an isolated peak in the Sierra Nevada is one. The Uruguayan rugby team stranded on the Andes when their plane went down is another. The crew of the shipwrecked French frigate *Méduse*—vividly and horrifyingly captured in the *Raft of Medusa*, a painting by the French romantic painter Théodore Géricault—is another. With so many examples of how far people will go to fight for their survival, the court's condemnation of Dudley and Stephens has a whiff of the armchair quarterback.

From the point of view of philosophers and ethicists, there may be no one correct solution to the moral dilemma of the men on the lifeboat.

Instead of thinking of yourself as one of the crew, imagine that you could observe the disaster unfold from above the drifting skiff, and that you could move the people below like pieces on a chessboard. Would you sacrifice one piece to save three others, or would you gamble all four on a hope—no matter how remote or unlikely that hope might be? Approached this way, the case of *Dudley and Stephens* can be thought of as a real-life example of the classic ethical dilemma known to philosophers as the trolley problem.

The trolley problem goes something like this: A trolley careens out of control toward a group of five people stuck on the track in a stalled car. Their doors are jammed shut. They are helpless and terrified and will surely die when the hurtling trolley smashes into their defenseless vehicle. But there is good news. A nearby switch will change the trolley's course from one track to another. All that has to happen is for someone to pull that switch. But there is bad news too. On that other track stands one person who is unaware of the trolley's approach. There is no time to warn this person to get out of the way. If the switch is pulled, this one person, an innocent bystander, will be killed before he or she even knows what is happening. Would you pull the switch to save the five people at the price of condemning the one person to death? Should you?

If you are counting noses in order to decide, five is more than one; so maybe you would pull the switch. But if you do so, you—the person who changed the course of the trolley and directed the hurtling mass of metal destruction at a person who was otherwise safe from harm—become the instrument of that person's death, a person who is completely innocent, a person who never agreed to the sacrifice you have unilaterally demanded. What has given you the power of life and death over this unsuspecting soul?

On the other hand, if you cannot bring yourself to take a single life even to save five, then maybe you do not pull the switch. In that case, events take their course, as if you had never been there. The one person lives, and the five perish. These five are equally innocent (let us assume) and also have not asked to die on those train tracks. They are victims of pure chance. Does it clear your conscience that the deaths of the five are accidental, not the deliberate act of another person, even though you could have saved them had you been willing to pay the price or, more precisely, make the one person on the other track pay the price?

The trolley problem is fascinating because it can be endlessly debated. The problem puts into opposition two classic, philosophical schools of thought. Utilitarians generally seek the greatest good for the greatest number, and so sacrificing one to save five will almost always be considered just. In contrast, Kantians generally consider it immoral to use a human being as a means to an end, and so sacrificing a person to save others will almost always be considered unjust.

If you found the trolley problem easy because of the utilitarian calculus, that one should obviously be sacrificed to save five, consider the case of organ transplants. Five people wait in a hospital for lifesaving organ donations, needing, collectively, a liver, two kidneys, a lung, and a heart. You happen to be in the hospital, and you happen to have healthy kidneys, lungs, liver, and heart. A transplant surgeon approaches you with a startling observation. If she harvested your organs, the lives of these five others would be saved. True, you would die, but the surgeon offers by way of consolation the fact that by sacrificing one (in this case you), she can save five. In this scenario does utilitarian justice lose any of its appeal?

While these ethical debates are fascinating, the judges in *Dudley and Stephens* did not have the luxury of toying with hypothetical questions and leaving them unresolved. In *Dudley and Stephens*, the court avoided the knottier conundrums by deciding the more prosaic question of whether what happened on the lifeboat fit the legal definition of murder—the intentional taking of another person's life. While the morality of the case may be tantalizingly uncertain, the facts were not in doubt. Captain Dudley, with the assent of Stephens, slit Richard Parker's throat and Parker died. The knife did not slip by accident. No compulsion forced Dudley's hand, other than a desire to save his own life. Dudley and Stephens intended to end Richard Parker's life, and they did so. Was that an intentional taking of another person's life? It was. The definition of murder settled the question.

Legally then, Dudley and Stephens could escape conviction only if they could mount a defense to excuse their conduct. Self-defense is a justification for taking another person's life, and so the court addressed this defense with another comparably prosaic question: did the killing fit the definition of self-defense? Self-defense is permitted to protect one's own life (or the life of another) from a person who is threatening it. There was no question that Dudley and Stephens were in mortal peril. Heat, cold, hunger, and thirst circled the men like wolves closing in for the kill. But was Richard Parker threatening their lives? No, he was not. So self-defense did not apply.

Dudley and Stephens exquisitely illustrates how in legal disputes philosophical questions take a backseat to simpler—some might say simplistic—questions about the definitions of legal terms. In this way, the law differs from philosophy and ethics. The judge's duty is to apply the rules that the law has established. Sometimes, these rules are a poor fit, but that does not change the duty of the court.

It is interesting to consider how the court that condemned Dudley and Stephens might have ruled on the trolley problem. We can't know for certain, of course, but if Dudley and Stephens were not justified in taking Richard Parker's life to save three lives (their own plus Brooks's), it would seem that this court, at least, would likely have ruled that pulling the switch to alter the course of the runaway trolley would be an act of murdering the person on the other track. True, the motive in pulling the switch would be to save lives, not to take the life of the person on the switched track, but Dudley and Stephens' motive was also to save lives. Killing Richard Parker just happened to be the only means they could think of to do that.

It is also possible, however, that the court might have found differences between the lifeboat and the trolley problem that would have led it to a different outcome. For example, Dudley and Stephens killed Richard Parker for their own personal gain: saving their own lives. In the trolley problem, the person who pulls the switch has no personal stake in the outcome other than a desire to save five lives, albeit at the price of another person's life. The court was very concerned that if it condoned Dudley and Stephens's act of killing Richard Parker to save their own lives, it might inadvertently open the door to all manner of crimes that one person or another thinks is necessary to saving his or her own life. Another possible difference is that the trolley is certain to kill the five people on the one track, while the court in *Dudley and Stephens* speculated that the death of the crew was not completely certain because rescue could, theoretically, have come at any moment.

Are those differences important? Are there others that might change the outcome? Answering those questions is the very heart of what judging is about and the first step toward figuring out for yourself how would you rule.

EPILOGUE

In nineteenth-century England, the penalty for murder was death; and so the prisoners Dudley and Stephens, having been duly convicted, were condemned to die by hanging. But Dudley and Stephens did not die on the gallows.

In acknowledgment of the extreme suffering that led Dudley and Stephens to commit their crime, the court added to its judgment a recommendation for mercy. At the time, the queen of England had the power to commute a criminal sentence (a power shared in modern America by the president of the United States and by the governors of the individual states regarding crimes within their respective jurisdictions); and through the action of the queen's advisers, the sentences of Dudley and Stephens were reduced to six months in prison. On May 20, 1885, a year and a day after they first set sail on the *Mignonette,* Dudley and Stephens were released from jail. They were free men, but they would never be the same again.

．　　．　　．　　．　　．

Questions

1. Are there any circumstances where killing a person who is not directly attacking you should not be deemed murder? Consider the following hypothetical cases. Concerned that the collective weight on a lifeboat might lead the boat to sink and cause all aboard to drown, three passengers throw a fourth off the boat. Murder? Does it matter how certain it was that the lifeboat would sink? Would it matter how the ejected person was chosen? For example, would choosing by lots be better than choosing by, say, weight or by relative weakness? What role does consent play? Next consider what difference it would make if the extra person were not on the boat but in the water trying to get on the boat. Would it be murder to prevent the fourth person from coming on the lifeboat if the other three feared that the new person's weight would cause the lifeboat to sink? Would it be murder to refuse to allow a person onto a lifeboat to avoid adding another mouth to feed from the small provisions on board and a concern that provisions

might run out sometime in the future? What if there were ample provisions and the fear of running out was unreasonable?

2. Was the six-month sentence that was ultimately imposed on Dudley and Stephens just? Should it have been more or less severe? How should the right punishment, if any, have been determined?

3. Brooks was not charged with murder, because he served as a witness for the prosecution. According to his own account, Brooks opposed Captain Dudley's plan to sacrifice Richard Parker but did nothing to stop it. After the killing was done, Brooks survived by partaking of Parker's body just like his shipmates. Should Brooks, through his inaction and acquiescence, be considered guilty of any crime?

4. Consider the trolley problem and programming self-driving cars. Imagine a self-driving car is winding its way down a narrow mountain road when it makes a hairpin turn only to discover five children on the road taking pictures of the scenery. The car's navigation system determines that the only way to avoid a collision that will kill the five children is to drive itself off the cliff and kill the driver. The navigation system also determines that if the car hits the children, all the children will die, but the driver will not be harmed. Should the navigation system be programmed to kill the driver and save the children or kill the children and save the driver? If you had the choice of buying a self-driving car with one system or the other, which would you buy? If you could choose the navigation system to install in other people's cars, which would you choose? If other people had the power, which navigation system do you think they would choose for you? Compare your answers with those found by social scientists Jean-Francois Bonnefon, Azim Shariff, and Iyad Rahwan.[1]

Read It Yourself

Regina v. Dudley and Stephens, 14 QBD 273 DC (1884).

2 Bringing a Gun to a Fistfight

Gabriel Mobley started his day early. His wife, a schoolteacher, was expecting their second child, so Mobley was working two jobs to get ready for the addition to their family. First, he worked at the pressure-cleaning business he owned. Later in the afternoon, he worked a second shift doing other people's taxes at the offices of his old high school buddy José Correa, who went by the nickname Chico. After working two jobs, Mobley was tired, so he jumped at the invitation to unwind after work with Chico and the rest of the tax-preparer crew.

Mobley followed the group from Chico's office to a local restaurant. For protection, Mobley always carried with him a Glock .45 caliber pistol. The Glock packed a punch. One round could easily drop a charging man. People don't mess with a man with a Glock. At least not more than once. At the restaurant, Mobley stowed the Glock in his car's glove compartment and went inside. He didn't like being unarmed; but although he had a license to carry a concealed weapon, Mobley didn't think he could bring his gun into the restaurant, where alcohol was being served.

By the time Mobley arrived, a group of women from the office were crowded into a booth, leaving him no place to sit, so Mobley pulled up a stool at the bar next to Chico and another coworker. Food and drink began to arrive. After a bit, Mobley and Chico slipped into the parking lot for a quick cigarette. When they returned, a pair of men were chatting up the women in the booth.

Chico didn't like the men's looks and thought the ladies were becoming uncomfortable with the unwanted attention, so he went up to the men and told them to move along. The men didn't much like Chico cutting in on their conversation. The exchange grew heated. Mobley tried to get everyone to keep it down. He didn't succeed. Voices rose, and the restaurant owner alerted his security guard that things might turn ugly. Chico insisted that the men leave. The men weren't budging.

The tension rose, and the standoff looked like it might bubble over into a full-on fight. The chances of the two men—one named Jason and the other Roly—did not look good. Jason was five feet, eight inches, and weighed 217 pounds. Roly was five feet, six inches, and 156 pounds. They weren't exactly lightweights, but they were significantly outsized by Chico and Mobley. At six feet, one inch, and weighig 285 pounds, Chico towered over both men. Mobley was even bigger, standing an imposing six feet, two inches, and weighing 285 pounds. Jason and Roly sized up the much bigger men and, apparently calculating their chances in a fight, backed down and returned to their table. The immediate crisis had passed, but Jason and Roly were not in a forgive-and-forget mood. They kept giving Chico the evil eye, and Chico, not one to be cowed by punks, returned their stares with icy defiance. The worst, however, appeared to be over.

Later in the evening, Mobley and Chico went to the bathroom; and when they came out, Jason and Roly were standing outside the restaurant with their faces pressed against the large plate-glass window. They banged on the window with their hands and pointed angrily at Chico.

Mobley decided it was time to go home. He told Chico that they should wait until Jason and Roly had cleared out and then they would go. After about ten or fifteen minutes, Mobley left the restaurant while Chico paid the bill inside.

Mobley went straight to his car and put on a heavy sweatshirt. Later he would say he was feeling chilly, but the sweatshirt was not the only thing he retrieved. Mobley also grabbed his gun from the glove compartment, tucked it into his waistband, and covered the weapon with the folds of the sweatshirt. There's nothing like cold steel pressed against your body and hidden underneath your sweatshirt to keep you warm on a Florida night.

Chico emerged from the restaurant, and Mobley, gun concealed under his sweatshirt, walked Chico to his car. But Chico didn't get in. Although they had talked about leaving, although this was their opportunity to get home without any more confrontation, and although they were just a few feet away from putting this night behind them, Mobley and Chico didn't leave. Instead, they decided to smoke one more cigarette. Bad decision.

Out of nowhere, Jason suddenly appeared and took a wild swing at Chico. His fist connected with Chico's right eye. Blood spattered onto clothes and sidewalk, but Chico didn't fall. At that point, Jason could have fled into the night with the same speed with which he had emerged, but he did not. Instead, Jason danced backward, fists raised, ready to finish the fistfight he had just started. Another bad decision.

Seconds later, Jason's companion, Roly, rushed to Jason's side. Mobley thought Roly was coming to help Jason with the fight. What happened next is not entirely certain. Mobley would later testify that he thought he saw Roly reach under his shirt. The move startled and scared Mobley. Was Roly was going for a gun? Mobley wasn't going to let Roly get the draw on him.

Mobley's hand plunged under his sweatshirt like a viper striking. He drew first and fired—five times in all. Four bullets in rapid succession struck Roly. Roly crumpled to the ground. Jason started to turn to flee, but a shot to the chest brought him down too. Jason collapsed on the asphalt and died. Roly lived long enough to make it to the hospital, but he died too.

After gunning down Jason and Roly, Mobley waited for the police and gave them a statement about what happened. He told them about Jason's surprise attack and Roly's move for a gun under his shirt. The police searched Roly's body. No weapons were found. Jason was clean too. Mobley had killed two unarmed men. Mobley was charged with two counts of murder.

In court, Mobley claimed that he shot Jason and Roly in self-defense. The laws of Florida defined self-defense like this: "A person is justified in the use of deadly force . . . and does not have a duty to retreat if . . . he or she reasonably believes that such force is necessary to prevent imminent death or great bodily harm to himself or herself or another or to prevent the imminent commission of a forcible felony." Mobley pointed out that Jason had, without warning or provocation, punched his friend Chico in the face. Although Jason was a much smaller man, the punch had cut Chico's eye and fractured his eye socket.

The prosecutors responded that Mobley could not claim the protection of the self-defense statute. He could not reasonably believe that these two much smaller, unarmed men threatened him or Chico with death or great bodily harm, or that gunning down Jason and Roly was necessary to prevent the imminent commission of a forcible felony. Jason's attack, while unprovoked and wrongful, did not cause great bodily harm. Chico just didn't seem all that hurt by the blow. At the scene, he had turned down an offer to be taken to the hospital. Instead, for medical care, he had just slapped an icepack on his eye. It was only later that Chico found out that the punch had fractured his eye socket. An injury that is barely noticed surely does not qualify as great bodily harm.

Roly and Jason were so much smaller than Mobley and Chico that the two larger men had little to fear in a fistfight. If weapons had been drawn, that might have changed the equation, but neither Roly nor Jason was armed. Whatever danger Mobley perceived was in his own head and did not qualify as reasonable.

Mobley admitted that he never *saw* a weapon on Roly or Jason, but he argued that he saw Roly reach under his shirt and *thought* that Roly was going for a gun or a knife. Jason had launched a vicious sneak attack. Who was to say that he and Roly were above pulling a gun? At a shoot-out, no one wants to be the guy who shoots second. Here is how Mobley testified in court:

Q. Okay. So, as soon as he [Roly] was coming towards you, you shot?

A. Yes.

Q. Why did you first pull your firearm?

A. Why[?]

Q. Yes.

A. By this time, you know, I didn't know what they had done—I didn't know what Chico had got hit with, and it was so much blood, I freaked, I was scared and I seen [sic] this other guy coming up from the back. And he reached up under his shirt. So, I was scared, I thought, they were going to shoot or kill us or stab us or something. So I was scared.

This testimony did not impress the prosecutors, who argued that Mobley had a gun and Jason and Roly didn't. In fact, they had no weapons of any kind. Whatever motion Roly might have made near his shirt that Mobley thought he saw, Roly clearly wasn't going for a gun he didn't have. Mobley never gave the men he killed any warning—no "stop or I'll shoot" or anything like that. Mobley and his friend Chico were never in real danger of serious bodily harm. They were bigger. They were stronger. Mobley was armed. Mobley could have defused the situation in any number of ways. He and Chico could have just walked away. Just drawing his gun—but not firing it—would probably have ended the confrontation, and everyone would have walked away alive. But Mobley didn't do that. Instead, he immediately pulled out his gun and, without warning or hesitation, started firing and didn't stop until both men were dead.

Was this self-defense or murder? How would you rule?

HOW THE COURT RULED

Mobley gunned down two unarmed men without giving them a warning or a chance to retreat when they saw his gun, and if that were all there was to the story, a murder conviction would be easy and uncontroversial. But that's not all there was.

Jason and Roly were not innocent bystanders who by chance crossed paths with Mobley. Although they had just met that night, by the time of the shooting the men already had a history together.

Jason and Roly had argued in the restaurant with two much bigger men. Most people won't pick a fight with men who outweigh them by a hundred pounds and tower over them by half a foot. And in the restaurant, Jason and Roly didn't: the smaller men backed down instead.

In the parking lot, however, the equation had changed. Out of nowhere Jason punched Mobley's friend in the face. Chico didn't go down, but blood was drawn. After this unprovoked, surprise attack, Jason didn't disappear back into the night. Instead, he danced defiantly before the two men he had just assaulted, fists up, spoiling for a fight.

Seconds later Jason's companion came rushing onto the scene. Mobley had no way of knowing what Roly was going to do, but when he saw Roly reach under his shirt, he panicked, thinking that Roly might be going for a gun.

The central question, said the court, was what would a reasonable person in Mobley's shoes *think* was about to happen. Was the danger over? What could give these two smaller men the courage to attack these larger men? Were Roly and Jason just going to go on their way after drawing first blood? Were they inviting a fistfight they would surely lose? Or was the violence about to escalate to a potentially lethal level?

Mobley came to his own conclusion. He grabbed his Glock and started shooting. In the judgment of the court, under the circumstances, this was a reasonable thing to do.

The law did not require Mobley, facing what seemed like a reasonably imminent threat, to shout warnings to the people who had attacked his friend and who seemed poised to attack him next. The law did not require Mobley to give the attackers a chance to retreat, which they could just as easily have used as an opening to attack again, this time with deadly force. Mobley had a split second to make a decision, and a reasonable person in Mobley's position would have reasonably concluded that lethal force would be necessary to protect his own life and that of his injured friend.

Yes, it would have been better for everyone if Mobley and Chico had not smoked that last, fateful cigarette. They knew trouble was brewing, and they had a clear chance to avoid it. But they weren't the ones who struck first. Foolish as it may have been, Mobley and Chico had every right to be in that parking lot and not be attacked. A prudent person might have decided that discretion in this situation was the better part of valor; but once the fight started—at Jason's instigation—Mobley had a right to fight back.

This was self-defense, concluded the court, not murder. Mobley must go free. Did the court get it right or wrong? You decide.

REFLECTIONS

Gabriel Mobley gunned down Jason and Roly. That fact was irrefutable and undeniable. The other events that evening are more doubtful.

Later, Mobley would say that he saw Roly reach under his shirt and feared Roly was going for a gun. Mobley's testimony raises two difficult questions: did Roly really reach under his shirt, and, whether he did or not, did Mobley really think Roly was going for a gun?

When one person kills another and claims self-defense, a common problem is that the story of the encounter is told by the person who did the killing. As the cliché correctly observes, dead men tell no tales.

Sometimes, the testimony of other witnesses can help, although even completely impartial eyewitnesses routinely make errors.[1] In this case, the only other witness was Mobley's friend Chico, who had just been punched in the eye. With his eye injury, he was hardly in a position to see what happened, and in any case, he was hardly an unbiased source.

That left Mobley's testimony as the only evidence of how the fistfight escalated to a gunfight, with only one side having a gun. How should that testimony be weighed? Let's consider the two questions about what happened that night in turn.

The first question is about what Roly did. He either reached under his shirt or he didn't. Mobley says he saw Roly reach under his shirt; but when Roly's bullet-riddled body was searched, he was unarmed. Roly had just run onto the scene where his buddy Jason had started a fistfight with two much larger men. What might have motivated Roly to put his hand under his shirt? Putting his hand under his shirt would have meant that his hand wouldn't be free to defend against an attack or to launch one, if that was his plan. Since Roly was unarmed, there seems to be little reason for him to reach under his shirt in the middle of a fight. Maybe Roly did reach under his shirt for some elusive reason, but it seems unlikely. Surely, Roly knew he was unarmed. A person doesn't reach for a gun that isn't there.

The second question requires a judgment about what thoughts were really in Mobley's head when he took out his pistol and opened fire. Mobley said that he thought he saw Roly reaching for a gun. As we've just discussed, the facts make it seem implausible that Roly did reach under his shirt; but is it implausible that Mobley *thought* Roly was reaching for a gun?

The fight lasted only a few seconds from start to finish, so it would be a fiction to dissect Mobley's thoughts as if they had streamed out one by one in an orderly fashion, with time for individual analysis. Nevertheless, on the night of the shooting, guns were clearly on Mobley's mind. When he left the restaurant after his heated encounter with Jason and Roly, Mobley went to his car and retrieved his personal weapon. It is not clear why he did this. Maybe he liked to be armed at all times, just in case. But maybe he wanted to have the gun handy in the event Jason and Roly returned. If it made sense to Mobley that he should arm himself, it would likely make equal sense to him that Jason and Roly would do the same thing. If so, Mobley was primed to be on the lookout for guns.

Confirmation bias is the tendency for people to seek out evidence that supports their preconceptions and to discount evidence that contradicts them. In other words, people see what they want to see and hear what they want to hear. This bias has been repeatedly demonstrated in laboratory experiments and observed among groups as diverse as witch hunters, scientists, physicians, and jurors, among many others.[2] With confirmation bias in play, it would not be surprising that Mobley—who was already thinking that a gunfight might break out—would interpret an ambiguous movement as a grab for a gun, just as he was expecting.

On the other hand, maybe Mobley made up the whole thing. When the police arrived in the parking lot that night, Mobley was holding the gun that had just killed two unarmed men. Mobley had to be worried that police and prosecutors might decide that he had to answer for the deaths; and in fact, Mobley ultimately was put on trial for murder. What defense could Mobley offer for spraying half a dozen bullets into unarmed opponents? It wouldn't take a legal eagle to know that self-defense was Mobley's only chance to avoid spending the rest of his life in prison.

Jason and Roly were dead. Who was to say one of them didn't make a move that looked like a reach for a gun? If Mobley had been inclined to lie, it would have been a simple thing to invent a story and hope police and prosecutors and judge and jury bought it. Of course, with no witnesses to corroborate or refute Mobley's version of events, it's impossible to know what really happened that night.

This is the hard reality of many disputes. Sometimes, the evidence available isn't enough to definitively establish the truth. Nevertheless, uncertainty or no, decisions are required. In the case of Gabriel Mobley, the court believed his story and set him free; but another court with other judges could just as easily have dismissed his self-serving account and condemned him to a life in prison. It's a lesson in why judging is hard, and why facing the judgment of other people in a lawsuit can be terrifying.

•　　　•　　　•　　　•　　　•

Questions

1. If you were the prosecutor in Gabriel Mobley's case and had a chance to cross-examine him, what questions would you ask in order to call into question his story that he drew and fired his gun because he thought he saw Roly reaching under his shirt for a weapon?

2. In this case, Mobley and Chico could easily have avoided the fight had they not stayed in the parking lot. It seems that Mobley sensed the danger of staying, because he retrieved his gun before meeting Chico for a smoke. The laws regarding self-defense vary from state to state, especially when it comes to questions like whether a person has a duty to avoid a fight, or whether a person can claim self-defense if he or she initiated the confrontation. In Florida, where this case took place, there is a law known as the Stand Your Ground Law, which essentially states that if a person is in a place he or she lawfully has a right to be, the person need not retreat in the face of danger but instead can fight back without losing the right to claim self-defense. What do you think about the wisdom of this law? Should a person have a duty to avoid a fight if possible? Under what circumstances should self-defense not be available as a defense?

Read It Yourself

Mobley v. State, 132 So. 3d 1160 (Fla. App. 2014).

3 Don't Lie to Me

Sheppard Scott's last day on earth was January 24, 2005. He never saw the sun rise.

At 4:30 A.M., Scott and his girlfriend, Yalandria Narcisse, pulled into the drive-through of a fast-food chain restaurant. While the young couple waited to order, two men standing outside a nearby convenience store eyed them from a distance. One man was wrapped in an orange jacket emblazoned with the logo for the Baltimore Orioles baseball team. The other wore a gray hooded sweatshirt. They had no business with Scott or Narcisse, but that didn't stop them from staring. The young couple had something they wanted, or so they thought.

While Scott and Narcisse waited for their turn to pick up their order, the two men sidled up to Scott's side of the idling car and asked whether he had any weed. According to Narcisse, Scott said he didn't. That was not the answer the men were looking for. One of the men muttered something to Scott. Narcisse didn't hear what the man said, but Scott did, and he instantly lit up with outrage.

Narcisse asked Scott what happened, and he told her that those punks had just called him a "bitch-ass nigger or something." Those were fighting words, and Scott was raring to go.

Scott scrambled out of the car and got in the face of the two men. He was part of a gang, Scott told the men, so they should back off. It was two to one. Scott was unarmed. Who knew what the two men were packing? Eyes locked. Hearts pounded. Fists clenched. The staring contest lasted a second or two, and then it was over. Scott won. The two men retreated, and Scott got back in his car. Gang membership had its perks and privileges, or so it seemed.

Scott and Narcisse got their food and headed for the drive-through exit. They were almost gone when Scott heard a voice yell from behind, "Hey, homey."

Scott was in a car in the driver's seat. The man was on foot, some distance away. No one will ever know what would have happened had Scott simply put the car in gear and hit the accelerator. He and Narcisse might have forgotten that morning's unpleasant experience and lived their whole lives never once thinking that, in that fraction of a moment, just by moving his foot from one pedal to the other, Scott had made a choice that changed their lives forever. The engine was running. The road ahead was clear. All Scott had to do was press the gas pedal and go. But he didn't.

Scott stopped the car. He stuck his head out the window to see who had yelled at him, although surely he must have guessed. The man in the gray hoodie came up to the car. He mumbled something that Narcisse couldn't make out and stuck out his hand for Scott to shake. Maybe it was an apology. Maybe it was a peace offering. Maybe it was one man saying to another: "No hard feelings." Whatever the man in the gray hoodie said, Scott, still seated in the car, reached out to accept the man's hand—bygones sealed with pressing flesh. The two men never connected.

Instead of taking Scott's hand, the man in the gray hoodie pulled a gun and started firing. Multiple shots at point-blank range. Scott never had a chance. He died on the spot, and the shooter fled into the night.

The police investigation that followed the shooting homed in on Darius Antoine Mays. The police brought Mays in for questioning.

Under interrogation, Mays repeatedly claimed that he had nothing to do with the shooting. He said he wasn't even at the convenience store that morning. If the cops didn't believe him, he could prove it. All the police had to do was give him a polygraph test. The lie detector would show, Mays said, that he was telling the truth.

The police weren't making progress, and they couldn't hold Mays forever. They didn't have any reliable witnesses to put Mays at the scene. They needed to get him to crack before he lawyered up and stopped talking. The police liked the idea of giving Mays a polygraph test, but there was just one problem: there wasn't a polygraph examiner available. So they improvised.

The officers wheeled in a polygraph machine and connected wires to Mays's body. They flipped some switches, some lights flashed, and they started asking Mays questions, including the critical question of whether he was there at the scene of the crime on the morning the shooting took place. Mays denied everything. He was innocent. The police had the wrong man.

When they had finished asking their questions, the officers printed an official looking report, while Mays waited and wondered what would be the verdict of the machine. The officers huddled over the paper and grimly shook their heads. Mays strained to see what they were looking at. The officers shrugged and handed him the paper. Machines don't lie, but people do. All the time. Mays had failed the test. The polygraph proved, the police told him, that he was a liar. The official report that Mays was holding in his own two hands conclusively showed that Mays was guilty.

The polygraph report could not have been more damning, with the exception of one detail that the police neglected to mention to Mays. Everything about it was a fake. The polygraph test was fake. The examiner was fake. The readings were fake. The report was fake. Everything a fake and a lie, and everyone in that room knew it—everyone except for Darius Mays.

The police waved the manufactured report in Mays's face. Lie detectors don't lie. He had failed the test—the test that he himself had asked for. That meant he was guilty. He needed to say something and say it fast or he was looking at doing some very hard time.

Mays was baffled. How could he have failed the test? He had been so sure that he would pass. But he had seen everything with his own eyes, the machine, the wires, the lights, the readings, and then the report that said in black and white that he was guilty. Up to that moment, Mays had steadfastly maintained that he was not at the convenience store on the morning of the shooting. His will buckled, and then it broke. Mays told the police that he was at the convenience store the morning of the shooting. He admitted he had been wearing a gray sweatshirt but vigorously denied that he was the shooter. The man in the orange Orioles jacket had done the shooting. Who was this man? Mays didn't know. It was just someone he had met that day. Mays was there, but he was innocent.

That was enough for the police. With Mays's admission that he was the man in the gray sweatshirt, and the testimony of other witnesses who said the shooter was the man in the gray sweatshirt, the police turned the case over to the district attorney, who put Mays on trial for murder.

At his trial, Mays changed his story back to what he had said before taking the fake polygraph test. He denied being at the scene of the crime at all. He openly admitted that he had told the police he was there, but he explained that he had lied to the police. When he saw the polygraph report that said he was lying, Mays testified, he felt so confused and defeated that he told the police whatever they wanted to hear just to get the ordeal of the interrogation over with.

Mays tried to win over the jury with candor. He admitted to the jury and to the court that he was in a gang. He had sold drugs on the streets. He had done a lot of things wrong, but cold-blooded murder wasn't one of them. He begged the jury not to send him to jail for a crime he had not committed.

The jury didn't buy it and came back with a verdict of guilty. Mays appealed.

The big weakness in Mays's case was that he had changed his story. He told the police he was at the convenience store. He told the jury that he wasn't. Same event. Two different versions. Nothing damages a person's credibility more.

On appeal, Mays argued that his incriminating admission that he had been at the scene wearing a gray sweatshirt should be thrown out. The police tricked him into saying that with their fake polygraph test. That charade was bad enough, but the police made it even worse by fabricating a false report, which they showed to Mays. The report looked like real evidence, but it wasn't. Mays believed, wrongly, that polygraphs were always accurate, so when he saw that report, he believed the report had to be true and his own memories false. He was tired, scared, and confused.

The police had acted like criminals, using fraud to gain a confession that wasn't true.

The police responded with a shrug. Yes, they had tricked Mays with the polygraph report, but no one made him admit that he had been at the scene of the crime. Those words came out of his mouth of his own free will. Only Mays knew for sure the truth of where he was. If Mays hadn't been standing outside the convenience store in a gray sweatshirt the morning Sheppard Scott was gunned down in cold blood, the police contended, no amount of fake polygraph reports would have gotten him to say that he was. The trick had teased out the truth. The police's lies had exposed Mays's lies. No innocent person admits to being at a crime scene that they weren't really at. Mays said he was there because he was.

So those are the facts and those are the arguments. Did the police violate Mays's rights by fabricating a polygraph test, or was this just good, clever police work to crack a tough case? How would you rule?

HOW THE COURT RULED

Your mother may have told you that honesty is the best policy, and while that might be good advice in life, it is not something the law requires of police officers interrogating suspects. Police can lie and deceive as much as they like, within limits.

Making up facts to play upon the psychological weaknesses of people held in interrogation rooms is considered fair in the effort to extract confessions and other incriminating statements. The only limit is when police deceptions become "coercive." In other words, only when the lies the police tell are likely to elicit statements that are involuntary and unreliable do they cross the line.

That's exactly what Darius Mays claimed happened to him. He innocently believed polygraph tests were 100 percent accurate. He believed the police had performed an honest polygraph test. And he believed that the report with the fake test results was real. It never occurred to him that the whole thing—the polygraph test, the report—was just an elaborate hoax. He didn't think police officers did that sort of thing, or if they did, the law wouldn't let them. He was wrong.

Trickery alone is not enough to make an interrogation unlawful. Why? "Because subterfuge," the court explained, "is not necessarily coercive." Some kinds of lies are likely to elicit false confessions, but that's a small minority. The lie has to be "shocking and outrageous" to be coercive.

What are some examples of "shocking and outrageous" lies by police that courts won't condone? Surprisingly, examples are hard to find. For example, telling a mother that confessing to a crime was the only way to retain custody of her children and preserve her government benefits was found to be over the line.[1] By threatening her children, the officers' deception ran the risk that a mother might say anything—even confess to a crime she did not commit—to keep her family intact, and that risk was too great.

What's not shocking and outrageous? In general, officers' lies about evidence that the police claim to have are fair play. So there's no problem with the police telling you that they found your fingerprints at the scene of the crime, when they have found no such thing; no problem telling you the police have an eyewitness who has identified you as the perpetrator, when no such witness exists; and no problem telling you while you're being transported in an ambulance that it looks like you're dying and you might not make it to the hospital, so you should come clean while you still have a chance to clear your conscience. All of those lies are just fine. They're not shocking. They're not outrageous. They're good police work.

In light of the great latitude the law gives police officers to deceive people under interrogation, the trick of the fake polygraph test and fake results was relatively mild.

What's more, the court noted, the polygraph trick did not cause Mays to completely break down. Yes, he admitted to being at the crime scene, and yes, he admitted to being the man in the gray sweatshirt—two facts he had previously denied—but his spirit wasn't so crushed that he confessed to the murder itself. By continuing to maintain his innocence, reasoned the court, Mays demonstrated that the fake polygraph didn't get him to admit to *anything and everything* that the police wanted him to say.

The police had not forced the polygraph test on Mays. He had asked to take the test, and the police had obliged, albeit with a fake test instead of a real one. Either way, the police didn't make Mays do anything he didn't want to do.

Coercion is the line police cannot cross, and the court concluded that, while Mays may have been tricked, he was not coerced. The fact that Mays made only a few incriminating statements was enough to convince the court that this particular subterfuge was not the kind of misrepresentation that was likely to produce false confessions, and this fact was all the law required. Therefore, the incriminating statements that put Mays at the scene of the crime stood. Along with the other evidence that the man in the gray sweatshirt was the one who had gunned Sheppard Scott down, Mays's damaging admissions led the court to uphold his conviction for murder.

Did the court get this one right or wrong? You decide.

REFLECTIONS

Perhaps the most celebrated sentence in American legal history is the Miranda warning. Established by the U.S. Supreme Court in 1966 as a constitutional requirement, and made famous by countless detective and courtroom dramas, the Miranda warning summarizes people's legal rights, of which police officers are obligated to advise people when they take them into custody. Americans may only dimly recall the words of the national anthem, but many can recite the Miranda warning from memory: "You have the right to remain silent. Anything you say or do can and will be used against you in a court of law. You have the right to an attorney. If you cannot afford an attorney, one will be appointed for you."

When the *Miranda* decision was first handed down, law enforcement officials across the country howled that informing suspects of their legal rights would choke off confessions; and confessions, they argued, were essential to catching criminals and making the justice system work. If criminals knew that they could choose not to talk to police, everyone would clam up and many a guilty person would go unpunished. The worst fears of these law enforcers, however, never came to pass. Even with handcuffs on and the threat of criminal punishment looming, many people cannot resist the instinct to try to talk their way out of trouble—such is the skill of police interrogators. Very often those in custody accomplish, like Darius Mays, the exact opposite.

The impact of the *Miranda* decision on law enforcement has also been limited by exceptions and limitations placed on the rule. For example, to invoke the privilege of avoiding self-incrimination, a person must expressly claim it. Simply standing mute in the face of police questioning is not sufficient. In that case, a person's silence might be used against him or her.[2] Moreover, the Miranda warning is not necessary when public safety is at stake. For example, if a suspect might have hidden a gun in a supermarket just before the police apprehended him, the police are permitted to question the suspect about the location of the gun without reading him his rights.[3]

Police interrogators might not tell you, but the act of speaking to law enforcement officers can expose even the innocent to the possibility of criminal charges that would be impossible had they said nothing at all. Many laws make it a crime to make a false statement to a law enforcement officer.[4] At first blush, it might seem that these laws should cause no concern for anyone who is telling the truth, the whole truth, and nothing but the truth; but sometimes "truth" can be a matter of perspective or interpretation, and many times our memories are not as precise as we would want or hope.

If a statement to law enforcement is not demonstrably accurate, criminal charges for lying to police are possible even if you're completely innocent of the crime the police originally brought you in to talk about. Martha Stewart, a rich and famous celebrity, a media mogul with magazines, television shows, and numerous lines of products bearing her name, learned this lesson the hard way when she was investigated for insider trading. She made the mistake of sitting down with federal investigators to talk things over. The federal investigators couldn't make the insider trading charges stick, but prosecutors charged her with making false statements to the investigators. Stewart denied making the statements that the investigators attributed to her, but it was her word against the word of the FBI, and in a swearing contest between federal law enforcement agents and a criminal defendant—even a defendant as famous as Martha Stewart—it's no surprise that the jury accepted the FBI's version of events. And so Martha Stewart went to jail for a crime she could have entirely avoided had she not talked to the police in the first place. Cases like Martha Stewart's are the reason that many defense lawyers tell their clients— both guilty and innocent—never to talk to the police. There's just too much risk.

As Darius Mays's case illustrates, the playing field between interrogators and the interrogated is not at all level. The police can hold a person, barrage him with questions for hours, and tell extravagant lies to get him to talk; and if he does talk, then as the Miranda warning bluntly puts it, anything he says can and will be held against him.

What's the case for allowing the police to engage in behavior that would be considered questionable, unethical, or even criminal if done by anyone else? For one thing, proving guilt can be hard. In many cases, there are no rock-solid witnesses or smoking-gun documents. In the shooting of Sheppard Scott, the person who had the best look at the killer was the victim, and he was dead. His girlfriend was at the scene, but it was dark and she was scared and so she wasn't able to make a positive identification. If anyone were going to pay for the crime, a confession was the only way.

Another argument for the police's right to lie is that lies by the police are harmless because they ensnare only the guilty. Innocent people, according to this logic, cannot be taken in if the police falsely claim to have witnesses or evidence against them. Innocent people know they are innocent, and so they also know that the claims must be false. Only the guilty can be fooled by police lies, because only the guilty have to worry that they left behind a trail that the police have picked up.

But is that logic right? If you are innocent, isn't it still *possible* that the police have—or *think* they have—evidence against you? Even assuming every witness is perfectly honest all the time, perfectly honest people make mistakes. Someone might honestly, but mistakenly, believe that the person they saw was you when it wasn't. Or worse, some witnesses might make up accusations for reasons of their own, such as to get better treatment from law enforcement, to reduce a criminal sentence, to deflect suspicion, to protect a loved one or business associate, to eliminate a rival, or to exact revenge. In other words, if the police say they have evidence against you, the fact that you are innocent doesn't mean you know for sure that they're lying. If you are an honest person and trust the police, hearing officers in uniform with badges and guns say they have proof of your guilt could shake your confidence in everything you think you know. And for some people in some circumstances, that shaken confidence might be enough to cause them to question their own judgment and memories and to confess to things that may not be exactly true.

Whether that is what happened to Darius Mays is impossible to tell. What we know is that before the fake polygraph test, Mays denied being at the scene of the crime; and after the fake test, he admitted it—at least while he was in the interrogation room. In court, he recanted. Without the police's deception, and without the courts' condoning of the deception, Mays would never have made the statement and would never have been convicted for the killing of Sheppard Scott. The root of the problem is that in many cases it can be exceedingly difficult to know when a person is lying. This is true for the guilty. This is true for the innocent. And it is true for the police.

.   .   .   .   .

.

Questions

1. Is it fair that police are generally allowed to lie to suspects when it's a crime for suspects to lie to police?

2. The modern polygraph test was developed in the nineteenth century and purports to determine whether a person is lying, by measuring changes in certain vital signs, such as breathing, blood pressure, heart rate, and sweat. Despite the polygraph's promises, most courts and most states have determined that polygraph tests are too unreliable to be admitted as evidence in court.[5] Nevertheless, law enforcement officers often see the test as a useful tool for extracting confessions, even if only from those who naively believe in the test's lie-detecting powers. Given that there is no scientific or legal consensus that polygraph tests are reliable, should law enforcement be prohibited from using them because their results are untrustworthy, or is their continued use still worthwhile, even if they are mainly traps for the uninformed?

3. Mays claimed that the fake polygraph test coerced him into saying he was at the scene of the murder when he was not really there. The fact that Mays did not confess to the murder convinced the court that Mays wasn't really coerced by the fake test. What do you think of this reasoning? Is it possible for a person to be

coerced to say some false things while still retaining the fortitude to resist saying other, much more serious, falsehoods? Must coerced confessions always be all or nothing?

4. How should courts go about figuring out under what circumstances a person is likely to make a false confession? What factors would make sense to consider?

Read It Yourself

People v. Mays, 174 Cal. App. 4th 156 (2009).

4 Show Me Yours

Steven Warshak was a small business owner with big ambitions. Mostly he sold herbal supplements, which he called nutraceuticals. His flagship product was Enzyte, which, according to Warshak, increased the size of a man's erection.

One might think that a product like Enzyte basically sells itself, but Warshak didn't want to leave his success to chance; so to get the word out, he turned to television ads to inform the masses about his miracle potion. The ads featured a trademarked character sporting a huge grin called "Smilin' Bob," who let it be known that a little bit of Enzyte went a long way toward making the men who used it stick out in their communities. Sometimes, Mrs. Bob would show up in the ads, and her smile was just as big as her husband's.

Cute cartoons are one thing, but convincing skeptical consumers to entrust their most private part to an unknown product would take the weight and authority of science. To boost their potency, Warshak's commercials pointed to a scientific study that found that, after three months of regularly taking Enzyte, men saw their girth grow by 12 to 31 percent—a prodigious augmentation by anyone's measure. The only shortcoming in the study was that it was completely made up.

Warshak also touted Enzyte's 96 percent customer satisfaction rating in sales pitches, brochures, and his Internet ads. Another impressive statistic, certainly, but this number, too, suffered from the imperfection of being a complete fabrication.

Finally, Warshak advertised that Enzyte was the brainchild of "Dr. Frederick Tomkins, a physician with a biology degree from Stanford[,] and Dr. Michael Moore, a leading urologist from Harvard," who had collaborated in the search for the perfect supplement to "stretch and elongate." The impressiveness of the good doctors' academic credentials matched the impressiveness of their scientific breakthrough, both of which were tempered only by the fact that the scientists were, like so many of Warshak's extravagant claims, entirely fictitious.

For customers enticed by the prospect of enlarged expectations but not entirely sold on the idea of buying over the telephone or Internet, Warshak generously offered a free trial in exchange for some basic information and a credit card number. There was just one small thing. Once their data was in Warshak's system, customers would keep receiving the supplements whether they ordered more or not, and Warshak would keep charging their credit cards whether they wanted him to or not. The only way to stop the charges was to contact the company directly and navigate an ordeal roughly equivalent to Hercules cleaning the Augean stables. At first, Warshak didn't disclose this detail, and when that deception seemed too much even for Warshak, the automatic orders found brief and obscure mention in the marketing materials sent to the customer, but only after the customer had placed the first order and was already in Warshak's clutches.

Propelled by Warshak's creative business methods, demand was huge, and business boomed. After a few years, Warshak's company grew to fifteen hundred people and nearly a quarter of a billion dollars in sales per year. Warshak's supplement was most potent indeed—at least for producing profits. The supplement, and the tactics used to sell them, also proved equally effective at attracting complaints from upset customers. These complaints, in turn, brought Warshak and his business to the attention of law enforcement.

To build the criminal case against Warshak, the government turned to one of the most fertile sources of information in this technological age:

email. Like most people, Warshak trusted a private company to provide him and his business with email. This was the chink in the armor that law enforcement decided to exploit.

The government investigators started small. They went to Warshak's email provider, a company called NuVox Communications, and asked NuVox to keep copies of all of Warshak's email messages—oh and by the way, the government told NuVox, don't tell Warshak. We don't want to tip him off. NuVox complied with the government's request and started copying all of Warshak's email, without Warshak being the wiser.

A few months later, government agents returned to NuVox, this time with a subpoena ordering NuVox to turn over all the email it had copied from Warshak's account. A few months after that, the government was back again, asking for any email that it might have missed the first time around. In all, the government extracted about twenty-seven thousand email messages from Warshak's email provider—without Warshak's knowledge. About a year later, Warshak found out about the email snooping the hard way: he was indicted for 112 counts of fraud and other crimes, with his own email a big part of the evidence against him.

Warshak cried foul. He complained that by taking his email without his knowledge or consent, and without a valid search warrant issued by a court based on a showing of probable cause, the government had violated his rights under the Fourth Amendment to the U.S. Constitution. The Fourth Amendment says that "the right of the people to be secure in their persons, houses, papers, and effects, against unreasonable searches and seizures, shall not be violated, and no Warrants shall issue, but upon probable cause." The government didn't get a warrant, Warshak argued, so its search and seizure of his email were illegal.

Not so fast, replied the government. The Fourth Amendment protects only *private* papers. If you expose your personal information to the public, the government can grab it without a warrant, and that's what Warshak did by using a third-party service to host his email. In its terms of service, Warshak's email provider NuVox reserved the right to access its customers' email for certain purposes. The terms of service said NuVox "may access and use individual Subscriber information in the operation of the Service and as necessary to protect the Service." That was pretty broad and open-ended. If Warshak had no problem with his email provider going through his email "in the operation of the Service," the government argued, then the email was not very private, so Warshak could hardly complain when law enforcement went through his email in the same way.

To support its position, the government cited precedent from the highest court in the land. In a case called *United States v. Miller,*[1] the U.S. Supreme Court ruled that people don't have a reasonable expectation of privacy in their bank records, checks, or deposit slips because bank depositors allow bank employees to see and work with this information. If it's okay for bank tellers to see a customer's bank records, the Supreme Court decided in *Miller,* then it was okay for the government to see them too— without a warrant. In the words of the Supreme Court: "The depositor takes the risk, in revealing his affairs to another, that the information will be conveyed by that person to the Government. . . . [T]he Fourth Amendment does not prohibit the obtaining of information revealed to a third party and conveyed by him to Government authorities, even if the information is revealed on the assumption that it will be used only for a limited purpose and the confidence placed in the third party will not be betrayed."

The government argued that the *Miller* case stood for the general rule that if a person voluntarily provides information to a third party, the government can get that information from that third party without a warrant. The Supreme Court seemed to adopt that broad principle in a later case called *Smith v. Maryland.*[2] In the *Smith* case, law enforcement went to the telephone company and installed a device called a "pen register" on a suspect's telephone line. A pen register records every number dialed on a telephone line, but doesn't record the contents of the call. In that case, the Supreme Court held that installing the pen register wasn't even a search because when people make phone calls, the numbers they dial are transmitted to the telephone company; and like the banks in *Miller,* once the telephone company has the information, the telephone company is free to provide it to the government, no warrant required.

Miller and *Smith* were problems for Warshak, but Warshak was up for the challenge. He argued that email was different from bank records. They were more sensitive and more confidential, and therefore, email deserved more protection from government intrusion. He also pointed out that pen registers recorded the numbers that were called, but not the calls themselves, and that in his case law enforcement didn't just look to see the names of the people he was emailing but, rather, read the email messages themselves.

So who should win? Did Warshak give up his claim to privacy in his email by entrusting his most private communications to a third party, thereby running the risk that his email provider would turn his email over to the government without his knowledge or consent? Or did the government overreach by pressuring the email provider to hand over Warshak's email without getting a warrant? How would you rule?

HOW THE COURT RULED

Warshak played fast and loose with the truth and with his customers. The records that the government seized proved that fact beyond a reasonable doubt, as confirmed by the jury that convicted him. But even crooks have rights.

The Fourth Amendment forbids unreasonable searches. This meant the court had to answer two questions: was pressuring Warshak's email provider to turn over email a "search"; and if it was, was the search "unreasonable"?

A "search"—as that word is used in the Fourth Amendment—occurs when the government infringes upon "an expectation of privacy that society is prepared to consider reasonable." In other words, searches require two things: (a) a person must expect privacy, and (b) society must consider that expectation to be reasonable.

Did Warshak expect privacy in his email? Absolutely. His email was a record of his whole life. His personal life. His business life. Everything. There was no way Warshak expected that information—some of it highly incriminating—to be anything other than completely private. As the court put it: "People seldom unfurl their dirty laundry in plain view."

If Warshak expected privacy in his email, was his expectation reasonable? For this question, the court observed that in the early twenty-first century, email was one of the main ways people communicate with each other about anything and everything. As the court stated: "Since the advent of email, the telephone call and the letter have waned in importance, and an explosion of Internet-based communication has taken place. People are now able to send sensitive and intimate information, instantaneously, to friends, family, and colleagues half a world away. Lovers exchange sweet nothings, and businessmen swap ambitious plans, all with the click of a mouse button. Commerce has also taken hold in email. Online purchases are often documented in email accounts, and email is frequently used to remind patients and clients of imminent appointments."

Although email was a relatively new mode of communication, older modes of communication had been protected by the Fourth Amendment. Police can't listen in on telephone calls without a warrant.[3] They can't raid post offices and start tearing open letters.[4] Email messages, concluded the court, were like telephone calls and letters, and therefore, reading email is a search under the Fourth Amendment. So Warshak won step one. The government had "searched" his email.

The second step was to consider whether the search was unreasonable. Warshak had agreed to a contract that allowed his email provider to access his email under certain conditions (as much as anyone agrees to the terms of service of online companies—but that's a different question). If Warshak didn't keep his email messages private from the email provider, then maybe his email wasn't so private after all. The government argued that Warshak's email was just like the bank records in the Supreme Court's *Miller* decision. If he wanted to keep his email private, he should not have allowed a third-party company to have access to it.

The court disagreed. Unlike a bank depositor giving bank employees access to his bank records, Warshak never gave his email provider blanket permission to read his email. Just because the email provider *could* read Warshak's email didn't mean that it did, and the access granted was extremely limited. The terms of service said that the email provider "*may* access and use individual Subscriber information in the operation of the Service and as necessary to protect the Service." "May access" is not the same as "will access." The court saw this as analogous to renting a room in a hotel. Just because cleaning crews enter to make beds and tidy the room doesn't mean that people in hotel rooms have agreed that government agents may also enter at any time without a warrant. The same goes for tenants whose landlords reserve the right to enter their apartments to fix leaky plumbing or perform other emergency repairs. The landlords' right to enter doesn't give the government a blank check to do the same. The terms of service, therefore, didn't eliminate Warshak's expectation of privacy in his email.

But what about the *Miller* case? In *Miller*, the Supreme Court held that giving a bank access to your banking records meant the government had the right to access those records too. Wasn't Warshak's email provider just like the bank?

The court didn't think so. In the court's view, *Miller* involved "simple business records," not the potentially unlimited confidential communications an email account might store. Moreover, banks used depositors' account information for their own purposes in the ordinary course of business—namely keeping track of how much money each depositor had. Email providers are different. They are intermediaries. They hold and transmit email for other people, not for themselves. They are not intended recipients. They have no reason to access the contents of email in the ordinary course of business. They would read a customers' email only in the most extraordinary circumstances. To operate, banks need to know your account balances and where your money is coming from and going to. Email providers don't need to read your email to deliver their services. This difference was enough to convince the court that the rule in *Miller*, while perhaps fine for banks, should not apply to email providers. Searching private email without a warrant was not reasonable.

Warshak, the court concluded, was not the only one who broke the law. The government had violated Warshak's rights under the Fourth Amendment by seizing his email without a warrant. That was the good news for Warshak.

The bad news was that the court also concluded that the government agents had acted in "good faith," meaning that they made a reasonable and understandable mistake in light of the complexity and novelty of the law about seizing email. In the future, email seized without a warrant would be excluded from prosecutions, but not in this case. Because the government made a reasonable mistake, it could still use the email to put Warshak in jail, which is exactly what happened.

Warshak, fraud though he was, struck a blow for the privacy of email for all the people of the United States—all except himself. Did the court get this one right? You decide.

REFLECTIONS

A person's home is his or her castle. The cliché is an old one. One of the earliest writers to inject that phrase into common parlance was Sir Edward Coke, who in 1644 published the third installment in his seminal review of English law titled *Institutes of the Laws of England*. Although it was a crime to resist the power of the English monarch, Coke noted, even the sheriff should not intrude upon the sanctity of the home, because "a man's house is his castle, *et domus sua cuique est tutissimum refugium* [and each man's home is his safest refuge]; for where shall a man be safe, if it be not in his house?"[5]

This refrain was picked up a century later by Sir William Blackstone in his *Commentaries on the Laws of England*, a magisterial and hugely influential summation of the common law. Blackstone wrote, "And the law of England has so particular and tender a regard to the immunity of a man's house, that it stiles it his castle, and will never suffer it to be violated with immunity: agreeing herein with the sentiments of ancient Rome, as expressed in the works of Tully [an abbreviation for Marcus Tullius Cicero, the famous Roman lawyer and orator]; *quid enim sanctius, quid omni religione munitius, quam domus unusquisque civium* [what is more sacred, what more strongly guarded by every holy feeling, than a man's own home]?"[6]

The rhetoric regarding the sanctity of the home reached its most eloquent expression in 1763, in a speech to Parliament by the British prime minister William Pitt. Pitt declared, "The poorest man may in his cottage bid defiance to all the forces of the crown. It may be frail—its roof may shake—the wind may blow through it—the storm may enter—the rain may enter—but the King of England cannot enter."[7]

Yet despite the lofty rhetoric, intrusions into the homes of the subjects of England were common in the eighteenth century and were particularly hated by England's colonists in the increasingly restive Americas. Professional police forces as we know them today did not come into being until the nineteenth century and so were unknown in the eighteenth century as the American Revolution percolated up and down the Atlantic Coast. Instead, citizens were at the mercy of agents of the king, who could invade any home at any time by securing a "writ of assistance," which required nothing more than the flimsiest suspicion to authorize the ransacking and carrying off of goods and papers, many of which were never to be seen again by their owners. These searches were often baseless, always invasive, and more often than not directed at punishing and intimidating dissidents rather than solving true crimes.[8]

After the Americans had won their revolution, the revolutionaries, now governors themselves, recalled the indignity of the abusive searches and seizures they had endured at the hands of arbitrary agents of the English Crown. With power in their hands, they repudiated the blanket authority of government to invade people's private affairs without cause and enshrined that repudiation in the Fourth Amendment to the U.S. Constitution.

The Fourth Amendment stands as a rejection of arbitrary government power over the private affairs of the people, but it is framed very much in the language of its time. The Amendment speaks of houses, papers, and effects; but in the twenty-first century, the great store of people's private information has migrated from papers locked in houses to bits and bytes stored in cell phones, computers, and servers. The question raised in *Warshak* is: how should the Fourth Amendment apply to modern times?

Applying the Fourth Amendment's general prohibition against unreasonable searches to new technologies is a challenge. Consider just a few dilemmas:

- A state requires that all people arrested for serious crimes provide samples of their DNA to be tested against a criminal database. Is that a search? Is it reasonable?

- Law enforcement secretly attaches a GPS tracking device to a person's car and uses the GPS to monitor everywhere the vehicle goes. Is that a search? Is it reasonable?

- Law enforcement sets up surveillance of a house on a public street and points a thermal-imaging device at the house to track the movements of all the people inside. Is that a search? Is it reasonable?

Take a moment and decide these cases for yourself. What do you think is reasonable?

For the DNA case, the Supreme Court ruled that taking the DNA sample was a search because it required invading the person's body (even if only with a swab on the inner cheek). The search, however, was reasonable. The intrusion was minor, and the reason for the intrusion (ensuring accurate identification of the arrested person) was significant.[9]

For the GPS case, the Supreme Court ruled that attaching the GPS tracker was a search because it was a physical intrusion onto a person's property. Was the search reasonable? The Supreme Court decided that it didn't need to answer the question at that time, so the question remains an open one.[10]

For the thermal-imaging case, the Supreme Court determined that although the device was nonintrusive (it emitted no rays or beams and measured only the heat emanating from the house), the device exposed "details of the home that would previously have been unknowable without physical intrusion" and, therefore, was a search. Because the search was of a home, it was unreasonable without a warrant.[11]

These cases, and others like them, challenge the courts to define what is reasonable and what is unreasonable in an era when technology is transforming how much we can know about other people and how we can come to know it.

In the early twenty-first century, outside of the home there is probably no more intimate and personal item than the modern cell phone. In 2014, the U.S. Supreme Court tackled the question of whether searching a cell phone requires a warrant under the Fourth Amendment. How would a court composed of elderly judges, many of whom were born before color television, let alone the advent of the Internet, handle this sensitive question?

Modern cell phones, the Supreme Court observed, "are now such a pervasive and insistent part of daily life that the proverbial visitor from Mars might conclude they were an important feature of human anatomy."[12] The cell phones of today are not really phones but miniaturized computers with the capacity to store every message the owner has ever sent or received, every web page the owner has visited, every picture the owner has taken, every book read, every note written, and even every location the owner has been. The cell phone potentially is a complete catalog of the innermost thoughts and actions of its owner. Therefore, to search a cell phone, the Supreme Court held, the police need permission from a judge by first obtaining a warrant.[13]

The ransacking of desk drawers that the authors of the Fourth Amendment feared and hated has given way in importance to forensic analysis of cell phones, computers, servers, and intercepted telecommunications; to surveillance drones; and to other technological innovations that only a few years ago were the stuff of science fiction. The privacy debates of the future will be less about physical spaces and more about digital troves where people store their most personal information. The challenge for the Fourth Amendment and the judges who interpret and apply it will be to adapt the eighteenth-century principles that animated the amendment to twenty-first-century technology and the realities of how contemporary people live and record their lives. Judging and judgment will play a crucial role in the success or failure of this transition.

. . . . .

Questions

1. The government relied heavily on the terms-of-service agreement Warshak had with his email provider. How many people read these terms-of-service agreements, and among those who do, how many people really understand them? If it is the case that these agreements are very rarely read and even more rarely understood, does it make sense to use them as a tool in deciding the reasonable expectation of privacy that society is prepared to accept when it comes to searches and seizures by the government? If the terms of service should *not* be used as a benchmark, what alternatives might exist?

2. The court distinguished *Miller* (the bank records case) with two arguments: email is more sensitive than "simple business records," and email providers don't use email content for ordinary business purposes in the same way banks use depositor information. How persuasive are these distinctions? Bank records can show the names of everyone you paid money to and everyone who paid money to you. Why should that information receive less protection than email; or put the opposite way, why should email receive more protection? Also, email providers frequently use email content for ordinary business purposes, such as serving advertisements and filtering spam. Why should those uses be treated differently than banks' keeping track of depositors' account information? If the case for treating bank records and email differently is weak, should *Warshak* have come out the other way or should *Miller* be overruled; or are there other alternatives?

3. Warshak's complaint was that his email was searched without a warrant. A warrant is an order from a judge authorizing law enforcement to search and seize property (or in the case of an arrest warrant, a person). The requirement that law

enforcement first obtain a warrant before executing a search is justified by the argument that judicial officers are more neutral, detached, and disinterested and, therefore, will more accurately balance the need for law enforcement to ferret out criminals and the right of the people to be free from government intrusions and surveillance. Police officers caught up in the heat of prosecution lack this bigger-picture perspective. The warrant requirement is an eighteenth-century idea. In the twenty-first century, does the warrant requirement effectively maintain the balance between law enforcement and privacy? Is there an alternative system that might be better?

Read It Yourself

United States v. Warshak, 631 F.3d 266 (6th Cir. 2010).

5 Dead Dogs Don't Bark

The crime was murder. The place was the Pink Poodle nightclub in San Jose, California. The victim was Kevin Sullivan. The time was the night of August 24, 1997, and the means a savage beating.

The police worked fast and concluded that the murderer was Steve Tausan, one of the nightclub's bouncers and a member of the San Jose Charter of the Hells Angels Motorcycle Club. Not satisfied with catching just the perpetrator, the police suspected that other members of the Hells Angels had concealed evidence of the murder. That made them accomplices after the fact.

The police's challenge was figuring out how to connect these other Hells Angels members with the killer. Working with the district attorney, the police submitted an affidavit to a judge seeking permission to search the homes of suspected members of the Hells Angels. They wanted to look for video of the beating, notes from a Hells Angels meeting that took place after the murder, and "any evidence of membership in, affiliation with, activity of, or identity of, any gang, including but not limited to, any reference to 'Hells Angels.'"

The judge issued warrants to search two homes, one belonging to James Souza, the other to Lori and Robert Vieira. Souza and Robert Vieira were not model citizens. Souza had been arrested for weapons and narcotics charges. Vieira had prior weapons-related convictions. Going into their houses could be dangerous. The police needed to be prepared for the worst.

Complicating matters, the police learned about a week before the searches that both Souza and Vieira owned dogs. Souza owned a Rottweiler and had hung an ominous sign that said, "Warning: Property Protected by Guard Dog." Word on the street was that Souza's Rottweiler attacked without provocation. The number of dogs that Vieira had and their breeds were unknown. For the searches to succeed, the dogs would have to be dealt with.

The police planned a simultaneous, two-pronged attack on Souza's house: One team would go through the front door. Another team would take a side gate to secure the backyard. The week passed. The day arrived. It was go time.

At the appointed hour, the police knocked on Souza's door, but no one answered. Maybe no one was home. Maybe Souza was going for a gun. The police outside couldn't know for sure. They had to move. The police broke the door down by force and pushed their way inside.

Meanwhile, the team at the side gate was stymied by a lock that their bolt cutters couldn't cut. Their radios crackled. The first team was already in. No one was home. The second team abandoned the side gate to join the first team. They entered the house through the shattered front door.

The house secured, two officers made their way to the backyard. The backyard was a mess. Miscellaneous objects and machinery littered the yard, making it hard for the officers to have a clear line of sight on the whole area. Nervous, the officers kept their weapons drawn. These weapons weren't standard-issue sidearms. They were MP5 automatic rifles. If a gunfight broke out, the police were not going to lose.

What happened next happened very quickly, and only the two officers were there to witness it. Here's how one of the officers told the story: "The [R]ottweiler suddenly appeared around the corner, approaching from the west at a distance of about ten to fifteen feet. It looked at me, gave a low growl, and started advancing toward me. I feared that the dog was going to attack me and I immediately discharged my firearm pulling the trigger twice."

The dog died instantly. A small white dog was also in the backyard, but the officers let this one live because they didn't think the small animal posed any threat.

Meanwhile, at the Vieira house, things didn't go much better. Three large dogs guarded the backyard. The officer in charge of the operation hoped that they might be able to sneak in without alerting the dogs. If the dogs did appear, his plan was to poke at them through the fence with his shotgun to scare them off. If that failed, he would "engage" the dogs to make sure that he and his team were safe.

As the officers tried to sneak in the back gate of the Vieiras' property, the three dogs ran to the gate, teeth bared, barking and growling and snapping at the officers on the other side of the fence. An officer tried to stick his hands through the gate to cut the lock, but one dog snapped at him, and he pulled back.

The officers tried yelling at the dogs. The team leader pushed one dog back with the barrel of his shotgun, but the dogs would not retreat. Their barking grew louder and more intense. If this went on much longer, the Vieiras were sure to notice and the police would lose the element of surprise. The dogs had to be silenced. But how?

The team leader solved the problem with the tool most readily at hand. He pointed his shotgun at one of the barking dogs and shot it. The dog collapsed into a bloody heap. One dog was down, but the other dogs did not retreat. The barking became wild and frenzied. This was not what the officers had hoped for. The team leader took aim again, this time at a second dog, and fired two quick rounds. The dog went down instantly. The third dog, seeing his companions shot and bleeding, now standing alone against the men and their metal stick that blasted thunderous death, turned and fled.

Although shot at point-blank range, somehow the first dog wasn't dead. The wounded animal tried to get back to its feet. Maybe the dog was trying to flee. Maybe it was getting ready for one last attack. The police were not going to take any chances. The team leader aimed at the dog's head and fired. The dog went down, and this time it stayed down.

The noise from the shootings woke Robert Vieira. He emerged from the house at the second floor balcony just as the officers made it through the gate. Guns drawn, the police told him to freeze and put his hands above his head. An officer broke through the front door with a battering ram, and then the police proceeded to search the house.

James Souza and the Vieiras filed a lawsuit against the San Jose police department for the killing of their dogs. The police officers objected to the lawsuit. They had come to the Souza and Vieira houses to execute a lawfully authorized search warrant to establish gang connections in a murder case. Souza and Robert Vieira were known to be dangerous men, the police argued, and so it was imperative that the police approach their residences in stealth. Speed was also critical, to avoid allowing one man to get word to the other that police might be on their way. Finally, the safety of the officers, argued the police, had to come ahead of the lives of dogs. If the dogs had not been dealt with, one could easily have injured the officers. That was an unacceptable risk.

Souza and the Vieiras didn't think that the police should have a license to kill their beloved animals. They argued that the police could have found some other way to subdue the dogs short of shooting them. Dogs weren't just a piece of property, like a lock that could be cut or a door knocked down, inanimate objects to be casually destroyed to clear the way for police to enter a home. Locks and doors could be replaced. The dogs were part of their families. Killing the animals should have been a last resort. Souza and the Vieiras demanded that the police pay for the pain and suffering they inflicted when the officers who came to their houses decided that the best way to handle the dogs was by putting bullets in their brains.

Were the police justified in killing the dogs, or did they act unreasonably and use excessive force, so that the police should have to pay for the damage they did when they shot Souza's and the Vieiras' dogs? How would you rule?

HOW THE COURT RULED

Under the Fourth Amendment, searches and seizures must be reasonable (or as lawyers often prefer to put it, not unreasonable). A seizure of property occurs if the police interfere with the owner's control of the property. Destruction of property is the ultimate interference. Therefore, under the

Fourth Amendment, the police must have a good reason before destroying people's property.

In this case, the police offered three reasons for shooting the dogs. First, the searches were part of a murder case, so the need for successful searches was especially great. Second, the people to be searched were dangerous, so stealth and speed were paramount. Finally, the dogs were not fluffy lap-dogs lolling in ladies' purses. They were big, they were vicious, and they were very upset about the police intruding on their territory. The officers' lives were at stake.

On the other hand, the police knew at least a week in advance of the searches that they would have to deal with these dogs. They had time to make plans for subduing the animals if they were loose on the property. For example, the police could have considered pepper spray or tranquiliz-ers, but they didn't. The plan they had—hoping the dogs wouldn't show up—was feeble at best. And the plan of poking the dogs with a shotgun if they did appear, and hoping they would retreat, had no reasonable chance of success. The police's lack of planning had created the danger that they then had to defend against by shooting the dogs.

If the officers had been truly surprised by the dogs, the analysis might be different. Police officers are afforded wide latitude to react to volatile and unpredictable situations. But the police had a week to come up with a reasonable strategy for dealing with the dogs, and they didn't even try. This utter lack of any real planning was unreasonable, and so the court ruled that the police violated the Fourth Amendment when they shot the dogs.

Souza and the Vieiras would never get their dogs back, but the police officers would have to pay something for their loss. Did the court get it right or wrong? You decide.

REFLECTIONS

Police do dangerous work. Their business is finding bad people, the kind of people most citizens do their best to avoid, and that takes them to places and puts them in situations where their lives can be at risk. When police officers put on a badge, they know that there may be times when they will have to make split-second decisions where their lives—and the lives of others—may hang in the balance.

Given the dangers they face, the police need to be able to react quickly and decisively to potential threats. The luxury of hindsight makes it easy to second-guess a decision from the safety of armchairs far removed from the urgency and danger of the moment, and police officers afraid of lawsuits questioning their judgments might shy away from taking the risks the public needs them to take to keep the streets safe. Recognizing that officers need room to make tough decisions in difficult circumstances, courts normally defer to the judgment of the police.

At the same time, the police wield enormous power. Alone among citizens, police are authorized to apply force to compel others to follow their commands. They can put their hands on the bodies of other people, hit them with sticks, spray their faces with toxins, and even gun them down, all with the authority and approval of the government. With this power to apply physical force comes the possibility of abuse.

Consider the case of Eric Garner, who on July 17, 2014, stood outside a storefront on a street corner in Staten Island, New York, when a number of police officers approached him. The officers suspected that Garner might be selling loose cigarettes, a misdemeanor.

Garner was a big man, standing six foot three and weighing 350 pounds. His size must have made the officers worry about what damage a man like that could do if he wasn't happy, and on that afternoon Eric Garner wasn't happy.

Garner was tired of being hassled by the police. "Every time you see me," he told the officers, "you want to mess with me. I'm tired of it. It stops today."

But crime suspects don't get to tell the police what to do. One officer came up behind Garner and tried to grab his arms. Garner pulled his arms free. That was it. A fight was on, and police don't lose fights. An officer put Garner in a chokehold, while the others swarmed over Garner from all sides.

Garner fell to his knees. An officer pushed his face to the sidewalk. "I can't breathe," gasped Garner. And then it was over. Garner lay on the ground, unmoving. The officers secured Garner's hands in handcuffs. The danger was over. They relaxed. Everything was good, except one thing.

Garner still wasn't moving. The officers called for an ambulance. An hour later Eric Garner was pronounced dead.

The death of Eric Garner was an extreme case, but it illustrates the power of the police. Only the police could swarm over a man on a street corner, choke him from behind, and wrestle him to the ground in broad daylight in front of multiple witnesses. And for what? Selling loose cigarettes and pulling an arm free from a surprise grab from behind? Because the police have such tremendous power, the law and the courts must enforce limits on that power.

That line is drawn according to whether the police's use of force was reasonable. What is reasonable, naturally, depends very much on the information available at the time of a decision, and so reasonableness has to be judged from the perspective of the police officer facing danger, real or perceived, as events are unfolding in real time. But even with this generous benefit of doubt, police can and do go too far.

Killing a person is far more serious than killing a dog, and therefore it requires much more serious justification; but the principle at play in both cases is the same: the force used by the police must be reasonable in light of the objective to be achieved. Trying to figure out how much force is reasonable is tricky and often turns on the specific details of a particular encounter. Some factors that courts typically consider are the severity of the crime at issue, whether the suspect poses an immediate threat to the safety of the officers or others, and whether the suspect is actively resisting arrest or attempting to evade arrest by flight. Importantly, "the reasonableness of a particular use of force must be judged from the perspective of a reasonable officer on the scene, rather than with the 20/20 vision of hindsight."[1]

This rule of reasonableness has replaced blanket rules that previously gave law enforcement even greater discretion in using force against suspected criminals. There was a time, for example, when the common law authorized the killing of any suspected felon who resisted or fled lawful authority. Now, deadly force can be legally applied only if a suspect poses a significant threat—a threat of death or serious physical injury—to the officer or others.[2]

In the case of Souza's and the Vieiras' dogs, the police invoked the exigencies of the search. In other circumstances—say, the police had been in hot pursuit of a fleeing, armed, and dangerous murderer and a barking dog stood in their way—their plea likely would have found sympathetic ears. But killing these dogs was the product of, not a split-second decision, but a failure to think ahead when there was plenty of time for thinking. A reasonable person plans ahead.

Balancing the police's need for space to make difficult decisions on the spot, against the people's right to be free from excessive force, can be difficult. Reasonableness, as slippery as that concept may be, is the place where the law has drawn the line between legal and illegal force by the police. While simple enough to state, the rule of reasonableness can be dauntingly difficult to apply in specific cases, which is where the judgment in judging comes in.

·   ·   ·   ·   ·

Questions

1. In this case, no one challenged the reasonableness of the police's decision to break down doors to search the houses. Should pets be entitled to greater protection than inanimate objects like doors, or should the destruction of property, whether it is a dog or a door, be evaluated by the same standard? If you think the standards should be different, how would you describe the standard for pets versus the standard for nonliving property?

2. What would have happened if one of the dogs had injured one of the police officers during the search? Would the officer have been justified in shooting the dog in that case, despite the lack of advance planning on the part of the police? Should the injured officer be able to sue the dog owner for damages from the dog bite?

Read It Yourself

The San Jose Charter of the Hells Angels Motorcycle Club v. The City of San Jose, 402 F.3d 962 (9th Cir. 2005).

6 When Is Fruit a Vegetable?

Tomato: a fruit or a vegetable? It seems like a debate better suited to the dinner table than the august halls of the U.S. Supreme Court. But when money is at stake, lawsuits are often close behind, and so the profound philosophical question of the proper taxonomy of the beloved tomato came to court because one family didn't want to pay a tax.

To the delight of children and the consternation of parents, the Tariff Act of 1883 required that a tax be paid on all imported vegetables. Imported fruits, however, could enter the country free of charge. Whether a tomato was a vegetable or fruit, therefore, meant the difference between a hefty tax bill and sweet and juicy freedom from taxation.

The parties to the dispute were Edward Hedden, a member of the oft-maligned profession of tax collectors, and the Nix family, importers of delicious and, in their estimation, tax-exempt tomatoes. To get their produce into the country, the Nix family had paid the vegetable tariff on their tomatoes under protest, and they appealed to the courts to get their money back.

The Nixes had dictionaries on their side. Fruits, these dictionaries instructed, were "that part of plants which contains the seed, and especially the juicy, pulpy products of certain plants containing the seed."

Tomatoes have seeds. Tomatoes are juicy and pulpy. Tomatoes, therefore, are unambiguously and indubitably fruits.

To the Nixes' appeal to authority, Hedden the tax collector countered that *everyone* knows that tomatoes are vegetables and not fruits. Dinner tables across America would be turned upside down and have to be reset if the court ruled otherwise. No dictionary is needed to know whether a tomato is fruit or vegetable. *Tomato* is a common and ordinary word and should be given its common and ordinary meaning, the meaning that ordinary people in their ordinary way of speaking ordinarily give it. Should native speakers be slaves to dictionary definitions? In common parlance, tomatoes are vegetables. And that, in Hedden's opinion, was all that needed to be said about the matter.

Thus, the age-old debate about the true status of tomatoes ripened for resolution. Is a tomato a fruit or a vegetable? How would you rule?

HOW THE COURT RULED

The question for the court was: what did the Tariff Act of 1883 mean when it said "vegetables" were to be taxed. Since the word *vegetable* had no special meaning in trade or commerce, to interpret the meaning of the word the court began by looking for the word's normal and ordinary meaning.

Vegetable is a common English word, and the judges on the court were English speakers, well read, learned, well acquainted with the meaning of common words in their native tongue. Nevertheless, while not substitutes for the judges' understanding of what words mean, the justices acknowledged that dictionaries are "aids to the memory and understanding of the court," and very often they are the first places courts look when the meaning of a word is in dispute.

The court could not disagree that the dictionaries favored classifying tomatoes as fruits. "Botanically speaking," the court observed, tomatoes are fruits. They grow on vines. They contain seeds from which new tomato vines grow. These are the qualities of fruits, and if this were a scientific question rather than a legal one, the court would unhesitatingly have found tomatoes to be fruits.

But this was a court not a classroom, so the question was whether the lawmakers who wrote the Tariff Act considered tomatoes to be among the "vegetables" they sought to tax. Notwithstanding the Nixes' dictionaries, the court believed that, in common parlance, tomatoes are most definitely vegetables. Moreover, tomatoes were not the only fruits that were commonly, but erroneously, called vegetables. Cucumbers, squashes, beans, and peas all contain seeds, but they too are commonly called vegetables. The common person, after all, is not a botanist.

To clinch its analysis, the court looked to the dinner tables of ordinary folk. Tomatoes, the court observed, are traditionally served as accompaniments to the main dish, side by side with potatoes, carrots, beets, cauliflower, and cabbage. All of these are considered vegetables. In contrast, fruits, according to the court, are served as dessert, after the main course is complete. Tomatoes rarely, if ever, occupy this place of honor.

Those who enjoy tomatoes as a delicacy for dessert may have begged to disagree with the court's culinary pronouncement, but in the end the court ruled that "common knowledge" proved that, even if botany and dictionaries might say otherwise, tomatoes were vegetables—or at least that's what the lawmakers intended in the vegetable tariff. So the Nixes could not get their money back from the taxman, which probably comes as a surprise to absolutely no one.

REFLECTIONS

One of the most common tasks for courts is to decide what the words in a law mean. This seems like it should be simple and straightforward, but that's often not the case. Some words are inherently vague (like "unfair" competition). Other words are clear enough in the common case (cars are "vehicles") but harder to figure out in other contexts. (Are bicycles "vehicles"? Are skateboards? Baby strollers? Remote-controlled toy cars? Drones?)

When interpreting a statute, courts tend to follow a predictable pattern of analysis. The first and often decisive step is to read the statute as written and attempt to give each word the meaning that a native speaker using the words in an ordinary way would naturally understand. If the words are clear, the analysis ends. This is often referred to as identifying the words' *plain meaning*. Although the court in the tomato case gave short shrift to the dictionary definitions, contemporary courts rely heavily on dictionaries as authoritative sources for the plain meaning of words.

Still, dictionaries are not the be all and end all. Some words have technical meanings that are not captured by generic dictionaries. Other words have specialized meanings that are apparent only from their context. And dictionaries themselves often present multiple definitions for the same word; and in cases when differences in the definitions could affect the outcome of a legal case, the courts must figure out which definition to endorse.

If doubts about the meaning of a statute remain after studying the words themselves, courts try to figure out what the lawmakers intended, also known as the *legislative intent*. Sometimes, this intent can be discerned from looking at the statute as a whole. For example, in a law that radically reforms the national health care market by creating subsidies for people to buy health care insurance, it is unlikely that an ambiguous fragment of one sentence on one page of the thousand-page bill would be meant to preclude large numbers of people from receiving the very subsidies the law spent hundreds of pages creating.[1] In that case, the context clarifies what might otherwise be an ambiguous meaning.

Courts can also find evidence of the legislative intent by looking at such things as committee reports and bill analyses prepared by legislators or their staff, or even, albeit less reliably, the speeches of lawmakers for or against a bill.

Finally, when all else fails, courts give statutes the meaning that makes the most sense. This last method of understanding a statute is sometimes called taking into consideration *public policy*, or which reading would do the most good, at least in the minds of the judges who are interpreting the statute.

In the tomato case, the court did not have to go past step one of the analysis, because the court concluded that it is well known that the vegetable category is widely regarded as including tomatoes. That was enough to answer the question, and so that's where the court stopped.

. . . . .

Questions

1. The court acknowledged that, scientifically speaking, tomatoes are in fact fruits, not vegetables. When should a court adopt precise, scientific definitions of words, and when should it embrace less accurate but more widely shared understandings?

2. In concluding that tomatoes are commonly understood as being included in the vegetable category, the court relied on a number of observations: normal people regularly referred to tomatoes as vegetables, other seeded plants are often called vegetables, and tomatoes are often served in meals at the same time as other vegetables. It is possible, however, that some of these observations are not universally true. The court noted that tomatoes are not eaten for dessert like other fruits, but how does the court know that to be the case? Presumably, the judges relied on their own personal experiences in making these observations. Is it appropriate for judges to rely on their personal experiences in this way, or should judges be required to base decisions only on evidence presented in court? What would evidence of how people normally use the word *vegetable* look like?

3. The court concluded that a tomato was a vegetable and not a fruit, but it reached that conclusion in a case that called for an interpretation of the word *vegetable* in a particular statute, specifically the Tariff Act of 1883. If the word *vegetable* appears in a new law written today (for example, concerning the types of food that can be served as subsidized school lunches), how much weight should the court's decision in this case be given in deciding whether tomatoes should be considered fruits or vegetables under this hypothetical new law?

Read It Yourself

Nix v. Hedden, 149 U.S. 304 (1893).

7 Private Parts

It must have been a hot tip that brought the deputy from the county sheriff's office to the doors of this particular nightclub on that particular night. *Scandals* was a popular watering hole, offering drinks, company, and fun with a racy edge, albeit served with a shortage of modern thinking about gender equality. Topping the bill that night was a "lingerie fashion show," where local women would strut their stuff before the eager eyes of *Scandals'* patrons. The dauntless deputy braced himself for the distinct possibility of direct exposure to a brazen display of criminal activity, took his place in the crowd, watched, and waited.

Soon enough, the lingerie fashion show got under way, and Pamela Parenteau strode onto the catwalk. Sporting a sultry lace brassiere, Parenteau sashayed up and down, basking in the hoots, hollers, and delight of all in the crowd. All but one.

The sheriff's deputy was not, to put it mildly, having a good time. He stared at Parenteau's uninhibited performance, and where everyone else may have seen feminine beauty, the deputy saw a crime shamelessly being committed right before his wide-open eyes. The deputy focused on Parenteau's chest—for purely professional reasons, of course—and thought he spied a nipple poking out from underneath her bra. He had seen enough, more than enough. When Parenteau had finished her run and retired to a changing room in the back, the courageous deputy, without calling for backup, made his move.

He burst into the dressing room and demanded that Parenteau hand over the clothing she had worn on stage. Why did he need her undergarments? Evidence, of course. Scared and confused, but not wanting to defy an officer of the law, Parenteau turned over the apparently contraband apparel. The evidence of the dirty deed securely in hand, the deputy placed Parenteau under arrest for the crime of public indecency.

The Ohio law that firmly stood as the thin veil protecting the moral sensibilities of the good citizens of Hamilton County stated, "No person shall recklessly do any of the following, under circumstances in which his or her conduct is likely to be viewed by and affront others, not a member of his or her household: (1) Expose his or her private parts." Parenteau was charged with violation of this statute.

At Parenteau's trial, the court weighed the sartorial evidence. First, and certainly most damning, was the lace brassiere, which undoubtedly received the greatest attention. In her defense, Parenteau pointed to a square of pantyhose fabric and told the court that, mindful of the possibility of protrusion in her admittedly thin and lacy attire, she had taken the prudent precaution of inserting the fabric under her bra to prevent revealing anything more than modesty would allow. Why, then, was there only one square of fabric before the court when, clearly, two at a minimum would have been required? The second square, Parenteau hypothesized, must have fallen to the floor, and the arresting officer, not realizing its significance, must have neglected to impound it in the shuffle and confusion that followed the deputy's unexpected sequestering of the rest of her scanty outfit. If the officer saw anything that night in *Scandals'* darkened hall, Parenteau proclaimed, he saw it only in his imagination.

Parenteau argued that she should be acquitted on that fact alone. But there was another, equally challenging obstacle for the prosecution. Even if her nipple had slipped into the officer's eagle-eyed view, the law required two more elements. First, the slip must have been "likely to . . . affront others." There was, Parenteau argued, no affronting. Parenteau would likely have caused more affront to the *Scandals* crowd if she had taken to the stage in a burka rather than in an overly revealing brassiere.

Affront was needed—on this point, the statute was clear—and the prosecution had just the man. To supply evidence of affront, the state called to the stand the arresting officer himself. Did he, solemnly asked the prosecutor, enjoy the show? The deputy, with unflappable stoicism and the decorum befitting his station as an officer of the peace and a defender of the public's morals, replied that no, he did not.

The final piece of the case against Parenteau required the state to prove that the offending exposure was of her "private parts." On this ground, too, Parenteau pressed, saying that the state's case wasn't up to snuff. Breasts, she argued, are not "private parts." Private parts were to be found lower down on the human anatomy.

The state waved away Parenteau's argument and replied that the statute should be understood in its most commonsense form. Long-standing tradition established that a woman's breasts, especially her nipples, should not see the light of day in decent company, so the statute should be read to include Parenteau's breasts as private parts that must be kept under much more than see-through, lacy wraps.

Parenteau's arguments fell on deaf ears in the trial court, and so she was convicted. Undeterred, Parenteau appealed her case. It became the job of the appellate court to address Parenteau's three arguments urging the court to find that she was not guilty of this crime against decency for which she had been convicted. She had kept her breasts securely concealed with fabric inserts, Parenteau steadfastly maintained on appeal. Even if she hadn't, no one was affronted, not even the deputy, who at most said only that he did not "enjoy" the show, not that he was "affronted" by it. Finally, even if her breasts had hung out in all their spectacular, mammary glory to the chagrin and embarrassment of the puritan sensibilities of the assembled crowd, her breasts were not private parts whose display was proscribed by the law. She was, Parenteau firmly declared, an innocent woman.

Was Parenteau innocent or guilty? How would you rule?

HOW THE COURT RULED

Laws against public nudity have been a part of the legal fabric of America since the country's inception. Yet the same modest motivations that impel legislators to enact bans on the display of excessive amounts of skin also on occasion inhibit precise, anatomical description of the areas of the human body prohibited from public view. This proclivity for the polite euphemism can sometimes present a legal puzzle of just the kind posed by Pamela Parenteau's case.

Two of Parenteau's arguments to the appellate court turned on questions of fact—in other words, questions of what really happened that night on the *Scandals* stage during the lingerie fashion show. Did fabric squares really conceal the most intimate part of her breasts? And if they did not, did anyone in the audience really experience any affront?

Questions of fact are always difficult for judges on appellate courts. These judges don't get to see the witnesses, hear their testimony, and assess their credibility firsthand. They have only a cold record to review and must contend with the reality that at least one judge and jury found the evidence to be enough to convict.

In contrast, Parenteau's last argument about what really is or is not a "private part" as those words are used in the statute did not depend on what any witness said in her trial. That question is about the meaning of words in a statute, and figuring out what words mean is the bread and butter of appellate judging.

So the court bypassed Parenteau's first two arguments and homed in on the third. With the legal question thus focused, the court explained that, in its view, "the resolution of this case is quite clear (though perhaps not transparent)." Breasts are not "private parts."

To begin its analysis, the court turned to dictionaries for guidance on the meaning of *private parts*. The *American Heritage Dictionary* defined *private parts* as "genitals." The *Oxford English Dictionary* agreed, defining *private parts* as "the external organs of sex." Not content to leave any nook or cranny unexamined, the court consulted *Gray's Anatomy of the Human Body* and independently verified that the female sex organs were all located in "the vaginal region"—in other words, nowhere near the female breasts.

Thus armed with these authoritative definitional sources, the court's conclusion followed with the inexorable logic of a syllogism. *Private parts* means genitals. Breasts and genitals were, as the court keenly observed, "two separate things." Parenteau was accused only of showing off her breasts, not her genitals. Therefore, she was not guilty. Parenteau's conviction had to be set aside. To the relief of all aficionados of lingerie fashion shows throughout the state, the breasts of Ohio were unchained.

Parenteau's virtue was restored and her reputation cleansed of the stain of the crime of which she had been wrongfully convicted.

As for the arresting deputy, the law reports do not say whether he ever returned to *Scandals* to revisit the scene of this almost-crime to ensure the enforcement of this particular law, but if he did, the court's ruling would compel him to concentrate his gaze on other parts of the anatomy.

Did the court get it right? You decide.

REFLECTIONS

As in the case of the classification of tomatoes as a fruit or vegetable, the resolution of Pamela Parenteau's conviction came down to interpreting a specific phrase in a statute. In Parenteau's case, the crucial words were *private parts*. That phrase, like many words and phrases, including the humble word *vegetable,* can mean different things to different people.

In the *Parenteau* case, unlike in the tomato case, the court deferred to dictionaries and a scientific treatise rather than the judges' own personal understanding of the phrase or a sense of the general public's likely interpretation. In part, this reflects a century in the development of judicial thinking and the rise of judicial deference to experts, including the linguists who write dictionaries.

The *Parenteau* case holds lessons for both rule makers and rule followers. For rule makers, the lesson is that precise words are better than imprecise ones. Euphemisms, circumlocutions, and idioms all run the risk of unexpected interpretations. The more exact the wording, the better.

But this is easier said than done. Human language is riddled with potential uncertainties. Ambiguity can rear up even in words and phrases that might seem obvious and clear. Take the word *night.* It's a common word, one that every child past infancy knows. But does *night* have a precise meaning? Consider, for example, a law that requires bicyclists to use a light when riding at "night." The law demands that we draw a line between day, when riding without a light is permitted, and night, when riding without a light is forbidden. The inevitable question, therefore, is: when exactly does "day" end and "night" begin? Does the night begin the moment the sun disappears over the horizon? Or does night begin only when the twilight afterglow of the setting sun has completely faded from the sky?

Almost any word can be put through the same microscopic analysis. It's the kind of hair-splitting that lawyers thrive on and that drives the general public crazy. And yet, words matter. Lives and livelihoods hang in the balance. Parenteau was convicted of a crime. The exact words of the law she supposedly broke were crucial, and they did not mean what the police officer who arrested her, the prosecutor who prosecuted her, and the trial judge who tried her thought they meant. If Parenteau had not objected to the definition of those words and fought for a different interpretation, she would never have won the exoneration that she was entitled to.

· · · · ·

Questions

1. The court sidestepped the two factual questions that Parenteau's case presented. The court was able to do this because it ruled in Parenteau's favor on her third argument that involved only an interpretation of the words in a statute. If the court had ruled that female breasts were "private parts" under the statute, the court would have had to address Parenteau's two factual claims, that her breast was in fact covered and no one in the audience, not even the arresting officer, was in fact affronted by her performance. For questions of fact, appellate courts are much more deferential to the decisions of trial courts, overturning one only if the trial court has committed "plain error." In contrast, for questions of law, appellate courts freely substitute their own judgment with no deference to the trial court's decision, a standard of review known as "de novo." Why do appellate courts show deference to trial courts for questions of fact but not questions of law? Does this distinction seem reasonable?

2. The court relied on dictionary definitions to conclude that *private parts* meant genitals and not female breasts. The meaning of *private parts* was at least confusing enough to cause a police officer, a prosecutor, and a trial court judge to conclude that breasts fell within the statute's proscription. If a criminal statute is susceptible to more than one meaning, how should a court decide which definition to apply in a particular case?

3. Precise definitions of terms reduce ambiguity and therefore reduce the chances that a rule might be misinterpreted. Is it possible for definitions of legal

terms to be overly precise? What are some of the drawbacks and difficulties with trying to squeeze out all ambiguity from rules?

4. What would happen if Ohio amended the law to prohibit the public exhibition of women's breasts in addition to their "private parts"? Would such a law unlawfully discriminate against women if it allowed men to be topless in public but criminalized the conduct of similarly shirtless women? Should the First Amendment's protection for freedom of speech extend to protecting nude dancing?

Read It Yourself

State v. Parenteau, 564 N.E.2d 505 (Ohio Mun. 1990).

8 Is a Burrito a Sandwich?

Panera Bread was a restaurant that sold sandwiches, coffee, and soup, and what better place to find hungry customers than in a shopping mall located near a well-trafficked highway? White City Shopping Center in Massachusetts seemed to fit the bill and was eager to have Panera as a tenant. Each had something the other wanted. So the two struck a deal.

Panera was ready and willing to pay the shopping center's price for space in the mall, but Panera had one condition. Panera would make money only if hungry shoppers bought their food, but that might not happen if other sandwich places set up shop in the mall. So Panera demanded that the shopping center agree to keep out competing sandwich sellers. Shopping center gets rents. Panera sells sandwiches. Everybody wins. (Except maybe mall shoppers, who have fewer choices of places to eat, but they weren't part of this deal.)

Lawyers were called in to put the agreement down on paper, and this is how the final version read, "Landlord agrees not to enter into a lease, occupancy agreement or license affecting space in the Shopping Center or consent to an amendment to an existing lease permitting use . . . for a bakery or restaurant reasonably expected to have annual sales of sandwiches greater than ten percent (10%) of its total sales."

The shopping center didn't want to tie its hands too much with the no-sandwich-shop clause, and so the lease had a few exclusions. The agreement explicitly stated that the no-sandwich-shop restriction did not prevent the shopping center from bringing in "a Dunkin Donuts–type business," "a business serving near-Eastern food," "restaurants primarily for sit-down table service," "a Jewish delicatessen," or "a KFC restaurant."

A few years went by without incident, but Panera wanted even more protection for its upscale sandwiches and was willing to pay a premium to the shopping center for extended privileges. And so Panera and the shopping center renegotiated the lease to remove some of the exemptions and expand the no-sandwich-shop restriction. After some back and forth, the shopping center agreed that the no-sandwich-shop restriction "shall also apply (without limitation) to a Dunkin Donuts location and to a Jewish-style delicatessen within the Shopping Center."

Throughout their many discussions, however, there was one point neither Panera nor the shopping center thought to negotiate: what exactly is a sandwich—and this, as things turned out, put Panera and the shopping center on a collision course.

Panera thought its intentions had been crystal clear. It wanted to be the exclusive sandwich seller in the mall, so that sandwich-seeking shoppers would have to go to Panera to get their fix. That's why it negotiated the no-sandwich-shop clause in the original lease and then expanded that clause's reach in the amended lease. So it must have been quite a shock when Panera learned that the shopping center was secretly negotiating to bring Qdoba, a Mexican restaurant, to Panera's mall. Who doesn't like a good burrito? And so Qdoba's muscling in on Panera's territory must have felt like an existential threat. No one likes double-dealing. So Panera sued.

In court, Panera argued that the shopping mall had specifically promised that it would not allow into the mall any restaurant that sold "sandwiches" as a central part of its business. In Panera's view, Qdoba's tacos, burritos, and quesadillas were sandwiches, albeit with thin bread instead of thick and with fillings different from Panera's normal fare. By letting Qdoba into the mall, argued Panera, the shopping center had breached the lease and should be stopped. Immediately.

The shopping mall thought Panera's argument was half-baked. A taco is not a sandwich. Neither is a burrito or a quesadilla. To the shopping mall, nothing could be more obvious or self-evident. If common sense were not enough, the shopping mall called a celebrated chef, who confidently testified, "I know of no chef or culinary historian who would call a burrito a sandwich. Indeed, the notion would be absurd to any credible chef or culinary historian." Putting the icing on the cake, the expert opined, "A sandwich is of European roots. . . . A burrito, on the other hand, is specific to Mexico."

Panera didn't buy it. Sandwiches are bread and stuffing. So are tacos. So are burritos. So are quesadillas. They look different. They are prepared differently. But they are essentially the same: bread (however cooked) wrapped around other food.

Anyway, Panera argued, the shopping center knew full well that the whole purpose of the no-sandwich-shop clause was to protect Panera from competing restaurants, so Panera could make more money. The rents Panera had agreed to made sense only if Panera could capture all the revenue from the mall's market for quick and delicious finger food. The elimination of the exclusion for Jewish-style delicatessens demonstrated that both Panera and the shopping mall intended Panera's zone of exclusivity to be as broad as possible. The shopping center's fine slicing of the word *sandwich* made a mockery of their deal.

And so the great question came under judicial review: is a burrito a sandwich? How would you rule?

HOW THE COURT RULED

When it comes to interpreting contracts, the goal of the court is construe the contract as a whole in a reasonable and practical way, consistent with its language, background, and purpose. If the words the parties used in a contract are plain and unambiguous, then the court will give them their ordinary and usual meanings.

For the court, this was not a close question. The entirety of its analysis of whether a burrito is a sandwich fit into one, brief paragraph:

> Given that the term "sandwiches" is not ambiguous and the Lease does not provide a definition of it, this court applies the ordinary meaning of the

word. *New Webster Third International Dictionary* describes a "sandwich" as "two thin pieces of bread, usually buttered, with a thin layer (as of meat, cheese, or savory mixture) spread between them." *Merriam-Webster*, 2002. Under this definition and as dictated by common sense, this court finds that the term "sandwich" is not commonly understood to include burritos, tacos, and quesadillas, which are typically made with a single tortilla and stuffed with a choice filling of meat, rice, and beans.

One definition in one dictionary, with a dash of common sense, was all it took for the court to decide that Panera had no case. If Panera had wanted to include burritos, tacos, and quesadillas in the definition of *sandwiches*, then it should have done so explicitly by providing a definition of the word in the lease. Without such an explicit definition, Panera's interpretation of what constitutes a sandwich was, in the court's view, unreasonable.

Therefore, the shopping center's backroom deal with the Mexican restaurant did not violate the lease. Panera would just have to hope that people in the mood for sandwiches would not be led astray by the allure of tacos, burritos, or quesadillas. The courts would not intervene.

Did the court get this right? You decide.

REFLECTIONS

Take a moment, close your eyes, and imagine a sandwich. What did you see? Did you see what the court in the Panera case defined as a sandwich? Did you see "two thin pieces of bread"? Or was the bread thick, like a kaiser roll? Was the bread "buttered" as the court suggested it would be? Or did it have some other condiment, or did it lack any dressing at all? Did you imagine a thin layer of meat, cheese, or other savory mixture spread between the two thin slices, or did you think of a thick piling up of stuffing that you would have to squeeze with your fingers to fit in your mouth?

Once you have your personal image of an ideal sandwich firmly in mind, ask yourself: does everyone else who does this exercise see the same thing? And how would you know?

Consider the club sandwich. It has three slices of bread instead of two. Or consider the open-faced sandwich. It has only one slice of bread. And what about the wrap, a popular choice among the carb-conscious. It has only one very thin slice of bread wrapped all the way around the filling. Are these sandwiches? If not, why not? If so, why couldn't a quesadilla or burrito be a sandwich too?

The court in the Panera case relied on a single definition of the word *sandwich* found in a single dictionary. And while the definition describes some sandwiches, it is by no means clear that the definition reflects the full variety of things we call sandwiches. Sometimes the most obvious words are the hardest to define.

As with statutes, dictionaries form the basis for interpreting many a contract, but that is not the only possible approach. Consider the case of *Frigaliment Importing v. BNS International Sales*, where a court was called upon to determine what exactly is a "chicken."[1]

In *Frigaliment*, a seller contracted to sell and a buyer contracted to buy "US Fresh Frozen Chicken, Grade A, Government Inspected, Eviscerated." The chicken had to be a certain weight, but otherwise was left undescribed. The seller and buyer thought that they had a meeting of the minds (everyone knows what a chicken is, right?), but when it came time to exchange chickens for cash, they learned that they had a profound disagreement.

The buyer wanted young chickens, suitable for boiling and frying. The seller thought *chicken* meant any member of the species, including culinarily less desirable older birds that the seller called "stewing chickens" and which the buyer disdainfully dismissed as "fowl."

Unlike the court in the Panera case, this court immediately concluded that "the word 'chicken' standing alone is ambiguous." To figure out what the parties meant when they used the word *chicken* in their contract, the court went through an elaborate analysis.

First, the court looked for clues in the contract. The contract said that the birds had to be small (between one and a half and two pounds). The buyer argued that *small* meant that the chicken had to be young. But young and small are not the same thing, and while young chickens might all be small, old chickens can be small as well, so the contract was no help.

Next, the court considered the negotiations. Maybe the buyer and seller said something as they struck the deal that might shed light on their true intentions. But while the parties haggled over price and quantity, the intended item of exchange was blandly described without adornment as "chicken." So this too was no help.

Next, the court considered how people in the chicken business use the word *chicken*, a concept known as "usage of trade." The buyer offered three experts. These witnesses testified that in their commercial contracts they generally understood *chicken* to mean "a broiler" and not "a fowl," but they also admitted they normally used the more specific term *broiler* to avoid precisely the ambiguity that the buyer now faced.

The seller offered experts of its own. These experts testified that "fowl," "broilers," and "fryers" were all chicken. They pointed to Department of Agriculture regulations that described "chickens" as having many different classes. In addition, the seller pointed out that broilers could not be bought at the contracted price, and the buyer knew that, so the buyer must have known that when the seller said it would sell chickens, it meant fowl and not broilers.

The seller argued that the buyer's conduct showed that the buyer understood chickens didn't have to be young broilers, an argument sometimes known as looking at "the course of performance." The seller shipped what the buyer called "fowl," and the buyer accepted the shipment and sold it. This would have been strong evidence, except that upon receipt of the seller's shipment, the buyer immediately protested the quality of the chickens and demanded compensation. Far from showing acquiescence or agreement, the buyer's immediate protests demonstrated that the meaning of *chicken* was disputed from the beginning.

In the end, the court could not establish by an objective measure what exactly the seller and buyer had subjectively intended when they had signed the contract for "chicken." To resolve the lawsuit, the court concluded that it was the buyer's burden (as the plaintiff in the case) to prove that *chicken* meant broilers. Since the evidence was open to debate, the buyer had failed to carry its burden, and so the buyer lost.

The court in the chicken case cast its net far wider than the dictionary and its own notions of common sense. To discover the true meaning of the contested word, the court considered other aspects of the contract: the larger context, the parties' negotiations, the usage of trade, expert testimony, and the course of performance. Although this extraordinary effort resulted in little insight into what the seller and buyer were really thinking in this particular case, the exercise itself demonstrates that defining terms in the face of disagreement does not necessarily have to be left in the hands of the writers of dictionaries.

There are many ways to come to understand the meaning of a word, and it is useful to be aware of different ways to do it, because ambiguity lurks in many more words than people might think.

. . . . .

Questions

1. In the chicken case, the route the court took to interpreting a common word in a contract was very different from that of the court in the Panera case. Is that approach better or worse than the simpler, but less nuanced, approach of the court in the Panera case? When should courts use more searching inquiries? When should they rely on dictionaries and their own commonsense understandings?

2. In addition to relying on a dictionary definition of the word *sandwich*, the court in the Panera case also invoked "common sense." How effective is an appeal to common sense? Different people might have different views about what exactly is common sense. How widely shared must a belief be to qualify as common sense? How is one to know whether a belief is held widely enough to qualify?

3. Both contracts and statutes call for the interpretation of words. Supreme Court Justice Antonin Scalia and coauthor Bryan Garner, in their book *Reading Law: The Interpretation of Legal Texts*, observed that "if you seem to meet an utterance which doesn't have to be interpreted, that is because you have interpreted it already." What strategies might lawmakers and contract writers employ to reduce the amount of interpretation needed? Under what circumstances might lawmakers and contract writers prefer ambiguity?

4. The shopping mall owners' food expert argued that sandwiches were from Europe and burritos were from Mexico. In her article "Is a Burrito a Sandwich? Exploring Race, Class, and Culture in Contract,"[2] Professor Marjorie Florestal asks whether race, class, and culture played a role in the court's summary dismissal of Panera's claim that a taco, burrito, or quesadilla might qualify as a sandwich. What do you think? Could the idea of what a person thinks of as a "sandwich" be a product of that person's race, class, or culture?

5. Can you come up with a definition of *sandwich* that is better than the one the court used in the Panera case? Where do burritos, tacos, and quesadillas fit

under your definition? After you're finished, check out the *Atlantic* magazine's solution to the great sandwich-definition mystery, in "What Is a Sandwich? (No, Seriously, Though)": www.theatlantic.com/video/index/379944/what-is-a-sandwich-no-seriously-though/.

Read It Yourself

White City Shopping Center, LP v. PR Restaurants, LLC dba Bread Panera, 21 Mass. L. Rep. 565 (2006).

9 Haunted Contracts

Helen Ackley lived in an attractive, three-story clapboard house in Nyack, a charming, middle-class suburb of New York City nestled in picturesque rolling hills near the Hudson River. Ackley's house was a lovely Victorian home in a neighborhood of lovely homes. Serene, enchanting, cozy, the house was; but there was one thing about it that was a bit out of the ordinary: the house was haunted, or so said Helen Ackley.

No one knows when ghosts first began to walk the halls of Ackley's Nyack home, and the haunting might have remained entirely a private affair but for a contest in 1977 sponsored by *Reader's Digest*, a popular magazine of the time, which had solicited stories from readers about personal experiences with the paranormal in their homes. Helen Ackley had a story to tell, and tell it she did. In her submission to the magazine, Ackley recounted several close encounters with ghostly spirits over many years. She repeated her spectral-encounter claims in the local Nyack paper on two different occasions. Later, she would tell the *New York Times* about a time she came face to face with a being from the other side. "He was sitting in midair, watching me paint the ceiling in the living room, rocking and back forth," Ackley reported. "I was on an 8-foot stepladder. I asked if he approved of what we were doing to the house, if the colors were to his liking. He smiled and he nodded his head." Spooky stuff, indeed.

The haunting made Ackley's house something of a celebrity in the neighborhood. In 1989, Ackley's home was featured in an exclusive five-home walking tour of Nyack. The tour's brochure described her house as "a riverfront Victorian (with ghost)." Other than this bit of local notoriety, existence at the Ackley residence, both for the living and the undead, went on without notable incident.

In 1990, Ackley was ready to leave the placid waters of the Hudson and relocate to the warmer climes of Florida, so she put her house up for sale. At the same time that Ackley was looking to leave Nyack, Jeffrey Stambovsky was looking for a home for himself and his new wife, and the Ackley house struck him as the perfect place to settle down and raise a family. A contract was prepared. Papers were signed. Money changed hands. Everything went swimmingly—or so it seemed.

Then the Stambovskys learned about the ghosts.

Suddenly, the charming home by the river didn't seem so charming. The thought of living with ghosts was more than the Stambovskys could bear. They wanted out of the deal and their money back. Ackley refused. A deal is, after all, a deal—ghosts or no ghosts.

So the Stambovskys sued. In court, the Stambovskys claimed that they had been misled about the nature of the property they were buying. They had proceeded with the normal diligence of a normal home buyer. They had walked through the property to inspect it for defects and had conducted a title search to make sure that Ackley really had the right to sell the house. It never occurred to them to check for ghosts.

If they had known that the house was haunted, the Stambovskys explained, they would never have agreed to buy it. Ackley knew about the haunting. She had told her neighbors and even published an account in a national magazine. It was wrong, they argued, for Ackley to keep this crucial information to herself. Ackley had a duty to disclose defects in the property that she knew about and that a reasonable inspection would not turn up. The Stambovskys had no reason to look for ghosts. The haunting, therefore, caught them completely by surprise and materially changed the deal. The house was not what they thought it was, so they should get their money back.

For her part, Ackley was willing to tolerate ghosts, but not dishonorable people who failed to live up to their promises. When it comes to buying a house, the ancient rule was caveat emptor, "buyer beware." The fact that ghosts were in the house was well known. The neighbors knew. The story had been in a national magazine. Had hauntings been something the Stambovskys cared about, they could easily have discovered that phantoms inhabited the house. All they had to do was talk to a single neighbor. But they had not made any kind of inquiry at all. Shame on them. They should have done a better job of checking out the house before signing on the dotted line.

More to the point, Ackley argued, the house wasn't actually defective. Everyone knows that ghosts don't exist. It was a perfectly ordinary house, not haunted at all. To the extent a seller has any duty to disclose defects, surely that duty extends only to real defects and not to imaginary ones. There was no evidence that poltergeists were in the house, nor could there be. The Stambovskys couldn't possibly be worried about fictitious phantoms. The supposed concerns over spooks and spirits were likely trumped up to cover up the fact that the Stambovskys simply regretted buying the house. But regret isn't a reason to get out of a contract.

Should the Stambovskys get their money back? Ackley did not disclose that the house was haunted, or at least that she had publicly claimed it was. Did she breach a duty to deal with her buyers in good faith? Or should the Stambovskys be held to the contract they signed, either because it was up to them to fully inspect the property they were buying or because the house wasn't really haunted so there was no real defect for them to complain about? How would you rule?

HOW THE COURT RULED

The heart of the Stambovskys' claim was that Helen Ackley had sold them a house she knew was haunted without telling them about this material

· defect. The first question for the court, therefore, was whether the house really was haunted. This was a tricky question. The Stambovskys had not actually seen any ghosts, and a trial about whether ghosts are really real could degenerate into a farce. This was territory on which the court preferred not to tread. But how could the question be avoided? The court came up with a neat solution.

The court noted that Ackley had made numerous public statements claiming that the house was haunted. Without deciding whether ghosts are fact or fiction, the court held her to her word. Ackley said that the house was haunted; and therefore, the court would not allow her to deny that fact once it became inconvenient in a lawsuit. (The technical term for not letting a person change a previously taken position is *estoppel*. Ackley was estopped from denying the house was haunted.)

The court agreed that the doctrine of caveat emptor requires buyers to act prudently to assess the value of property before they buy it. But prudence does not require perfect knowledge or endless inquiries. In the court's opinion, the Stambovskys had acted more than reasonably. They had inspected the premises and conducted a title search, but a reasonable inspection could not be expected to search for, much less discover, the presence of ghosts. Indeed, it's not at all clear where the Stambovskys might have found a qualified inspector experienced in the detection of paranormal spirits. Quoting a song from the 1980s movie *Ghostbusters*, the court asked rhetorically: "Who you gonna call?"

It was true that the Stambovskys could have asked around the neighborhood to see if anybody had heard about otherworldly activity at the house. But in the court's opinion no reasonable person would undertake such an inquiry.

Ackley had created the situation that impaired the value of her house by telling the world that it was haunted. In the court's view, it was unfair for her to force the sale upon a buyer who didn't know about her claims and who had no reason to inquire whether the owner had ever publicly proclaimed that the house was haunted.

Therefore, the contract was rescinded, the Stambovskys got their money back, and Helen Ackley had to find another buyer for her house. Did the court get it right? You decide.

REFLECTIONS

Courts must resolve disputes in accordance with the facts and the law. Figuring out the law can be a challenging intellectual exercise, especially in the face of ambiguous requirements with multiple possible meanings; but figuring out the facts can, in some cases, border on the impossible.

In the *Stambovsky* case, the Stambovskys wanted their money back because the house they bought was haunted. Imagine what a trial might have looked like if the Stambovskys had been required to provide proof of ghosts in the house. Whether ghosts even exist would be a central question. Witnesses would be called to testify about whether they had ever personally seen a ghost. Some would say no. Some would say yes. Experts in the paranormal would be summoned to give their learned opinions based on study, research, and experiment. Some would say no scientific proof of ghosts exists. Others would disagree.

One might hope that for this question the weight of evidence would tip the scales of justice decisively to one side, but the outcome of a trial on the existence of ghosts might be hard to predict. According to one poll, 48 percent of Americans said they believed in ghosts, and 22 percent said that they personally had seen or felt the presence of a ghost.[1] In other words, for every person who says ghosts don't exist, there is another who says they do. The outcome of a trial over the existence of ghosts might be as predictable as a coin flip.

No matter the difficulty of the dispute, however, courts have no choice but to rule in favor of one side or the other. Even if the court were to declare that the evidence is hopelessly tangled, and that therefore a reasonable conclusion one way or another could not be reached, the court would still have to resolve the dispute by declaring one of the parties to be the winner.

In cases with challenging problems of proof, sometimes the courts draw a line between Truth with a capital *T* and a smaller truth that can be invoked for the limited purpose of resolving the dispute at hand. The *Stambovsky* case illustrates one tool that courts frequently turn to as a shortcut to this more local truth: the party admission.

The party admission is a statement by one of the parties to the lawsuit that the *opposing* party uses against him or her. Generally, statements made out of court, also known as "hearsay," are looked on with suspicion, so hearsay statements may be introduced in court only when they meet the requirements of a narrow class of exceptions. The party admission is one of those exceptions. The premise of the party admission is that it is safe to presume that people generally say things that put themselves in a favorable light, and that when they do not, then those damaging statements are much more likely to be true. Parties may try to explain away their unfavorable statements—maybe they made mistake, or a statement was taken out of context, or it reflected only part of what a person really thought—but such statements come into evidence and can be used against them. Words matter. People must live with the consequences of what they say.

This notion that people wouldn't say things that damage themselves unless those things were really true applies to witnesses generally, not just to parties to the lawsuit. When the principle is applied to witnesses who are not parties to a lawsuit, it's called an "admission against interest." The idea is similar. We expect people to say only favorable things about themselves. When they don't, that's unusual, and those self-damaging statements may be considered in a trial, even if they are technically hearsay because they were made out of court and not under oath. The difference between an admission against interest and a party admission is that a party admission could be anything, not simply something obviously damaging (although it usually is— why else would an opponent want to use it?), while an admission against interest must be damaging to the witness or else it is not admissible.

The party admission allowed the court to resolve the haunted house case. The court did not have to decide whether ghosts are really real as a matter of scientific and empirical fact. Instead, the court could take a shortcut. Helen Ackley said her house was haunted. That was against her interests in this lawsuit, so the court could conclude that, for this one dispute, she had to live with her earlier claims and the court could presume that the house was truly haunted. This presumption may have been just a truth with a little *t*, but it helped the court do justice with a capital *J*.

EPILOGUE

After losing her case in court, Helen Ackley put her house up for sale a second time. This time, however, she was careful to disclose in the advertisement that the house was haunted. What happened next must have surprised Ackley as much as any paranormal housemates might have done. It turned out that many people relished the idea of sharing a home with spirits. Buyers came out in droves and the value of the house skyrocketed, netting Ackley a quick sale and a tidy profit above the previous sale.

. . . . .

Questions

1. What could Ackley have done to make it more likely that a court would enforce the contract of sale with the Stambovskys? Is it reasonable to expect a home seller like Ackley to take those actions?

2. Would you live in a house that a previous owner claims to have been haunted? What if a person had died in the house? Would it matter if a person died from cancer as opposed to old age or some other cause of death? How would you feel living in a house where a person had been murdered? Some states require that sellers disclose deaths in houses to prospective buyers. Are those laws fair and reasonable?

Read It Yourself

Stambovsky v. Ackley, 169 A.D.2d 254 (NY 1991).

James Barron, "Phones Ringing (Eerily?) for Nyack Spook Home," *New York Times,* March 20, 1990, www.nytimes.com/1990/03/20/nyregion /phones-ringing-eerily-for-nyack-spook-home.html.

Mark Kavanagh, "The Ghost of Nyack," last edited on December 5, 2010, www .ktransit.com/Kavanagh/Ghost/ghost-background.htm.

10   That Jet Won't Fly

The deal seemed too good to be true, but the offer was right there on television, in full, living color, streaming into his living room, a commercial from
one of the biggest companies in the country. And while you can't believe
everything you see or read, wasn't there truth in advertising—so maybe it
was true after all? There was only one way to find out. John Leonard, teenager and budding entrepreneur, was going to buy himself a fighter jet.

In October 1995, the makers of the Pepsi and Diet Pepsi soft drinks
wanted a new marketing campaign to capture the imagination of the all-
important teenage demographic, which at the time Pepsi liked to call the
"Pepsi Generation." Pepsi drinkers in their teenage years would become
Pepsi drinkers for life, or so the thinking went. And what better way to
attract new customers than by giving away free stuff?

Pepsi's marketing team went to work. They dreamed up a promotion
where Pepsi customers would buy soft drinks and collect "Pepsi Points"
from specially marked packages. The Pepsi Points could be redeemed for
prizes. The plan seemed foolproof. Pepsi sells more soft drinks. Its most
loyal customers earn fun prizes. What could go wrong?

For the Pepsi Points promotion to succeed, Pepsi needed to win the
hearts and minds of teenagers, and to do that, Pepsi needed to get their

attention. The company's marketing gurus thought they had come up with just the thing. What would be the ultimate teenage fantasy? (No, not *that*.) How about something that would blow away the indignity of school buses and the tedium of classes? What about flying to school in a—wait for it—fighter jet? That spark of marketing creativity became the focal point for a dramatic and eye-catching television commercial. To make sure it worked with the target demographic, before for turning it loose for a national run, Pepsi tested the commercial on the television airwaves in Washington State, where young John Leonard happened to live. The commercial went something like this:

The scene opens on a quiet suburban street. A paperboy rides his bike, tossing newspapers onto the porches of neat, two-story houses with well-kempt lawns and well-trimmed hedges. The sun glints brightly through the trees as birds sing a peaceful song in the background. All is well in this well-ordered world. Maybe too well. Maybe too ordered. A whiff of staleness hangs over the idyllic scene.

The paperboy tosses a paper onto the stoop of one particular house, and the crack of a military drum signals that the serenity of this suburban scene is about to be shaken up. Across the bottom of the screen splash the words "MONDAY 7:58 am," like in a spy movie. Martial music begins to play as the camera cuts to an interior bedroom and turns to a good-looking teenage boy preparing to leave for school, dressed in a shirt bearing the Pepsi logo, naturally. The snap of the drums rattles again as the words "T-SHIRT 75 PEPSI POINTS" slide across the bottom of the screen. The teenager heads out of his room and down the hallway sporting a leather jacket. Again the drum sounds, and more words appear, this time: "LEATHER JACKET 1450 PEPSI POINTS."

As the teenager emerges from his house, a flash of brightness from the sun assaults his eyes. Without missing a beat, he pulls out a pair of sunglasses. More drums and another subtitle follow: "SHADES 175 pepsi points."

A deep-voiced narrator intones in an authoritative baritone: "Introducing the new Pepsi Stuff catalog." The cover of the catalog fills the screen.

The commercial continues. Three young boys sit in front of a high school building. One pores over the Pepsi Stuff catalog like he's looking at a centerfold, while his companions smile and sip Pepsi from cans.

Something rushing overhead pulls their attention skyward. The boys stare up, awestruck, as a foreboding shadow passes by. Gale force winds create a tornado of paper in a nearby classroom, disrupting the dull lesson and stirring the first signs of life in the hapless students trapped at their desks.

The source of this storm is finally revealed. A Harrier jet swoops down and lands next to a bicycle rack just outside the school. The force from the jet's exhaust rips the pants off of an unsuspecting teacher. The voiceover states, "Now, the more Pepsi you drink, the more great stuff you're gonna get."

The cockpit opens. Who is piloting this fantastic, flying, metal beast? It's the teenager from the opening scene, beaming from the cockpit like he just won the lottery. He's not wearing a helmet, and his hair is flowing freely in the breeze. Laughing, he shouts, "Sure beats the bus!"

The military drum kicks in one last time, and across the bottom of the screen appear the words "HARRIER FIGHTER 7,000,000 PEPSI POINTS." The music hits a crescendo and the words "Drink Pepsi—Get Stuff" splash across the screen as the commercial comes to a close.

The Pepsi marketing team had worked their magic. With a commercial as exciting and appealing as that, how could red-blooded American teen-agers resist imagining themselves sitting in that cockpit, soaking up the astonishment and admiration of principals, peers, and teachers? Of course, the reverie was pure fantasy. A person would have to drink Pepsi night and day for more than a lifetime to accumulate the required seven million Pepsi Points—soaring teenage dreams once again cast against stony adult reality. But there is a difference between the truly impossible and the merely extremely difficult, and in that difference lies opportunity for those with the spirit, initiative, and resourcefulness to seize it.

John Leonard had just such a spirit. "Adventurous" is how he described himself. Leonard studied the Pepsi Stuff catalog, where he learned two interesting things. First, the catalog made no mention of the Harrier jet advertised in the television commercial—but that omission did not dis-courage this dauntless member of the Pepsi Generation, because the jet was plainly advertised in the television commercial. More importantly, he noticed that Pepsi Points could be purchased for ten cents each. In other words, the seven million Pepsi Points needed for the Harrier jet could be had for a mere seven hundred thousand dollars. While seven hundred thousand dollars is a lot of money, a Harrier jet cost at the time close to twenty-three million dollars. Seven hundred thousand was a steal. All he needed was the money.

Leonard did what any entrepreneur with an arbitrage opportunity would do. He cobbled together a group of investors. Flush with cash, Leonard filled out the required form in the Pepsi Stuff catalog, included a handful of Pepsi Points from the few sodas he had bought, sent in a check for the necessary amount, and politely requested that Pepsi send him the Harrier jet they promised in the commercial. Then he waited for his jet to arrive. It didn't come.

Pepsi assumed that Leonard's application was a joke. The idea that Pepsi would give a teenage kid a military fighter plane was ridiculous. Instead, they sent him some coupons for free soda. Leonard was not amused. Strongly worded letters were exchanged. Lawsuits followed.

Leonard made a straightforward argument. In its commercial, Pepsi said that you could get a Harrier fighter jet for seven million Pepsi Points. Pepsi had posted those words right on the screen, just like it had for T-shirts, sunglasses, and leather jackets. Pepsi's promise could not have been clearer.

Leonard had done everything Pepsi had asked by sending in the required number of Pepsi Points in the form of a check for ten cents a point, as Pepsi itself had specified in its Pepsi Stuff catalog. Maybe Pepsi had thought no one would ever claim the jet—seven million Pepsi Points was certainly a formidable number—but Leonard had taken Pepsi's challenge and met it. Pepsi should do the right thing, honor its promises, and hand over the jet. (Cash in lieu of the jet would probably be okay too.)

In the language of the law of contracts, Leonard argued that the commercial was an offer and his submission of the check for the Pepsi Points was an acceptance. A binding agreement had been formed between the two of them. The court, Leonard urged, should make Pepsi keep its word.

Pepsi countered that the ad was a joke. No one could seriously believe— not even Leonard—that Pepsi would hand over a twenty-three million-dollar military fighter to a teenager to fly around his neighborhood, and certainly not for only seven hundred thousand dollars.

The commercial was just a fanciful advertisement, not an offer to enter into a contract that Leonard could unilaterally accept. Pepsi pointed out that the commercial referred people to the Pepsi Stuff catalog, and the catalog made no mention of jets, Harrier or otherwise.

Leonard shot back that the commercial was like a reward poster. If you hang a sign and tell people that you will pay a reward if they do something for you—like find a wayward puppy or return a lost wallet—then if someone does what you ask, you have an obligation to pay the posted reward. Pepsi challenged people to submit seven million Pepsi Points. True, Pepsi might have thought that it would be impossible for anyone to accumulate that many Pepsi Points. True, Pepsi might have sincerely believed that a teenage boy had no business owning a fighter jet. But Pepsi's opinions were beside the point. Once Pepsi made the offer, then like the person who posts the reward, Pepsi had to pay if someone performed the specified task. Leonard had performed. Now it was Pepsi's turn.

Thus, the argument was joined. How would you rule?

HOW THE COURT RULED

John Leonard had two ways to win his case. First, he could prove that the television commercial was an offer to enter into a contract that he accepted, thus forming a binding agreement. Alternatively, he could prove that the commercial was like a reward that he had claimed by performing the task Pepsi set out for him. The court took up each argument in turn.

Not every ad is an offer to enter into a contract. In fact, most aren't. Stores sell out. Prices fluctuate. Markets are in a constant state of flux. Retailers change prices and inventory strategies every day, sometimes every minute or every hour. The law accommodates this commercial flexibility by treating most advertisements as merely invitations to negotiate. The ad entices a customer to come to the store, and then the customer and the seller work out a mutually agreeable deal at the moment the customer is ready to buy and the seller is ready to sell. That's how most ads work—but not all.

If the advertisement makes clear that the seller is committed to the transaction with no room for negotiation, then the ad will be considered an offer. In that case, if a customer accepts the offer, the seller must go through with the sale. If a car dealer, for example, runs an ad offering to sell brand-new cars worth fifty thousand dollars for only one thousand dollars to the first ten customers who arrive at the dealer's lot next Saturday at 9 A.M. sharp, the dealer will not be able to change his mind and limit the sale to the first five who arrive. Even so, while offer-advertisements are possible, they are rare and decidedly the exception, not the rule.

What about Pepsi's commercial? Was it specific enough to be an offer? The court thought not. By referring to the terms in the Pepsi Stuff catalog, the commercial made clear that there was more to the deal than what flashed across the TV screen. Indeed, the commercial did not explain how a person could redeem Pepsi Points for prizes at all. That information was only in the catalog.

The catalog, however, made no mention of the Harrier jet from the commercial. Even if it had, the catalog still wouldn't have been a firm offer, because it lacked words limiting who might accept the offer, such as "first come, first served." Therefore, neither the commercial nor the catalog was specific enough to support a contract. So Leonard's offer-and-acceptance theory was out.

What about the reward theory? Rewards are claimed by performing the task the person posting the reward requests. If, in the throes of grief at the disappearance of a beloved cat, a stricken owner announces to the world that she will pay one thousand dollars for the feline's safe return, and then when someone shows up with the cat in one hand, and the other hand held out for the reward, the owner isn't allowed, in a more sober moment, to renege because she never liked the cat all that much anyway. Extravagant offers of reward, even if later regretted, will be enforced, like it or not.

The most famous example of this legal principle at play, and a staple of first-year law-school classes, is the case of the carbolic smoke ball. A flu epidemic was ravaging London, and one company arose amid the suffering to sell a surefire device to ward off the dread disease: a carbolic smoke ball. The smoke ball was a rubber ball filled with carbolic acid attached to a tube that you stuck up your nose, ostensibly to clear out the flu virus. The company ran an ad claiming that no one—*no one!*—had contracted influenza after using their carbolic smoke ball three times a day for two weeks. And so sure were the manufacturers of the effectiveness of their wonder product that they printed an ad in the London newspapers, pledging that if anyone used the carbolic smoke ball as directed and did get sick, they would personally pay that person one hundred pounds in cold, hard cash.

You can probably guess what happened next. Louisa Elizabeth Carlill saw the ad, bought the magical smoke ball, used it religiously for two months, and then got sick with the flu. She demanded the one hundred pounds the Carbolic Smoke Ball Company had promised in its advertisement, but the company didn't want to pay.

The company tried to argue that the ad was just an ad, an invitation to enter into a contract, but not an enforceable promise without some further agreement on the company's part. The court would have none of it. The ad, the court ruled, was an offer of reward, and Carlill had justly claimed the reward by doing what the Carbolic Smoke Ball Company had challenged its customers to do and had said was impossible: contract influenza after using their product as directed. The ad induced Carlill to purchase the company's product and use it daily for two months, and so the company had to live up to the extravagant promises of its ad.

Leonard seized on the Carbolic Smoke Ball case, strenuously arguing that just as Carlill got her hundred pounds, he should get his Harrier jet. Pepsi had set out a challenge in its commercial, just as the Carbolic Smoke Ball Company had, and he had met the challenge and earned the reward Pepsi had promised.

Not so fast, said the court. The commercial itself did not explain what a person had to do to claim the Harrier jet as a reward. Yes, the Pepsi commercial stated that seven million Pepsi Points were required, but it also referred to the Pepsi Stuff catalog, and the catalog made no mention of Harrier jets. Moreover, the catalog itself imposed extra terms through the requirement of the submission of the order form. Since the jet was not in the catalog, reasoned the court, Leonard could not claim it by using the catalog's forms. Thus, the reward theory failed as well.

More importantly, aside from the technicalities of advertisement offers or the legal doctrines on rewards, the commercial was, the court observed, one big joke. No reasonable person could seriously believe that Pepsi would deliver twenty-three-million-dollar military jets to teenagers as a way of helping them avoid the indignities of going to school by bus. The commercial was a fanciful and absurdist fantasy at every turn, from the military music in the background, to the teacher whose pants were blown away, to the teenage boy jauntily piloting the plane to the lawn of his school. Buying a twenty-three-million-dollar jet for seven hundred thousand dollars in purchased Pepsi Points was a deal that was too good to be true. Any reasonable person would know that, and Leonard probably knew it too.

Soft drink companies don't give away military fighter jets, no matter how many of their sodas you drink. So Leonard did not get his fighter jet. The commercial was not a contract. It was not an offer of a reward. It was a joke.

Did the court get this one right or wrong? You decide.

REFLECTIONS

The paradigmatic model for how a contract is formed goes something like this. A competent adult walks into a market where rows upon rows of sellers vie for the buyer's attention, offering all manner of wares for sale. The buyer sees something that catches her eye. The buyer and seller discuss the price and any other terms of the transaction. They haggle, they bargain, they go back and forth, until all is agreed upon. The buyer gives the seller money or some other thing of value. The seller delivers to the buyer the good or performs the service. The transaction is complete.

Most modern consumer contracts bear only the faintest resemblance to this model transaction. Sellers are often large corporations, whose human decision-makers the typical consumer never, ever meets. For these goods and services, the corporations dictate the terms of every transaction. There is no negotiation. Usually, there is no one even to talk to. Consumers can either take it or leave it.

Credit cards, insurance, and software are just a few examples of common products sold with complex contracts with no room for negotiation. Every retail store sale comes with a long set of corporate policies, terms, and conditions. As simple a transaction as paying to park your car in a lot means having to accept preprinted terms that are spit out by an automated kiosk. If you don't like it, you can talk to the machine—and when you're done doing that, you either accept the terms or you leave.

Software is the paradigmatic example of the modern trend of taking the negotiation out of consumer contracts. Before a person can use software or access many services on the Internet, the person must agree to what is known as an end user license agreement, or EULA (pronounced YOU-la). The EULA sets out the terms and conditions that the person accepts in exchange for the right to use the software. Reject the EULA and the software closes. No negotiation. Game over.

The number of people who have read from start to finish every software EULA presented to them must be minuscule. (Have you ever read even one?) It's easy to understand why. EULAs generally run many pages of difficult-to-understand legal terminology. Some of the provisions can leave even experienced lawyers scratching their heads. For example, the EULA for Apple's iTunes music software has a provision requiring users to promise not to use the iTunes music application for "the development, design, manufacture or production of nuclear, missiles, or chemical or biological weapons."[1] That's quite a detailed requirement for software that is essentially a digital jukebox. What else might you have agreed to in some EULA? Who knows?[2]

These form agreements and their dense jungles of legalese are easy to ignore. Most people assume that they probably won't have any troubles, and for most people most of the time, that assumption proves true. But that doesn't mean these documents that people never read have no meaning, as John Leonard found out in his dispute with Pepsi.

In the *Leonard* case, Leonard felt that the bargain he struck with Pepsi was based on Pepsi's television commercial. The commercial said seven million Pepsi Points would buy him a Harrier jet. But there was fine print. The commercial made reference to the Pepsi catalog, and that catalog provided additional terms about what could be bought with Pepsi Points and how these items could be bought.

In his quest for his very own jet, Leonard could not escape the catalog's limitations and qualifications on the television commercial. By entering Pepsi's promotion, Leonard accepted Pepsi's terms. The lesson is that while limitations on the content of form agreements exist, consumers can't count on courts ignoring the fine print.

So next time you are confronted with a form contract as a hurdle before completing a consumer transaction, before you click *agree*—as you almost certainly will, because refusing would shut you out of large swaths of the modern economy—you may want to pause and remember that you may be held to those terms that you didn't read.

.   .   .   .   .

Questions

1. In this case, John Leonard did not spend much money out of his own pocket trying to acquire the Harrier jet. He purchased enough Pepsi products to acquire the minimum number of fifteen Pepsi Points (not even enough for a T-shirt); and for the other needed points, he sent in a check, which Pepsi duly returned. Would Leonard still have gotten nothing from the court if he had actually spent seven hundred thousand dollars to acquire the Pepsi Points and therefore been out of pocket a substantial sum of money? Even if Leonard had not been entitled to a Harrier jet, would he have been able to get anything from Pepsi?

2. The court ruled that the offer of a Harrier jet in the commercial was obviously a joke, and that because of all the fanciful elements in the commercial, no reasonable person could think otherwise. Could reasonable minds disagree about that conclusion? After all, the Harrier jet offer appeared in the same form as the offers of T-shirts, sunglasses, and leather jackets—all of which were real offers. How should a court decide whether no reasonable person could think something?

3. After Leonard brought his lawsuit, Pepsi modified the commercial to include the words "just kidding" underneath the words that declared a Harrier jet could be had for seven million Pepsi Points. Should this later-added disclaimer play any role in Leonard's lawsuit? For example, should adding the disclaimer be seen as an admission by Pepsi that, without the disclaimer, reasonable people might believe that the Harrier jet offer was real? Or should it be considered as merely an extra precaution to protect Pepsi from future frivolous arguments?

Read It Yourself

Leonard v. Pepsico, Inc., 88 F. Supp. 2d 116 (SDNY 1999).
Carlill v. Carbolic Smoke Ball Co., 1 Q.B. 256 (Court of Appeal 1892).

11 What Have You Done for Me Lately?

What is the value of saving a man's life? To the man, it's immeasurable. To his heirs, maybe not so much.

On August 3, 1925, a mill worker named Webb was working his regular shift at the W. T. Smith Lumber Company. He was clearing the upper floor of the mill of old pine blocks by tossing them out an opening onto the ground below. The blocks were big and bulky—seventy-five pounds each—but Webb was strong, and he was used to hard work.

On that August day, J. Greeley McGowin was out walking. And as luck (or maybe more aptly, cruel misfortune) would have it, McGowin's journey led him past the mill where Webb was methodically muscling the massive blocks out the window overhead. If McGowin had looked up, he might have seen the prodigious pine block in Webb's steady grip swinging toward the second-floor opening with a trajectory that put block and body on a collision course. With a moment to reflect, McGowin no doubt would have concluded that the weight of the block would crush and kill him instantly, and he would have taken immediate and rapid evasive action. But McGowin did not look up, and his destiny hurtled toward him with him none the wiser.

Webb, however, did look down. To his horror, he saw that McGowin innocently stood on the very spot where the pine block he was at that very moment heaving was sure to land. No one would have faulted Webb if he had let the block fly. The block was already in motion. Its momentum was impossible to stop. The block slipping from Webb's grasp, falling to the ground, and crushing McGowin would have been nothing more than the operation of the immutable laws of physics and motion. McGowin's death would be chalked up to tragic accident, a horrible case of being in the wrong place at the wrong time.

Webb wasn't going to let that happen, not if he had any chance to do anything about it. He could not stop the block from flying—it was too late for that—but using his great strength, Webb threw his weight against the block's momentum. As the block reached the peak of its swing, Webb, instead of releasing his fingers, redoubled his grip and dug in. The block went over the edge, and Webb, holding on with all his might, went with it.

In the seconds that followed, while Webb and block fell through the air, Webb twisted his body, gripped the block to his chest, and, turning the block, changed its course just enough to avoid McGowin. Through Webb's heroic act, McGowin escaped his brush with deadly peril completely unharmed. Webb was not so lucky.

The fall tore apart Webb's body. His right leg snapped on impact. Between the block and the ground, the heel of his right foot was torn completely off. Webb's mighty right arm was shattered. Webb lived, but these crippling injuries meant that he would never be able to work again.

McGowin was overwhelmed by Webb's selfless act of sacrifice to save his life. He visited Webb while Webb was recovering from his injuries to express his gratitude for a debt he could never repay. McGowin was a man of some means, and he was moved by the fact that Webb would never be the same man he was before the accident. This was a time before government disability and health insurance. Webb and his family faced destitution, with the main breadwinner unable to return to work. McGowin wanted to do something for Webb, so he promised him that he would pay Webb fifteen dollars every two weeks for the rest of Webb's life.[1] It was not a lot of money given the price Webb had had to pay to get it, but he was glad to have the help.

McGowin was a man of his word. He never forgot Webb or the sacrifice Webb had made for him. Every two weeks, McGowin dutifully sent Webb his fifteen dollars, until January 1, 1934—the day McGowin died.

McGowin was gone, but Webb was still alive, living with the same injuries he had sustained saving McGowin's life. McGowin had promised to make the payments to Webb for the rest of *Webb's* life, and Webb had every expectation that the payments would continue to come. They did not.

McGowin's heirs, it seemed, placed a much lower value on the service Webb had performed. Webb protested that McGowin had made him a promise that his heirs (or more precisely, McGowin's estate) had a legal obligation to honor. The heirs countered that there may have been a promise, but there had been no contract. Without a contract, McGowin's payments to Webb were gifts, which could be stopped whenever the giver decided to stop giving. And the heirs had decided the time had come to stop giving to Webb.

A contract, the heirs argued, requires that both parties promise to do something for each other. A one-sided promise with nothing in return is not a contract. It lacks consideration, a fundamental requirement for the formation of an enforceable contract. It was true that Webb saved McGowin's life, but, the heirs pointed out, that happened *before* McGowin promised to pay Webb his fifteen dollars every other week. When McGowin made his promise to Webb, Webb didn't make any promise back. Therefore, the heirs argued, there was no contract. No contract meant no legal obligation. No legal obligation meant they could stop the biweekly payments, and Webb was out of luck.

Webb protested that saving a man's life ought to count for something. McGowin thought that Webb's sacrifice was enough to commit himself to paying Webb a modest sum for the rest of Webb's life. If that was good enough for McGowin, it should be good enough for his heirs and for the courts.

The heirs stood on their legal point, a technicality to some perhaps, but also a cornerstone of the law of contracts: no consideration, no contract. Webb appealed to a sense of justice. He had provided a valuable (some might say invaluable or priceless) service in saving McGowin's life, for which he should get credit even though this act came before McGowin's promise and not after. As the litigants came to court, the Great Depression was in full swing. Money was tight all around. How would you rule?

HOW THE COURT RULED

McGowin's heirs were right. A promise without consideration—that is, something given in return—is not a contract. If they had been taking an introductory contracts class in law school, the heirs would have received top marks.

McGowin's heirs were also right that the promise that Webb wanted to enforce was made *after* Webb had rendered his services. But these weren't just any services. Webb had saved J. Greeley McGowin's life. McGowin might not have owed Webb a legal debt for his sacrifice, but he did owe him a moral one.

McGowin himself, observed the court, recognized his moral obligation to the man who had saved his life at the price of grievous and permanent injury to himself. McGowin's promise to pay Webb a small stipend so the man who saved his life would not be utterly destitute was not just a gratuitous act of spontaneous generosity. It was the fulfillment of a moral obligation. And this, for the court, made all the difference.

Webb's act of self-sacrifice was a gift to McGowin, and the law would have said nothing if McGowin had turned his back on Webb without further thought. In that case, McGowin would have had to answer only to his conscience. But if a person comes into the moral debt of another person by receiving a benefit he has not earned, and if that person makes a promise as a way of trying to repay a part of that moral debt, the court reasoned, then the law of contracts would not stand in the way of having that promise fulfilled.

Webb had paid a grievous price to earn McGowin's promised payments. That was sufficient consideration. McGowin's heirs, however correct they might be according to the letter of contract law, were wrong in the eyes of justice. The court ordered the promise fulfilled and ordered McGowin's heirs to fulfill it.

Did the court get it right? You decide.

REFLECTIONS

In 2005, Judge John Roberts was nominated to be chief justice of the U.S. Supreme Court. To become the country's top judicial officer, Roberts first had to win the support and confirmation of the U.S. Senate. At the time, one of the concerns of the senators was about judges overstepping their proper role of deciding cases in accordance with the law and instead intruding on the lawmaking role of Congress by creating new rules of the judges' own devising. To ease the senators' concerns, Roberts made this famous statement:

> My personal appreciation that I owe a great debt to others reinforces my view that a certain humility should characterize the judicial role. Judges and justices are servants of the law, not the other way around. Judges are like umpires. Umpires don't make the rules; they apply them. The role of an umpire and a judge is critical. They make sure everybody plays by the rules. But it is a limited role. Nobody ever went to a ball game to see the umpire. . . . I will decide every case based on the record, according to the rule of law, without fear or favor, to the best of my ability. And I will remember that it's my job to call balls and strikes and not to pitch or bat.[2]

Roberts went on to win confirmation by the Senate and to become the seventeenth chief justice of the United States. Comparing judges to umpires at a baseball game is an inspired analogy. In the sense that Roberts used the word, umpires are completely impartial and enforce rules as written without regard for who wins or loses. They are the very embodiment of fairness and the rule of law.

At the same time, in any particular baseball game, the strike zone is defined by what the umpire says it is. Coaches, players, and fans are not allowed to argue an umpire's decision about whether a pitch is a ball or a strike. If an umpire calls a ball a strike or a strike a ball, the call stands. This is a lot like how the legal system works.

Charles Evan Hughes, the eleventh chief justice of the United States, quipped, "We are under a Constitution, but the Constitution is what the judges say it is." Of course, the decisions of one judge can be appealed to other judges, unless of course, the judges making the decision are on the Supreme Court, in which case, theirs is the final word. We like to think that judges decide cases and umpires call balls and strikes correctly every time, but the world isn't that perfect. Judges are human beings, and to their judgments they bring their foibles, prejudices, preconceptions, and preoccupations, as well as their biases, blind spots, and errors.

The *Webb* case is a good example of the blurriness of calling balls and strikes in legal cases. The judges brushed past the settled law which says that contracts require a mutual exchange of value, and that past consideration does not support a future contract, and reached the novel result that Webb had an enforceable claim against McGowin's estate because of an undefined moral obligation. In ruling for the crippled hero and against the ungrateful heirs, did the judges evenhandedly apply the law, or did they go beyond the law to help out a sympathetic, but legally unentitled, plaintiff? Of course, there is no way to know what the judges were really thinking, and it's possible that they themselves didn't consciously know everything that influenced their decision. It is not the case that being a sympathetic litigant guarantees victory in every case, but it helps.

．　　．　　．　　．　　．

Questions

1. The court departed from the normal rule of contracts—which states that something of value must be given for a promise in order to form a contract—by ruling that McGowin owed Webb a "moral obligation." While Webb was certainly sympathetic and deserving, are there any dangers in the court's approach? How should courts be guided in deciding when an exception to a general rule is a reasonable accommodation for a sympathetic case?

2. Do you think the result of this case would have been different if the service Webb had rendered had been less heroic than saving McGowin's life by leaping out of the second story of a building and wrestling a seventy-five-pound weight away from the head of unsuspecting McGowin? For example, say Webb had changed a flat tire? What if he had merely said a kind word? Would those acts create a "moral obligation" too? How should a court determine whether an act creates a moral obligation or no obligation at all?

Read It Yourself

Webb v. McGowin, 168 So. 196 (Ala. App. 1935).

12 The Dancer Who Didn't Dance

Roland Parker was thirty-seven years old and lonely. He had graduated from college, but lived by himself in a one-room, attic apartment. Youth was largely behind him, and middle age loomed just ahead, far too close for comfort. He needed something that would give him purpose and unleash the person inside whom he felt he could be if only given a chance. Fiery passion smoldered within, ready to burst into flame. He just needed a spark. On a November day in 1957, Roland discovered that spark when he found himself in the Arthur Murray Studio, redeeming a certificate for three free dancing lessons.

Roland had never been a dancer, but these initial lessons uncovered a hidden ability. His dance teacher told him that he had "exceptional potential to be a fine and accomplished dancer." But if he wanted to realize his potential, he was going to need more lessons.

Maybe the instructor was just trying to upsell Roland from his free lessons. Maybe Roland had real dancing talent. Either way, Roland signed up for seventy-five hours of lessons at the not inconsiderable cost of one thousand dollars.[1]

That was a lot of money, especially because the dance studio had a firm no-refunds policy. In capital letters, set in bold type, the contract Roland signed stated, "NON-CANCELABLE NEGOTIABLE CONTRACT."

This didn't bother Roland. He didn't worry about refunds because he didn't plan on giving up. His instructor saw something in him, and Roland was determined to cultivate that talent until he became the best dancer he could be. Roland assiduously attended his dance lessons without fail, and his efforts were rewarded. His instructors heaped praise on his progress and encouraged him to keep working to improve even more—and, of course, to keep buying more lessons.

Roland was all in. Over and over again, he signed up for more lessons, and each time the contract he signed said in bold letters: "NON-CANCELA-BLE CONTRACT." Some of the agreements were even more explicit, saying additionally, in bold capital letters: "I UNDERSTAND THAT NO REFUNDS WILL BE MADE UNDER THE TERMS OF THIS CONTRACT."

Years went by and Roland continued to devote himself to his dancing lessons, happily signing up for more and more hours. Then, on September 24, 1961, tragedy struck. Roland was driving a car when he and another vehicle collided. Roland's injuries were severe. Perhaps most painful of all, he would never dance again.

At this point, Roland had, in his exuberance for lessons and his ambition to reach his full dancing potential, accumulated over twenty-seven hundred hours of prepaid, unused dance lessons that he had bought at a price of nearly twenty-five thousand dollars.[2] Because of the accident, Roland's dancing days were done forever. Because he would never take any of the thousands of hours of lessons he had paid for, Roland asked the dance studio where he had spent so much time (and so much money) for a refund.

The dance studio refused. Things got heated. Eventually, Roland filed a lawsuit to get his money back.

A deal's a deal, the studio argued, and pointed to the numerous times Roland had signed contracts that plainly told him his purchases were noncancelable and nonrefundable. The contacts could not have been clearer. Roland knew that prepaying for lessons was a risk. He could lose interest. He could run into financial trouble. The studio could go out of business. He could suffer a tragic injury, which regrettably is what happened. Sad as Roland's accident might have been, Roland understood the terms of his deal with the studio: once bought, dance lessons would not be refunded—used or unused. End of story.

Roland appealed to common sense. It never occurred to him that he might suffer a crippling injury that would forever keep him from pursuing his passion for dancing. He had expected a lifetime of lessons and was more than happy to pay for them, but now it was impossible for him to use what he had purchased. He was not trying to squirrel out of a deal just because he changed his mind about dancing or regretted spending as much as he had. Life itself had cut short his dancing days. A refund was only fair.

What should a court do? The printed contract was clear, but so was Roland's crippling injury. Did Roland assume the risk that he would never take all the lessons he had bought, or could changed circumstances that he could not reasonably anticipate—like his crippling car accident—free him from the contract that would otherwise bind him? How would you rule?

HOW THE COURT RULED

The general rule of contracts states that agreements must be enforced as written. To that extent, the dance studio had the law on its side.

Yet Roland's circumstances were unusual. Through no fault of his own, it had become impossible for him to take advantage of the dance lessons that he had bought and paid for. Sympathetic to Roland's plight, the court drew upon an exception to the general rule that bad deals must be enforced just as much as good ones: the doctrine of impossibility of performance.

The legal formulation of the doctrine goes like this: "A duty that requires for its performance action that can be rendered only by the promisor or some other particular person is discharged by his death or by such illness as makes the necessary action by him impossible or seriously injurious to his health, unless the contract indicates a contrary intention or there is contributing fault on the part of the person subject to the duty."[3]

Put less legalistically, this means that if all the parties to a contract understand something to be an essential part of the deal, then if that something becomes impossible through no one's fault, then the deal is off. And this cancelation of the contract can occur even if the understanding of what is essential is only implicit.

In this case, both Roland and the dance studio understood that when Roland was buying nearly three thousand hours of future dance lessons, he was doing so because they both believed that he would be physically able to dance. Because of Roland's car accident, that assumption was no longer true. Roland could never take another dance lesson. An essential assumption about the contract had failed.

It was true, as the dance studio pointed out, that part of the deal was that the contract could not be canceled and no refunds would be given. And that understanding *was* explicit. That was what the bold, capital-lettered warnings were for.

So the two understandings were in conflict. On the one hand, Roland and the dance studio understood that an essential condition was that Roland would be physically able to dance. On the other, they also both understood that no refunds would be given under any circumstances. The studio believed that the written understanding should trump the unwritten one. The court construed the studio's argument as saying that Roland had waived his right to rescind the contract based on the doctrine of impossibility.

The court rejected the studio's argument. In the court's view, the "no refunds" clause in the contracts did not demonstrate that Roland had waived his right to rescind under the doctrine of impossibility. Waivers have to be done knowingly, and what are the chances that Roland had ever heard about this arcane legal rule before his lawyers told him about it when he sued for a refund? If Roland didn't know about the doctrine of impossibility, and the contract made no mention of it, Roland could not have knowingly waived his rights.

The court's decision didn't mean that the "no refunds" clause was meaningless. If Roland had tried to get his money back simply because he changed his mind about learning how to dance or regretted spending so much money on lessons, the "no refunds" clause would have stopped him. But Roland didn't choose to be in a car accident. He didn't choose to suffer a crippling injury in that accident. And he didn't choose to have his crippling injury make it impossible for him to dance again.

If the dance studio wanted its customers to waive the benefit of the doctrine of impossibility, reasoned the court, the studio could have done so by explicitly calling out the legal rights that Roland was waiving. The studio wrote the contracts that it had its customers sign. If those contracts didn't do everything that the studio wanted, that was the studio's problem, not the customers'.

So Roland's dancing days may have been over, but he managed to waltz through the courts and emerge with the refund that the dance studio had refused him. Did the court get this one right? You decide.

REFLECTIONS

Most people consider contracts to be rock-solid commitments, enforced to the letter, without regard to circumstance. And in many cases, that's exactly what happens. The case of Roland Parker, however, illustrates that what courts enforce is not always necessarily exactly what is written on paper.

At the most basic level, the reason courts enforce contracts in the first place is because the parties to the contract agreed to be legally bound by the promises in contracts. No agreement, no contract. No contract, no court intervention.

Ideally, when two people come together to make a contract, they explicitly and expressly agree on each and every term and each and every assumption. But in the real world, it is the rare case where every possible contingency can be anticipated and accounted for in a contract. Life is too big, too complex, and too uncertain for that level of specificity.

Inevitably, therefore, contracts are based on assumptions that are not expressly included in the agreement. If these assumptions do not come to pass, then the question for the court is: what did the parties agree would happen in that situation? This is an especially tricky question when neither party to the contract ever considered the possibility that their shared assumption would turn out to be wrong.

The classic example is the case of *Taylor v. Caldwell*.[4] In *Taylor*, a music hall signed a contract to rent out its space for four days of concerts. A week before the concerts were to begin, the music hall burned down. The concert promoter sued the music hall for the profits he lost because the music hall owner did not make the music hall available as promised. The court held that the existence of the music hall was an implied condition in the contract. Neither party would have entered into the contract had there been no music hall—not the owner, not the renter. Because the music hall was gone, it was impossible for its former owner to perform the contract. The court decided that the music hall's existence was an essential assumption that had failed, and so both parties were excused from the contract. The music hall owner did not have to furnish the hall. The concert promoter did not have to pay for its rental. And more to the point for the lawsuit, because the contract was voided, the concert promoter could recover no damages from the music hall owner's failure to furnish the promised venue for the performance.

In *Taylor*, it was physically impossible for the music hall owner to perform the contract after the music hall burned down. Impossibility, however, is a high bar. Over time, courts relaxed the requirement of strict impossibility to allow defenses where changed circumstances made performing a contract either extremely difficult or pointless. In those cases, the legal rule is sometimes called either the doctrine of impracticability or the doctrine of frustration of purpose.

A textbook example of the expansion of the doctrine of impossibility so that it included impracticability and frustration of purpose, is the case of *Krell v. Henry*.[5] In that case, Paul Krell rented his London room to C. S. Henry so Henry could watch the coronation of the king of England. After the contract was made, but before the rental was to begin, the coronation was unexpectedly postponed. Henry wanted to rent the room only to watch the coronation. When he found out that the coronation was not happening, Henry didn't want the room anymore; but Krell wanted to be paid anyway. Henry refused to pay for a room that gave him a view of an empty street, and Krell sued for the money Henry had promised. The court sided with Henry, concluding, "It cannot reasonably be supposed to have been in the contemplation of the contracting parties, when the contract was made, that the coronation would not be held on the proclaimed days, or the processions not take place on those days along the proclaimed route." Because both parties assumed that the coronation would take place, the entire purpose of the agreement evaporated when that assumption turned out not to be true. And so the rental contract shouldn't be enforced, and Krell couldn't collect the rent from Henry. The purpose of the contract had been frustrated, so the deal was off.

Cases like *Taylor, Krell,* and *Parker* should not necessarily be seen as departures from the rule that contracts must be enforced in accordance with their terms. Rather, these cases, and others like them, recognize that not all the terms of an agreement are always written down. Some are unstated and simply assumed. And if the unstated assumptions are fundamental to the agreement (meaning that without the assumptions, there would have been no contract), and if those assumptions turn out to be wrong, then the only way to carry out the true agreement is to cancel the contract, wind back the clock, and put everyone back in the positions they were before they did the deal.

All three of these doctrines—of impossibility, impracticability, and frustration of purpose—rescind contracts when circumstances change after a contract is made and those changes fundamentally alter what the parties thought they were getting from the transaction. This is good news for dancers who can no longer dance, but bad news for dance studios that want to be sure that the money they receive in advance is theirs to keep.

.   .   .   .   .

Questions

1. The court allowed Roland to get his money back because of the doctrine of impossibility, but what about the studio's expectations that the money Roland had paid would be for the studio to keep? Does it matter how much of a hardship it would be on the studio to refund the money? Would it have made any difference if the studio had already spent the money it had received from Roland—for example, by building an extra practice room? In that case, would the studio still have to refund the money?

2. One challenge for the doctrines of impossibility and impracticability is how strict to be in saying that something is "impossible." For example, was it truly "impossible" for Roland to take his nonrefundable dance lessons? True, he couldn't dance as he had envisioned, but even though the case does not describe his exact condition, maybe he could have learned how to move around a dance floor in a wheelchair or a walker. Would the doctrine of impossibility apply if Roland had missed a lesson because he was stuck in horrible traffic? Could he get a refund for the lesson he missed on the theory that it was "impossible" for him to make it because of the traffic? Where should the line between the possible and impossible, and the practical and impracticable, be drawn?

3. Is it fair for courts to invalidate contracts based on unstated assumptions? How should a court determine whether something was really an assumption of a contract? How should a court decide whether an assumption is really fundamental to the contract?

4. If you were to advise a dance studio that wanted a strict no-refunds policy, how would you recommend they write the contract to prevent people like Roland Parker from suing for their money back under the doctrine of impossibility?

Read It Yourself

Parker v. Arthur Murray, Inc., 295 N.E. 2d 487 (Ill. 1973).

13 A Peerless Peer

The deal seemed simple enough. Raffles would procure 125 bales of fine cotton from India and deliver the goods to Wicklehaus, who would buy the cotton for a fixed price. There was, however, a wrinkle.

Raffles promised the cotton would set sail from Bombay aboard the good ship *Peerless*. Careful contract drafters that they were, the two businessmen specified in their agreement that the cotton was "to arrive ex *Peerless.*"

The journey from India to England was not without its perils, but fortune smiled on the voyage, and *Peerless* put into port in Liverpool with its cotton cargo intact. Raffles collected the cotton from the ship's hold and promptly delivered the goods to Wicklehaus. To his dismay, Wicklehaus refused the shipment. Raffles demanded to know the reason.

Wicklehaus explained that they had agreed that the ship *Peerless* would deliver the goods, and the *Peerless* Wicklehaus had in mind had set sail in October. The cotton Raffles was attempting to deliver was from another ship that also happened to be named *Peerless,* but it was not the one Wicklehaus had been thinking of. Raffles's *Peerless* sailed in December, two months later than Wicklehaus's *Peerless.*

Two ships named *Peerless*? Both sailing from Bombay bound for Liverpool within two months of each other? Raffles could hardly believe it; but it was so.

Raffles refused to go quietly. He had invested a great deal to bring the cotton from India to England, and he could not afford to lose his fee over a trivial technicality. What difference did it make, demanded Raffles, what ship carried the cotton? The contract was for cotton. Cotton is what Raffles had delivered. To the extent it mattered, the cotton had indeed been conveyed by a ship named *Peerless,* just as he and Wicklehaus had agreed.

Wicklehaus shook his head. The cotton had *not* come just as they had agreed. Wicklehaus had agreed to the shipment coming on the *Peerless* that sailed in October. Raffles, evidently, had in mind the *Peerless* that sailed in December. Wicklehaus felt that he was entitled to his understanding of the agreement. If Raffles did not perform as promised and agreed, as Wicklehaus understood the agreement, Wicklehaus was not obligated to pay him.

Raffles was enraged and brought suit to force Wicklehaus to pay for the cotton he had agreed to buy. The date the cotton sailed from India was not an important part of the deal. The ship that carried the cotton across the sea meant even less.

Why then had the contract made reference to the *Peerless* if the identity of the ship was unimportant? Raffles had an answer. They had named the ship in the contract in case it sank during the voyage and the cargo was lost. If the sea claimed the cotton in a shipwreck, Raffles explained, then the contract would be off and neither party would owe the other anything. The *Peerless* was identified by name so that they could each verify that the ship carrying the goods truly went down. As it turned out, *Peerless* did not sink—neither of them—and the cotton had made it safely to England. That was all that mattered.

Wicklehaus should not be able to wriggle out of the contract on a ridiculous technicality, argued Raffles. The possibility that there might be two ships named *Peerless* had never occurred to either of them. The deal was about cotton, and Raffles had delivered cotton just as he promised. He deserved to be paid.

Wicklehaus stuck to his guns. He would have gladly paid if Raffles had performed as they had agreed. Raffles sent the cotton by the wrong *Peerless*. The deal, therefore, was off. Raffles should get nothing.

Is Raffles right that this was a contract for cotton and that the naming of the ship was an irrelevant detail? Or is Wicklehaus right that because the ship was named in the contract, the precise identity of the vessel was an essential term? How would you rule?

HOW THE COURT RULED

Raffles and Wicklehaus agreed that Wicklehaus would buy Raffles's cotton that would sail from India to England on the *Peerless*. What they did not know was that two ships named *Peerless* would sail from and to the same ports at nearly the same time. Raffles had in mind the December ship, Wicklehaus the October one.

Raffles and Wicklehaus had both made a mistake—a mutual mistake in legal parlance. Although the contract specified a ship by name and route, an ambiguity lurked in what looked like clear language: which ship named *Peerless* did these men of commerce truly have in mind? Because of this latent ambiguity, the court reasoned, the two men never reached full agreement on the terms of the sale, even though they thought they had.

The essence of contract, of course, is agreement, and true agreement requires that both parties have in mind the same transaction at the time they exchange their promises. Through no one's fault, Raffles and Wicklehaus did not have the same *Peerless* in mind. Therefore, the men did not have a true agreement. Without a true agreement, no enforceable contract ever came into being.

Thus, Wicklehaus was right. He had no obligation to purchase Raffles's cotton, because their contract was defective at its inception. The *Peerless* had a peer, and that meant the two men did not have a contract.

Raffles kept the cotton he didn't want. Wicklehaus kept his money. The two men would have to strike a new deal or find new trading partners. A mistake and a strange twist of fate made this trade a bust.

Did the court get it right? You decide.

REFLECTIONS

The fundamental command of the law of contracts is this: the agreement of the parties should be enforced. The strange case of *Raffles v. Wicklehaus* illustrates the corollary to this rule: for an agreement to exist, both parties must have in mind the same thing. In legal parlance, this is called a meeting of the minds. No meeting of the minds, no contract.

The *Raffles* case shows how two people can use the same word and have completely different understandings of that word and, at the same time, be completely unaware that the other person has something different in mind. While the confusion over the two ships named *Peerless* is an extreme case of latent and unexpected ambiguity, many legal disputes can be boiled down to arguments over what words mean and whether an act or a thing falls within the definition of a particular word.

In *Raffles*, ambiguity sneaked into the agreement by virtue of a mistake. In other cases, ambiguity inserts itself by virtue of the limitations of language itself. Some words are by their nature imprecise: *reasonableness, materiality, significant,* and *substantial,* as well as many others common to contracts and other legal documents. The good news is that parties to contracts can guard against ambiguity by carefully defining their terms. The bad news is that careful definition leads to unwieldy agreements that are hard to read and harder to understand. And even with definitions piled on definitions, ambiguities and uncertainties often remain because the infinite possibilities of life can outwit even the most careful of contract drafters.

So now you know. One reason lawyers push for longer, more detailed agreements, to the chagrin and frustration of everyone outside the profession, is to guard against the surprise of a second ship named *Peerless* lurking out in the waters, waiting to scuttle the best-laid plans.

·   ·   ·   ·   ·

Question

1. The court invalidated the contract between Raffles and Wicklehaus on the grounds that they never really had an agreement because they were thinking of

different ships named *Peerless*. Was this the court's only option? For example, could the court have ruled that the identity of the ship was not material (i.e., not significant) to the agreement, that the agreement was for the purchase and sale of cotton, and that therefore Wicklehaus should have to buy the cotton that Raffles delivered, no matter how Raffles delivered it? Would that have been a better or worse result?

Read It Yourself

Raffles v. Wicklehaus, 2 Hurl. & C. 906 (1864).

14 And the Band Played On

On December 29, 2002, more than eighteen thousand eager fans packed into the Allstate Arena in Rosemont, Illinois, to hear a concert from one of the hottest bands in the country. With an eclectic mix of hard rock and post-grunge guitars, bass, and drums, the band Creed had released three multi-platinum albums and were at the apex of a meteoric rise from obscurity to rock-and-roll stardom. Four singles from their debut album had topped the rock music charts. The band had won a ridiculous number of awards, including the American Music Awards' Favorite Alternative Artist award—twice—and a Grammy for Best Rock Song, as well as two nominations for a Grammy for Best Rock Performance by a Duo or Group with Vocal.

Inspired by Creed's reputation for legendary live performances, Philip and Linda Berenz and their friends Wendy and Chad Costino were thrilled when they learned that the band was coming to Chicago, and they rushed to buy tickets to the show. As the Berenzs and Costinos packed into the arena with the throngs of other fans, they fully expected to experience a concert of a lifetime. Their wish was granted, but there was, as with so many fairy-tale wishes, an unexpected twist.

Three people were the heart of Creed. Mark Tremonti played guitar. Scott Phillips was the drummer. And the lead singer and front man for the band was Scott Stapp. The pressure of sudden fame and fortune had taken a toll on Stapp, and Stapp needed something to help take the edge off the highs and lows of life as a rock star. According to his memoir, *Sinner's Creed,* by this point in his life Stapp was "drinking all day, every day."[1]

The night of the concert, according to the Berenzs and Costinos, Stapp had gone on a drinking or drug-taking binge. They didn't know which; but either way, before the show even began, they alleged, Stapp passed out and an emergency medical team had to be called in to make sure that Stapp was all right.

At that point, the band had a decision to make. Stapp was not in good shape. The band could cancel the concert and give Stapp time to recover. But canceling would have meant refunding the concertgoers' money and a substantial hit to the band's finances as a result. The band considered and decided. The show must go on.

Stapp took the stage with his bandmates. Tremonti's guitar hit the opening riffs while Phillips's drums rapped out the beat. According to the Berenzs and Costinos, Stapp stumbled around the stage, mangling the songs they had come to hear, slurring his words to the point of incomprehensibility when he wasn't forgetting them entirely. Stapp could barely stand, and he spent most of the concert—such as it was—sitting or lying down. At one point, Stapp threw the microphone on the floor and ran off stage.

In his memoir, Stapp admitted that he was drunk that night, and that at one point he was on the floor singing from his back, but he claimed that he hadn't "fallen down drunk." Rather, he was making a point that he didn't trust his bandmates anymore. They didn't have his back, he wrote, so he was singing from his back.

If Stapp's performance that night was really a commentary on the damaged relationship between himself and his bandmates, the subtle message was lost on many of the concertgoers. After the concert, hundreds of disappointed fans demanded their money back.

Creed refused to issue refunds. The band felt an apology was enough. Two weeks after the disastrous concert, on January 12, 2003, Creed sent a letter to the fans who attended the concert. The band wrote:

Dear Creed Fan,

The band has heard that you are unhappy with the quality of the recent Creed show in Chicago.

We apologize if you don't feel that the show was up to the very high standards set by our previous shows in Chicago. . . .

For now we hope that you can take some solace in the fact you definitely experienced the most unique of all Creed shows and may have become part of the unusual world of rock and roll history! Again, we apologize if you didn't enjoy the show but remember, "It's only rock and roll but we like it!"

Have a great year!

Creed[2]

Talk is cheap, and the Berenzs and Costinos wanted something more substantial. They had spent good money to see a Creed concert, and in their minds what they got was nothing like a real Creed concert. Creed was legendary for giving amazing live performances. But that night, the concertgoers didn't get to hear their favorite singer sing their favorite songs. Instead, they watched their rock hero embarrass himself on stage by staggering around drunk. That wasn't a Creed concert. It was a freak show. An apology didn't cut it. They wanted their money back and thought everyone who attended the nonconcert should get their money back, too.

So the Berenzs and Costinos filed a class action lawsuit against Creed, the company that had sold them the tickets, and the concert promoter. More than anything, the plaintiffs claimed they were disappointed to see their rock idol laid so low. They knew that rock and roll was rife with drugs and alcohol, but they thought Creed was different. They had heard Stapp on television and radio telling the public that he did not drink or do drugs before going on stage. Naively perhaps, they had believed in his wholesome image when they bought their tickets. After the performance, the Berenzs and Costinos could only conclude that Stapp's clean-cut public persona was a lie, and that they had fallen for it.

The plaintiffs argued in court that Creed had tricked the public into buying tickets. The band had cultivated a reputation for putting on great shows. The band—and Stapp in particular—had publicly announced their distaste for drugs and alcohol. The band had promised to play Creed songs, and what the concertgoers got was worse than a bad version of amateur hour at karaoke night. This was fraud. This was breach of contract. This was unjust enrichment. Creed had taken the fans' money and for all practical purposes failed to put on the show they had promised. Giving the money back was the least they could do for their fans. It was the right thing. It was the honorable thing. More importantly for the lawsuit, the law required it.

In pressing their case, the plaintiffs drew an analogy between the band's performance and that of a portrait artist. If you hired a painter to paint a portrait that was a fair likeness, you would be entirely justified in refusing to pay for a painting that looked nothing like you. In this case, the ticket purchasers effectively hired Creed to play Creed songs, but the songs they heard that night, with their slurred words and forgotten lyrics, were nothing like the songs Creed had released on its albums and music videos. They were not a fair likeness. Creed had not delivered what it promised.

The plaintiffs also argued that if Creed had canceled the concert, there would be no question that the ticket holders would be entitled to their money back. In this case, given the lead singer's state of intoxication, the right thing for the band to have done would have been to cancel. They didn't formally cancel, but going on stage and not singing the songs the fans had paid to hear was, from the fans' perspective, the same thing as canceling the show.

Another way to look at it, argued the plaintiffs, was that Creed as a band had three parts: a guitarist, a drummer, and a lead singer. A band without all three wasn't Creed. In this case, one third of the equation had voluntarily taken himself out of the show by getting so drunk he could not perform his part. Without the lead singer, all that was left were guitar and drums—but that wasn't Creed. That wasn't the band that the audience had paid hard-earned money to see. It was as if Creed had never shown up at all.

Creed and its fellow defendants disagreed. Every member of Creed was on stage that night, the band argued. While it might not have been their best performance by any stretch, it was a performance. The plaintiffs thought it was a bad performance, but realistically there is no legal meas-ure to distinguish good performances from bad ones, especially in the world of rock and roll, where wild, drunken, drug-fueled shows are part and parcel of many a concert experience.

In the end, a band that promises to perform, Creed argued, only has the obligation to perform. It doesn't promise to perform well. It doesn't promise to perform to the satisfaction of the fans. It doesn't promise to perform songs that the fans want in the way that fans want to hear them. So long as the band takes the stage, even for one minute, the band has performed and earned its money, even if the audience leaves the show bitter and disappointed.

It is not that bands who put on bad shows suffer no consequences, but those consequences come in the form of alienated audiences who refuse to buy tickets in the future. The consequences shouldn't come in the form of lawsuits.

Frankly, Creed argued, even bad performances have value. Take this case. Yes, the performance may not have been great, but the fans, by being there to watch it, got to see a small part of rock history being made. They could hang on to their experience, remember and reminisce, share with their friends and family, and forever talk about the time they saw Scott Stapp stumble on stage. Who's to say that wasn't worth the price of admission?

In the end, Creed concluded, all the plaintiffs were really saying was that they went to a concert and didn't like the show. That's regrettable, and the band had apologized; but if anyone who didn't like a performance could sue the artists who had performed, there would be no end to lawsuits, because it's impossible to please all the people all the time.

The plaintiffs dismissed Creed's arguments as lame excuses for a lame performance. This wasn't just a bad concert. It was the worst concert they had ever seen, and with the lead singer drunk out of his mind on stage, it wasn't the concert that they had paid for. If you go to an opera and the lead tenor has laryngitis and can't sing, there's no opera. It would be a cruel joke to pretend that operagoers should be indifferent to whether the tenor chooses to sing or simply stand silently on stage while the supporting performers go about their business in the background.

So the case came on for argument. Let's concede for the sake of argument that Creed's lead singer was too drunk to sing. He stumbled, sat, and lay down on stage; his speech was a series of indecipherable slurs. Should the plaintiffs get their money back because the show they got was nothing like the show they paid for? Or should the plaintiffs leave the courthouse just as disappointed as they were when they left the concert hall—taking away nothing, because in show business you never know what you're going to get, and that's the risk you take when you pay to see a live performance? How would you rule?

HOW THE COURT RULED

The plaintiffs called upon the court to consider what it really means to put on a rock concert. All the parties agreed that if Creed had not shown up and not played a note, then the ticket holders who had paid to see a show would not have gotten what they bargained for and would be entitled under the law to get their money back. But that's not what happened. Instead, the band came on stage, but the show was a disaster. The lead singer was drunk. He sat or fell down. He could barely sing. What he did sing was a cruel parody of the songs the band had recorded on its albums. It was nothing like the shows the band had put on before. The band knew its performance was truly awful. It was so embarrassed that it issued a public apology. With a performance this bad, did Creed really put on a show at all?

Yes, the show was bad, but just how bad was it? And more importantly, who is to judge whether a show is so bad the audience should get its money back? This question gave the court serious pause.

One role of artists, the court observed, is to challenge the sensibilities of audiences, shake them loose from their conventional expectations, expose them to new ideas and modes of expressions. It is a cliché that new artistic endeavors often provoke an initial reaction of revulsion and disdain, and that, over time, many of these same works win over the public and change their conception of art. In other words, just because some or even all of the people in an audience might not like a performance doesn't mean that the audience didn't experience great art.

In this case, Scott Stapp may have staggered on stage drunk and rolled on the floor before staggering off again. Was this great art? Maybe no, but then maybe yes. How would a court begin to judge whether that performance was good enough?

The legal claim that the plaintiffs alleged was that they had experienced a breach of contract. A fundamental question in any contract is: what exactly are the terms that the parties agreed to? The plaintiffs contended that Creed had promised to play songs off of Creed's records in a style and manner that was similar to the recorded songs. The court, however, did not see where Creed had ever made that promise. It may have been true that the plaintiffs honestly believed that that was what the show was going to be, but the plaintiffs' personal beliefs couldn't be attributed to the band.

What Creed had promised was to take the stage and play music. And that's what the band did. They took the stage and played. Badly, perhaps, but courts are not rock critics. It is not for courts to judge the quality of a performance; they can judge only whether a promise was broken.

The fact that the lead singer might have been drunk at the time of the show didn't really change anything. Creed hadn't promised to be sober. If perfect sobriety were a legal requirement, there might be far fewer rock concerts in the world. Allowing artists the freedom to perform without fear of second-guessing by courts means that audiences have a chance to hear and see things that they might otherwise never see. Some of that will be terrible, maybe most of it. But some of it will be transcendent. The only way to find out is to let the artists take the stage without fear of legal liabilities.

The court, therefore, would not set itself up as the arbiter of quality in music. Nor would the court accept the idea that the audience's personal expectations or evaluations of a concert were legitimate standards against which to measure an artist's performance.

In the end, the court concluded that courts should limit themselves to objectively verifiable questions. Ticket purchasers pay to see a performance. If a performer shows up and goes on stage, the audience gets a performance, which is what they paid for. If they don't like the performance, they have every right to boycott future shows, complain to their friends, and never buy anything by the performer ever again. What they cannot do is go to court to get their money back. They paid for a show, and they got one.

So the plaintiffs' claims were dismissed. While Creed got to keep the money they made from the show, they also earned an ignominious place in rock history as the band that put on a show so bad that they got sued for it. The Berenzs and Costinos may have lost in court, but in the end their wish to see a show that they would never forget was granted.

Did the court get it right or wrong? You decide.

REFLECTIONS

Early on the morning of April 15, 1912, the luxury ocean liner *Titanic* sank in arctic waters, bringing a tragic end to its maiden voyage from England to America. As the ship took on water and panicked passengers rushed to flee, it became clear that not everyone on board was going to find a place on the few lifeboats the ship carried. Heroically, the musicians of the *Titanic* bravely manned their instruments and played music to soothe the terrified passengers, sticking to their posts until the very moment they and the ship went under the icy Atlantic waters. The *Titanic* orchestra's courageous decision to comfort the passengers rather than try to save themselves exemplifies the height of heroic commitment of artists to their craft.

The same can't really be said about Creed's Chicago concert. While the *Titanic*'s band had played on in the face of certain death to help maintain calm in a sea of panic, why didn't Creed cancel the concert if it was clear that the band was in no condition to perform? The plaintiffs argued that Creed was greedy. The band preferred to put on a horrible show rather than take a financial hit from refunding the fans' money. That may or may not be an accurate description of Creed's thinking at the time, but assume that the plaintiffs were right. Should the law protect a callous decision to deliver a pathetic performance just to put more money in the pockets of wealthy rock stars?

It is possible that Creed's decision to perform that night was worthy of condemnation; but in ruling on legal claims, judges must be mindful that they are identifying rules and principles that will be applied not just in the case at hand but also in future cases, where the sympathies might be very different.

The essence of a common-law system like the ones in England and the United States is that the rule in one case becomes the rule in future cases that have similar facts. This is known as the doctrine of *stare decisis*. While the doctrine has exceptions, every decision carries with it ramifications for future cases and for future litigants who will have to live with the rules handed down. The temptation to help a sympathetic person must be balanced against the danger of establishing a rule that will create more mischief than it cures.

In the Creed case, the judge was not concerned about Creed and its finances. The band had, after all, put on a horrible show. Rather, the judge worried about all the other artists in the world, and what it would mean to them if courts allowed disappointed audience members to demand their money back every time they didn't like an artist's performance. Artists have to make a living, and so they might be afraid that if they took any risks with their art, they could be bankrupted by lawsuits. If artists censored themselves out of fear of ruinous litigation, the world would be deprived of innovations that push the boundaries of art forward and uncover new territories of expression. Creed's terrible performance might or might not have deserved the court's protection, but the freedom of artists to invent new art certainly did.

The rule the judge applied—performers cannot be sued for poor performances—benefited Creed but was not for Creed's benefit. It was for the benefit of all artists who create new things and for the audiences who want to experience those creations, both good and bad. Protecting this principle meant exonerating the band, but it was the principle, not the band, that was paramount.

·   ·   ·   ·   ·

Questions

1. The judge in the Creed case was concerned about courts becoming arbiters of the quality of art. Are there any promises by artists that courts should enforce? What sorts of promises should courts enforce, and what sorts should courts stay away from?

2. What would the outcome of the case have been if the lead singer had been too ill to take the stage and his two bandmates had gone on without him? Would the outcome have been the same, because the audience paid for a performance

and got one; or would the outcome have been different because the audience paid for a performance by *Creed* and Creed could perform only if all three members were present? Would it make a difference if an understudy the fans had never heard of had come out to sing?

Read It Yourself

Berenz v. Diamond Road, Inc., et al., Case No. 03 CH 07106 (Cook County Circuit Court, IL, 2003).

15 Don't Do Me Like That

September 24, 1997, is a day that plaintiff John Doe (real name withheld) will always remember as the day that he got lucky and unlucky at the same time. Very, very unlucky.

John was in a long-term relationship with his girlfriend, whom we will call Mary (also not her real name). It was early in the morning, and the couple was feeling romantic. This wasn't their first time together, and everything seemed to be going well.

John was on his back, and Mary was on top of him, but Mary wanted to try something new, so she shifted positions. She didn't ask John if he was okay with the maneuver, and didn't tell him she was going to do it before she did. Mary put her feet on either side of John and began pushing herself up and down to generate more force. She didn't think this would hurt John, but it did. Big time.

Mary lifted her body and then dropped her weight down, but she did not, shall we say, stick the landing. Her body collided with John's at an awkward angle. Not all of his body exactly. Just the part that was sticking up. The result was a penile fracture.

The injury was no joke. The pain was instantaneous and excruciating. An ambulance rushed John to the hospital. John needed emergency surgery, immediately. The surgery, however, was only a partial success. John went through a painful and lengthy recovery. He took medicines. He got counseling. Despite his and his doctor's best efforts, John never recovered his ability to have sexual relations.

So John sued Mary.

The law of negligence, John argued, is clear. Every person owes every other person a duty not to engage in acts that unreasonably expose other people to foreseeable risks of harm. If a person unreasonably exposes another person to a risk of harm and causes that person injury, then the injured person may recover damages from the person who caused the harm.

According to John, Mary engaged in a risky maneuver that put him in serious jeopardy. She didn't tell him she was going to do what she did before she did it. He never consented to the maneuver. She did it for her benefit, not his. She took the risk, but he suffered the consequences. It was a classic case of negligence, so she should pay for his injuries.

Poor Mary. It never occurred to her that a bit of frisky play could result in a catastrophic injury to John. They were consenting adults doing what consenting adults do. They were just having fun. Nobody was supposed to get hurt. While she was very, very sorry about what happened to John, she didn't see how it would be fair for her to have to pay for what was an innocent accident. She was in the throes of passion. So was John. They did not discuss this particular maneuver at this particular moment, but then she wasn't doing anything that she could have imagined would crush John and his sex life with such devastating and permanent effect. Yes, she injured her lover, but an unreasonable risk of foreseeable harm this was not. It was a tragic accident that no one could have foreseen.

So in this sad case of star-crossed (or maybe leg-crossed?) lovers, who should prevail? How would you rule?

HOW THE COURT RULED

The cornerstone of the law of negligence is that every person has a duty to use reasonable care to avoid reasonably foreseeable injuries to other people. The amount of care required for any given situation is known as the standard of care. If you use less than the standard of care, you are negligent and the law will hold you responsible for the damage you cause. How much care the standard entails is, therefore, always a critical question in negligence cases.

The standard of care is often heavily influenced by what reasonable people in a similar situation do. If most doctors ask their patients if they are allergic to any medications before writing a prescription, then a doctor who neglects to ask that question will likely be found to have breached the standard of care if a patient has an allergic reaction that could have been avoided had the doctor done what everybody else usually does. The law of negligence and the standard of care encourage running with the herd.

When it comes to consensual sexual relations between adults, however, the court could not identify any generally accepted standards of what is acceptable and what is beyond the pale. The bedroom doesn't come with a rulebook. How is a judge or a jury to decide which intimate acts are reasonable and which are unreasonable? As the court put it: "In the absence of a consensus of community values or customs defining normal consensual sexual conduct, a jury or judge cannot be expected to resolve a claim that certain consensual sexual conduct is undertaken without reasonable care." In other words, courts have no expertise deciding what people should and shouldn't do in bed. With no standard of care for Mary to have breached, John's negligence claim could not succeed.

Even though the court ruled that negligence was not a viable legal theory, the court wasn't prepared to say that a person can do anything to another person without legal consequence just because the injury occurs in bed. While negligence—a lack of ordinary care—was too vague a standard for negligent intimate injuries, the court believed that a successful case could be brought if the person causing the injury acted recklessly. Recklessness is more than negligence. Negligence is when a person just makes a mistake. Recklessness is when a person knows that there is a very high chance that someone is going to get hurt but takes the chance anyway. Sometimes this is called deliberate indifference or conscious disregard of the risk of injury.

In John's case, Mary might have been negligent, but she wasn't reckless. She didn't know that what she was doing posed any risk to John, let alone have knowledge that her act carried a high probability of injury. Since she didn't know about the risk, she couldn't have consciously disregarded it. Therefore, Mary wasn't reckless, and John's case had to be dismissed.

Did the court get it right or wrong? You decide.

REFLECTIONS

The *Doe* case illustrates a critical, but often misunderstood, distinction between negligence and recklessness. The tort of negligence has four elements.[1] First, a duty of care must exist. Second, someone must have breached that duty of care. Third, the breach of the duty of care must have caused damage that was foreseeable. And finally, the breach of the duty must be the "proximate" cause of the damage, *proximate cause* being a legal term of art for consequences that follow naturally and directly from an act, without some other intervening factor.

At its core, the tort of negligence is about remedying injuries caused by careless people. Classic examples of negligence are drivers who don't pay enough attention to the road, or doctors who don't follow standard medical procedures, or drug manufacturers who neglect to do routine safety checks, or shop owners who ignore the need for a cleanup in aisle eleven.

Recklessness is different from negligence. A person is reckless if she demonstrates indifference to the potential harm to others under circumstances where it is clear that the safety of others is in jeopardy. A person can be held liable for negligence just by being oblivious to what a reasonable person would reasonably appreciate. For recklessness, in contrast, a person must know and understand that her action is highly likely to cause harm. It is by going ahead with the action, despite knowing the high risk of harm, that a person demonstrates the indifference required to prove recklessness.

Driving drunk is a classic example of reckless behavior. By dulling his own senses and impairing his own judgment with alcohol before getting in a car to drive, a person disregards the very high risk that he will cause an accident.

Recklessness is often confused with negligence because in both cases the injurer does not *intend* to harm the other person; but recklessness is more than negligence. Negligence can come from inadvertence, incompetence, unskillfulness, or a failure to take reasonable precautions. Recklessness is a conscious choice to run a risk, knowing that making that choice will put other people in serious danger.

Another reason recklessness and negligence are often confused is because the two concepts are often matters of degree, like the difference between warm and hot. As warm gets warmer and hot gets cooler, the line between one and the other blurs. The same is true with negligence and recklessness. Two cars can run a stop sign, and one driver might be found to be merely negligent because he was simply not paying attention, while the other driver might be found to be reckless because he was driving much faster and so ran a greater risk to others.

The difference between negligence and recklessness is important because the law often apportions liability based on what a person is thinking at the time she causes an injury. If a person consciously disregards the safety of others, the consequences will generally be more severe than if she simply makes a mistake. Naturally, the consequences will be harsher still if the person acted on purpose. When it comes to remedies against wrongdoers, state of mind matters very much.

.   .   .   .   .

Questions

1. In making his argument, John emphasized that, while he had consented to sex with Mary, he had not consented to the particular maneuver that resulted in his injury. When two people agree to sexual relations, under what circumstances should one partner have to ask the other person for express permission to do something different from what they are already doing? What would the result have been if John had sued Mary for sexual assault for engaging in an act that he had not consented to?

2. The court ruled that what goes on in the bedrooms of ordinary people is too diverse to permit a judge or jury to come up with an identifiable standard of care. What if Mary had tied John up or hit or choked him? Would that be actionable either as negligence or recklessness? If John consented, would that change the analysis? Should courts impose an outer bound on reasonable sexual activity, or should they stay out of all intimate acts because it is impossible to say what is "normal" and what is not?

3. To what extent should past acts be taken into account when determining the scope of consent and whether an act is reckless or merely negligent? For

example, if John regularly asked Mary to choke or hit him during intercourse, and if she were to choke or hit him without explicit permission, to what extent should Mary be allowed to argue that consent was implied by the prior conduct? What obligation does John have to expressly withhold consent from acts that he previously and regularly consented to, and how should he be required to express it? What duty does Mary have to ensure she has consent for everything she does?

Read It Yourself

Doe v. Moe, 63 Mass. App. Ct. 516 (2005).

16 The Five-Year-Old Defendant

Nobody knows for sure what happened that Monday afternoon on July 16, 1951. What we do know is that Naomi Garratt invited Brian Dailey, a boy of only five years and nine months of age, over to the house of her sister, Ruth. Ruth was quite a bit older than Brian. The law reports do not disclose Ruth's precise age, perhaps out of a sense of delicacy and politeness; but both Ruth and Naomi were fully grown adults, while Brian was only a child.

The two sisters and their youthful guest were relaxing in Ruth's backyard, and nothing seemed amiss until Ruth decided to rest her tired feet by sitting in one of the lawn chairs in the yard.

What is known for sure is that Ruth missed her mark and fell hard to the ground on her backside. The fall might have looked hilarious, especially to young eyes like Brian's, but a fall that might have been nothing but an irritating annoyance to most people was for Ruth Garratt a disaster. Ruth broke her hip and suffered other painful injuries.

What was disputed at the time and will never be known for certain was how exactly Ruth came to fall. Ruth was quick to point the finger at young Brian, and her sister, Naomi, backed her up. According to Naomi, Brian had played a terrible prank on poor Ruth. As Naomi told it, as Ruth went to sit in the chair, Brian snatched the seat away right out from under her. With the chair whisked out of position, Ruth crashed to the ground in a horrific heap.

Though not quite six, and likely still learning his letters, Brian told a different story. According to Brian, he had moved the lawn chair well before Ruth tried to sit in it, and in fact, he was sitting in the chair at the time Ruth made her fateful move. Brian could only speculate that Ruth must not have noticed that he had moved the chair. When Brian saw Ruth about to commit a serious error and sit where the chair had been, he moved as quickly as his little body would let him to slide the chair he was sitting on back into place to save Ruth from a fall. Alas, the chair was too big, and he was too small; the time was too short, and he was too late.

As the injured and indignant party, Ruth naturally embraced her sister's version of events, and so, though many decades his senior, Ruth went to the courthouse and filed a lawsuit against young Brian, seeking compensation for her injuries. Ruth alleged that Brian was guilty of committing a battery. A battery is the intentional infliction of a harmful bodily contact on another person. Ruth claimed Brian intentionally pulled the chair out from under her. Brian denied it.

It's not at all uncommon for different people to recall events very differently, and in other circumstances people might simply agree to disagree. But courts do not have the luxury of indulging uncertainty and doubt. Judges must make decisions and resolve disputes. With two irreconcilable stories, the judge hearing the case in the trial court had to choose to believe one version or the other. The judge sided with Brian. A battery requires an intent to touch another person in a harmful or offensive way, and the boy didn't mean to do any harm; or as the trial judge put it in legalistic fashion:

> The preponderance of the evidence in this case establishes that when the defendant, Brian Dailey, moved the chair in question he did not have any wilful or unlawful purpose in doing so; that he did not have any intent to injure the plaintiff, or any intent to bring about any unauthorized or offensive contact with her person or any objects appurtenant thereto; that the circumstances which immediately preceded the fall of the plaintiff established that the defendant, Brian Dailey, did not have purpose, intent or design to perform a prank or to effect an assault and battery upon the person of the plaintiff.

The case, however, was not over. Ruth appealed.

To the appellate court, Ruth pointed out that even if Brian had not intended to play a prank on old Ruth—a point Ruth contested, but of which she failed to convince the trial judge—Brian had admitted that he had in fact moved the chair that Ruth had tried to sit in. Maybe Brian didn't specifically intend to cause Ruth harm, but he did intend to move the chair, and he shouldn't have been monkeying with Ruth's chair in the first place.

It is common knowledge, Ruth argued, that moving a chair that a person is about to sit in is virtually guaranteed to cause an accident. This fact was so simple, so universal, so obvious, even a five-year-old would know it. Actions have consequences, and if the natural and probable consequence of an action is injury to another person, the law should infer that the person who did the act (such as moving a chair) also intended to cause injury (such as causing Ruth to crash down on her bottom). It shouldn't matter that a person did not subjectively mean to cause the injury itself. The boy should not escape justice by playing the innocent. He moved the chair on purpose. Any reasonable person would know that this put Ruth at risk, and even if Brian didn't mean to play a prank, he knew full well that moving Ruth's chair would likely lead to her injury. Because of that knowledge, justice required that Ruth receive compensation for the damage Brian caused.

Brian's lawyer protested on his behalf. The boy wasn't even six, and Ruth was making all sorts of assumptions about what is logical and obvious. The trial court had specifically found that Brian hadn't meant to cause anyone any harm. A battery is an "intentional" infliction of harm. Since he didn't intend to cause harm, he couldn't have committed a battery against Ruth or anyone else. Whatever else he might have known about moving chairs and the consequences that might follow was irrelevant.

The questions for the court were these: Is it even possible under the law for a boy of not quite six to commit an intentional wrong like battery? And even if it is possible, was Brian guilty of battery because he knew that Ruth was likely to get hurt when he moved the chair, even though he hadn't specifically intended any harm?

Now those questions are posed to you. How would you rule?

HOW THE COURT RULED

Brian's tender age of not quite six made no impression on the court. If a person breaks the law and injures another person, that person, however small or young, is liable for the damage he causes. As the court put it, the rules of the law of torts are the same for all, "whether five or fifty-five."

The only question that gave the court pause was whether Brian's actions met the requirements for battery. Battery requires an intent to touch another person in a harmful way. But *intent* is a tricky word. *Intent* can refer to the thoughts and plans that are in a person's mind. This is their "subjective intent." It can also refer to what a reasonable person would think if he or she did the same thing as the defendant. This is called "objective intent." Objective intent does not require proof of a person's subjective state of mind. Rather, objective intent is inferred from what the courts believe a reasonable person in the same situation doing the same thing would be thinking.

The trial court had specifically found that Brian did not *intend* to hurt or play a prank on Ruth. But that did not end the case. Just because Brian did not subjectively intend to injure Ruth or play a prank on her didn't mean that Brian didn't know what he was doing. If Brian knew "with substantial certainty" that moving the chair would cause Ruth to fall and get hurt, he would be responsible for her injuries, even though he might not have subjectively intended to cause them.

But what could young Brian really know with "substantial certainty"? For the court, that was a question of proof. As the plaintiff, Ruth had to prove that Brian knew what would happen if he moved her chair. Brian's knowledge, of course, like that of adults, would depend on his "experience, capacity, and understanding." Naturally, those qualities in toddlers would be much less well developed than in adults; but kindergarteners, observed the court, are not totally without experience in the world. They've sat in and fallen out of chairs and may even have seen chairs pulled out from under others or had chairs pulled out from under themselves. If Ruth could show that Brian knew that moving the chair would lead her to fall, Brian would be guilty of battery and liable for Ruth's injuries. Knowledge of the consequences—even without a specific intent—was enough for liability.

So who should win the case, Ruth or Brian? For the appellate court reviewing the decision of the trial court, it wasn't entirely clear. The judge in the trial court had found that Brian did not intend to harm Ruth, but he had said nothing about what Brian knew or didn't know with substantial certainty. From what the trial court had written, it was likely that the trial court thought Brian too young and too innocent to have the state of mind necessary to inflict a battery on Ruth. But the trial court did not expressly consider the boy's knowledge, and without knowing about Brian's knowledge, the appellate court did not have enough facts to say whether Brian should be liable or not.

The solution for the appellate court was to send the case back to the trial court to ask the trial court judge to make an express finding about whether Brian had known with substantial certainty that Ruth would try to sit down where the moved chair had once been, and that she would suffer injury as a result. If he did know, Ruth would win. If he didn't, Brian would win. The law was clear. Knowledge was enough for liability. The rest were questions of fact, which could be determined in due course by the trial court.

Did the court get it right or wrong? You decide.

REFLECTIONS

Appellate courts and trial courts perform different functions, and understanding the difference is crucial to understanding how the legal system works and why the *Garratt* case ended the way it did.

The primary function of trial courts is to establish what happened between the parties to the lawsuit. Trial courts do this by receiving testimony from witnesses and by reviewing documents and other evidence (things like pictures, videos, and physical objects, such as computers or a murder victim's bloody clothes). In many cases, evidence exists that supports both sides of the dispute. The parties tell different versions of events. Witnesses have different recollections. Documents are ambiguous. The trial court's job is to sort through the conflicting accounts, weigh all the evidence as a package, and come to a conclusion about who did what. This process is sometimes called finding facts, and trial courts are sometimes called the finders of fact.

Appellate courts sit above trial courts in the legal hierarchy, but they don't do the same thing. Appellate courts don't hear witnesses or receive documents to figure out the facts of a case. Appellate courts rely on trial courts for that. Instead, the job of an appellate court is to determine whether the trial court made some kind of mistake based on a review of the record that was placed before the trial court. There are two kinds of mistakes: mistakes of fact and mistakes of law.

A mistake of fact occurs when the trial court concludes that something is true when it is really false, or concludes that something is false when it is really true. When it comes to weighing conflicting evidence, however, trial courts are in a much better position to figure out what to believe and what to disbelieve. The trial judge and jury see the witnesses and hear their testimony in person and in real time. Consequently, appellate courts show trial courts a lot of deference on their findings of fact, reversing their decisions only for clear errors that are apparent from the record.

A mistake of law occurs when the trial court misinterprets or misapplies a legal rule. Since trial courts do not have special insight into the law in the same way they do into the facts, appellate courts show no deference to trial courts on their conclusions of law. Instead, appellate courts review legal questions de novo, meaning the appellate courts apply their own independent judgment in determining what the law is.

These principles were in full display in the *Garratt* case. In *Garratt*, the trial court found as a matter of fact that young Brian had not intended to injure Ruth Garratt. The trial court concluded that, under the law, if Brian did not intend to injure Ruth, Brian could not be found responsible for committing a battery.

In the appeal, the appellate court accepted the trial court's determination that Brian had not intended to injure Ruth. That was a finding of fact, and therefore, the trial court's judgment on this point was entitled to significant deference. In contrast, the appellate court did not accept the trial court's conclusion that the lack of a specific intent to injure precluded finding Brian liable for battery. Instead, the appellate court concluded that the law, correctly understood, stated that even without a specific intent to cause injury, Brian could still be liable for battery if he knew with substantial certainty that moving Ruth's chair was highly likely to lead to her injury. To apply this rule of law to Brian, however, the appellate court needed to know whether Brian did in fact know that moving Ruth's chair was highly likely to lead to her injury. That was a question of fact that the record did not answer. Since trial courts are the right place to find facts, the appellate court sent the case back to the trial court. If Brian knew that moving the chair would cause injury, he would be liable for battery. If he didn't, he would not. The appellate court had laid out the legal rule. It was up to the trial court to figure out what really happened.

The *Garratt* case illustrates the division of labor between trial and appellate courts. Broadly speaking, trial courts find facts, and appellate courts announce the law. Because legal decisions require that the law be applied to the facts, many cases can be resolved only through a back-and-forth between the appellate and trial courts.

. . . . .

Questions

1. The court drew a distinction between "intending" to cause another person harm and "knowing with substantial certainty" that one's actions would cause an injury. What do you think about this distinction? Is there a clear difference between intending an outcome and having knowledge that your actions are highly likely to produce an outcome? Can you think of examples where a person might know with substantial certainty that his actions will hurt another person, but in which that person doesn't intend to cause the injury? Is there a moral difference between actions taken with one mental state (intent) and actions taken with the other (knowledge)?

2. The court in this case concluded that all persons can be sued for their actions regardless of age. Should age ever matter? Or should all legal distinctions be based on each individual person's knowledge and intentions? Are there cases where bright-line rules based on age make sense? Are there cases where bright-line rules based on age don't make sense? How should we decide when to use a bright-line rule and when to leave decisions up to the maturity of each individual person?

3. In the case of *Nielsen v. Bell*,[1] the Supreme Court of Utah concluded that children under five years old were too young for the law to consider their actions to be negligent—that is, the law could not determine that a child under five had performed below the standard of reasonable care. Is this a reasonable rule? What if a child under five were to dart into the street and cause an oncoming car to

swerve and crash, injuring the driver? Would it be fair to say that the child had been negligent and was therefore responsible for the injury? Or should the rule be, as the Utah court suggests, that children of that age can never be negligent? What if the car were to fail to swerve in time, and it hit the child? In that case, is it reasonable to say that the child's negligence contributed to the accident; or if the law states that a toddler can never be negligent, is it fair to hold the driver solely responsible for the accident?

Read It Yourself

Garratt v. Dailey, 279 P. 2d 1091 (Wash. 1955).

17 Don't Forget to Duck

It should have been just a friendly game. It was only preseason, after all, and opening day for the official baseball season was still months away. Play some ball. Have some fun. Stretch out, and get back in shape. With nothing at stake, no one had to worry about anything. But when players face off on the field, it is not always possible to take the competitiveness out of the competitors.

It was January 5, 2001. The Rio Hondo Community College Roadrunners were playing the Citrus Community College Owls. José Luis Avila was on the mound for the Roadrunners. Since this was just a preseason game, everything was casual. There weren't even any umpires on the field.

As the game wore on, a pitch got away from Avila and hit an Owls batter. The Owls immediately leapt to their feet in protest. For a moment, flared tempers verged on violence, but the Owls' limited their fury to shouts and angry gestures. The Owls players returned to the bench, calmed for the moment, but by no means appeased.

As luck would have it, Avila came up to bat the very next inning. He squared up in the batter's box and faced the Owls pitcher. The pitch came in hard and fast and nowhere near the strike zone. By the time Avila computed the trajectory of the ball, it was too late to do anything but turn his head and brace for impact. The ball smashed into his skull with such powerful force that it cracked open his batting helmet. Avila immediately dropped to the ground. The Roadrunners' trainer and manager ran to his side. The world swam in and out of focus. Avila felt dizzy. His head throbbed in pain.

Maybe Avila should have left the game then and there, but his manager told him that he had to walk to first base. Avila managed to stagger down the line, but his head was still spinning. He complained to his first-base coach, but the coach told him to tough it out. Avila stayed in the game and on his feet and somehow made it to second base. The dizziness got worse. Numbness began to set it. By this time, his injuries were apparent even to the opposing team. An Owls player called out that the Roadrunners needed a pinch runner, and finally Avila staggered off the field to the bench. Later, he learned that he had suffered a significant concussion.

Avila blamed everyone for his head injury. He blamed his manager for not taking him out of the game sooner and for not attending to his injuries. He blamed the helmet manufacturer for making a helmet that didn't better protect him from the force of the speeding ball.

Most of all, Avila blamed the Owls for not controlling their pitcher. The pitch that hit him wasn't just an errant throw as sometimes happens. It was a deliberate attack, planned in advance, calculated to injure him, purposefully done in retaliation for the batter that Avila had hit—entirely innocently—the inning before. The wayward pitch that Avila had thrown the inning before was an accident. The precisely targeted pitch that broke Avila's helmet and gave him a concussion was payback.

Avila sued Citrus Community College for negligently failing to supervise and control its pitcher. The pitcher played for the college and threw the ball at Avila's head in an effort to help the college's team—however misguided that decision might have been. The manager and coaches for the Owls could see that tempers were running hot, yet they stood on the sidelines while their player purposely gave Avila a brutal concussion. They might as well have stood by while the pitcher beat him with a bat. They were the responsible adults, they should have seen the risk, and they should have done something to keep it from happening.

The community college didn't challenge Avila's contention that the college was responsible for the pitcher's actions, and the college didn't challenge the contention that the pitch that hit Avila was intentionally thrown. Instead, the community college argued that *even if* the pitcher purposefully aimed at Avila's head, Avila couldn't bring a lawsuit because beaning batters was just a part of the game of baseball.

Baseball, the college argued, is an inherently dangerous sport. A hard ball travels around a compact field at high speeds. The rules of the game mitigate some of the dangers by requiring batters to wear helmets, but the only way to squeeze all risk out of baseball would be not to play at all.

Avila was an experienced ballplayer. He knew that when he stepped onto the baseball diamond, he was taking a chance that he would be hit by a ball and be hurt, potentially seriously hurt. Avila voluntarily chose to play a dangerous game and so, argued the college, he assumed the risk that he would get injured. When the risk materialized, the only person he could blame was himself.

Avila took no issue with the community college's general points. Yes, baseball had dangers, and yes, accidents happen, and that's just part of the game; but as Avila saw it, that's not what happened to him. He was not the casualty of a random accident. He was the victim of a vicious assault that took place in front of and with the implicit or explicit approval of the college's managers and coaches, who had done nothing to protect him.

Intentionally hitting a batter, Avila argued, was not part of the game. The official rules of baseball clearly and unequivocally prohibited pitchers from aiming at batters. Pitchers get thrown out of games for hitting batters on purpose. Managers get thrown out for letting their pitchers break that rule. By stepping into the batter's box, Avila didn't agree to let opposing pitchers bean him and give him concussions whenever they felt like getting revenge for whatever grievance, real or imagined, that the pitchers might have. That would be crazy. More importantly, the rules of the game did not allow it.

Avila was not asking the community college and the Owls to drain the spirit of the game by making it excessively safe. He was asking that they not do anything to make the game more dangerous than it needed to be, by abiding by the rule not to intentionally hit batters. Avila accepted the risk of injury from a truly wild pitch. Accidents happen. What he did not accept, and what he did not think was right, was that the community college and the Owls astronomically increased the risks of injury by authorizing one of their players to intentionally injure another player by purposefully throwing a hardball directly at his head.

So, was the community college responsible for Avila's injury because its player intentionally hit him with a pitch? Or was Avila left without any recourse because he voluntarily put himself at risk by choosing to play a dangerous game? How would you rule?

HOW THE COURT RULED

For Avila to win his claim against the community college, he had to show that the college's pitcher owed him a duty not to throw the baseball at his head.

Most of the time, players injured when playing a game can't sue for their injuries. The general idea is that if you agree to play a physical game, you also agree to the risk that you might get hurt playing that game. The name for this legal rule is the assumption of risk doctrine, which basically says that where a person voluntarily accepts a known and appreciated risk, that person cannot later sue if that risk materializes.

The assumption of risk doctrine plays a role in any recreational activity that carries danger of injury, like skiing or skydiving. In sports, the assumption of risk doctrine means that a person cannot sue for injuries that result from risks "deemed inherent in a sport." Getting hit by a wild pitch would be an example of an inherent risk of baseball. Throws routinely get away from pitchers. Pitches come in at batters at speeds approaching one hundred miles per hour. The strike zone is only inches away from where the batter stands. Avila was a pitcher himself; he knew perfectly well that not every pitch flies straight, and that occasionally batters get hit by the ball. And when it happens that a pitch hits a batter, the risk that the batter might be seriously hurt is obvious and well known. Regrettable, yes, but undoubtedly part of the game.

But Avila hadn't gotten hit by a wild pitch. The pitcher didn't miss his intended target. He hit it squarely and with devastating force. The target just happened to be Avila's head instead of the strike zone. Getting a concussion from a pitch *intentionally* aimed at the batter's head, argued Avila, was most certainly *not* an inherent risk of the game of baseball.

The court began its analysis of this argument by noting that pitchers frequently throw the ball at or very near batters. They do this for lots of reasons. For example, to fool batters about where the ball will go next, pitchers need to move their pitches around, both inside and outside the strike zone. Sometimes that means throwing the ball very close to the batter's body. But there's more. Sometimes, throwing directly at the batter— *on purpose*—is precisely part of a pitcher's strategy. As the court put it, pitchers throw directly at batters "to disrupt a batter's timing or back him away from home plate, to retaliate after a teammate has been hit, or to punish a batter for having hit a home run." Throwing at batters is so common, the court observed, that baseball lingo is peppered with colorful terms to describe the tactic: "brushback," "beanball," and "chin music," among others.

The court was also impressed by the fact that many of baseball's most respected professional players and managers have openly talked about the important role that intentionally throwing pitches at batters plays in the sport. Past and future Hall of Famers like Don Drysdale, Early Wynn, Bob Gibson, Pedro Martinez, and Roger Clemens have thrown or threatened to throw at batters to gain an advantage in a game. Beaning batters is, according to these baseball luminaries, as much a part of the game as the home run and the double play.

The court acknowledged that, technically speaking, the official rules of baseball at the professional and collegiate levels prohibit pitchers from intentionally throwing at batters. In the court's view, however, breaking the rules of a game should be punished by the rules of the game, not by courts of law. It would be perfectly acceptable for an umpire seeing a pitch intentionally aimed at a batter to eject the pitcher from the game, or for the league to suspend the offending player. The courts, on the other hand, should stay out of disputes over the rules of games.

The court was also worried about what it would mean for baseball if Avila could sue the Owls for hitting him in the head with a pitch. If injured batters like Avila could bring lawsuits over being hit by a pitch whenever it was unclear whether the pitch was intentional or wild, pitchers would have to worry that throwing any pitch close to the batter's body might lead to an accusation that they did it on purpose. If pitchers missed their spot, they could be hauled into court on a charge that the throw was intentional. Maybe pitchers would win those lawsuits, but maybe they wouldn't. Their fates would be in the hands of juries, and even with an almost-certainly winning case, facing a trial can be frightening and intimidating, because, just like in sports, you can never be sure who will carry the day until it's over. As the saying goes, that's why they play the game. And even if pitchers were to win their cases, they would still have had to spend time, money, and worry fighting the claims. That might be enough to make pitchers think twice before throwing an inside pitch, and the court didn't want the threat of litigation to inhibit the game that way.

Sensing that its decision could open the door to all sorts of violent conduct—razor blades at football games, for example—the court tried not to leave sports players with a blank check to attack each other on the field. If a player does something that is "totally outside the ordinary activity involved in the sport," the court clarified, then that player could be sued in court. If, for example, the Owls pitcher had stormed the Roadrunners' dugout and clubbed Avila with a baseball bat, he would not have been legally immune to charges for his conduct. But hitting Avila with a pitch—even a pitch aimed at his head—was not "totally outside" what might be expected in an ordinary baseball game.

So the pitcher was safe and the batter was out (of court). The pitcher who took it upon himself to punish Avila for pitching poorly the previous inning could not be sued. When he stepped into the batter's box, Avila assumed the risk that a pitcher might come after him, and that's all that happened. So Avila took nothing from his lawsuit, except maybe more headaches to add to his head injury. Did the court get it right? You decide.

REFLECTIONS

Sometimes the most important facts shaping a court's decision are not the details of what happened to the parties in the case at hand. The *Avila* case illustrates how future consequences for other people can decisively influence the outcome of the current controversy.

In *Avila*, the court was called upon to set a rule for liability in baseball. Should pitchers who intentionally injure batters have to pay for the damage they cause? José Avila's case was the most favorable for batters. He hadn't done anything wrong and was the victim of a vicious attack that had done real damage. The trouble for Avila was that his was not the only case on the court's mind.

The court was also worried about future pitchers locked in disputes with future batters. The possibility of liability itself influences behavior. Often that is a good thing. If concern about legal liability leads people to avoid dangerous behaviors, that means less risk, and less risk means fewer injuries. Everyone wins. Usually. But not always.

Risky behavior is not always a bad thing. Or put another way, excessively cautious behavior is not always a good thing, and the rules that courts establish could tip the scales too far.

So while Avila represented injured batters, the court also considered the concerns of the pitchers who weren't represented in the lawsuit, the pitchers who hadn't taken intentional aim at a batter's head, but who wanted to play aggressive baseball while not worrying about lawsuits. Avila urged the court to impose liability on pitchers for their intentions, but proving or disproving the thoughts in a person's head can be excruciatingly difficult and fraught with uncertainty.

This uncertainty can lead to what courts call a chilling effect. A chilling effect occurs when the danger of legal liability discourages people from engaging in legitimate actions. In the contest between pitchers and batters, pitchers should be able to throw close to batters as well as away from them. But close pitches that go awry and hit batters could lead to lawsuits if the batter alleges that the pitch was intentionally aimed at the batter, whereas away pitches have no chance of provoking a lawsuit. This asymmetry between inside and outside pitches might lead pitchers to favor throwing outside pitches. If that happened, the game of baseball itself would be fundamentally altered.

Or at least that's what the court thought in the *Avila* case. Considering the interests of potential litigants not before the court comes with a challenge. The advantage of the adversarial system is that zealous advocates on opposing sides will vigorously argue their positions. This gives courts the benefit of weighing the strongest arguments (at least in theory—poor advocates certainly exist). For the potential future litigants who are not present, however, courts have less information. To some extent, courts rely on their own speculation about what these absent parties might think or do; but the personal speculation of judges, untested by the adversarial system, is susceptible to error. As another source of information, interest groups in big cases in front of the most important courts will submit friend-of the-court, or amicus, briefs that describe what these interest groups believe would be the effects if the courts rule one way or the other. The representations and predictions in amicus briefs suffer from not being tested through cross-examination, but this limitation is balanced somewhat by the fact that opposing amicus briefs often come from groups with opposite interests.

When courts are setting out the rules of law, their concern goes beyond the parties before them. Knowing this, well-counseled litigants argue for a rule of law by pointing, not just to their own self-interest, but also to the larger interests of everyone affected by the rule. The ideal rule produces just results not only in an individual case but also in all the other situations where the rule might be applied. It can be hard to know whether a rule will achieve that lofty goal. As a judge, sometimes you just have to take your best guess.

· · · · ·

Questions

1. The rules of baseball clearly prohibit intentionally throwing pitches at batters. Is the court right that intentionally hitting batters with pitches is really an inherent part of baseball, when the rules established by the organizers of the game prohibit it? How should ordinary fouls be distinguished from acts that are "totally outside the ordinary activity involved in the sport"?

2. The court was highly influenced by the fact that numerous high-profile baseball players admitted to intentionally hitting batters to gain some advantage in the game, and by the fact that baseball had nicknames for this particular type of misconduct. Are those good reasons for immunizing pitchers for intentionally injuring batters? For example, baseball has a name for when a team rushes out on the field to attack the other team's players. It's called "clearing the bench," and one can imagine that clearing the bench might gain some tactical advantage, such as intimidating the opposing team. If a team "clears the bench" and injures other players by punching, kicking, or jumping on them, as sometimes happens when brawls break out, should that be considered part of the game or "totally outside the ordinary activity involved in the sport"? How should a court tell the difference?

3. The court noted that baseball pitchers have traditionally thrown pitches directly at batters for many reasons, including "to disrupt a batter's timing or

back him away from home plate, to retaliate after a teammate has been hit, or to punish a batter for having hit a home run." By denying Avila's lawsuit, the court implicitly condoned throwing high-speed balls at batters for these reasons. What do you think of a pitcher aiming to hit a batter "to retaliate" or "to punish" the batter? Are those legitimate reasons to hit another person? Are those motivations that the law should support by immunizing pitchers from legal liability for injuring someone with a pitch that was intentionally aimed at the batter?

4. The court worried that if pitchers were exposed to lawsuits for hitting batters, that would inhibit how pitchers play and could ruin the game of baseball (or at least fundamentally change it). Do you think the court was right in its prediction? How do you know? How might baseball have changed its rules if the court had concluded that batters could sue pitchers for intentionally hitting them with pitches? Would those changes make the game better or worse?

Read It Yourself

Avila v. Citrus Community College Dist., 131 P. 3d 383 (Cal. 2006).

18 The Worth of a Chance

Leslie Herskovits was sick, very sick, only he didn't know it. Yes, he knew he wasn't well. He had pains in his chest and a pesky cough he couldn't shake, but those are common enough ailments, no cause for serious alarm. To be on the safe side, he went to see a doctor. The doctor ordered x-rays, but found nothing amiss, and sent Herskovits home. His coughing fits continued and got progressively worse. He returned to the doctor for help. The doctor prescribed cough medicine. Other than occasionally taking more chest x-rays, the doctor didn't prescribe any stronger treatment, and a year went by with no improvement.

The spring of the following year, Herskovits and his wife left their Seattle home for an extended vacation in search of warmer weather, hoping that heat and a change of environment might ease Herskovits's symptoms. It didn't work. So he and his wife returned home to Seattle and sought out another doctor for a second opinion.

This time the diagnosis was swift and dire. Within three weeks, Herskovits's new doctor gave him the bad news: he had cancer. A few weeks later, Herskovits went in for surgery and had one of his lungs removed. Twenty months later, at the age of sixty, Leslie Herskovits was dead.

Stricken with grief over the loss of her husband, Herskovits's bereaved widow sued his original doctor. The doctor had ordered x-rays of Herskovits's chest but totally missed the cancer that was growing in his lungs. If he had done his job right, the widow contended, the doctor would have seen the cancer and gotten Herskovits into treatment. Because of the doctor's carelessness, Herskovits had gone more than a year before receiving a correct diagnosis and finally starting treatments that might have saved his life if only he had gotten them earlier. Proper medical care came too late. It was the doctor's fault that a beloved husband was taken away from his wife before his time.

The doctor took issue with this perspective. Herskovits was already very sick with cancer when he came to see the doctor. Yes, he had failed to correctly diagnose it, but the doctor did not cause Herskovits's cancer, and it was the cancer that killed him. Herskovits lived for nearly three years after the missed diagnosis. Even if the doctor had spotted the cancer the first time Herskovits had come in, there was no way to know whether Herskovits would have lived a day longer than he did. For all anyone knew, Herskovits might have died even sooner from the effects of the cancer treatments, which are very hard on the body.

Herskovits's widow brought in an expert witness. The expert testified that if Herskovits's original doctor had made the correct diagnosis of lung cancer when he first saw Herskovits, then the latter's chance of surviving for five years would have been 39 percent. Because the diagnosis was delayed, opined the expert, Herskovits's chance of surviving five years fell to only 25 percent.

An expert also testified on behalf of the doctor. In his opinion, an earlier diagnosis of Herskovits's lung cancer would not have saved his life. It wouldn't even have lengthened it. With the kind of cancer Herskovits had, and the stage to which it had advanced by the time he had seen the first doctor, his death within several years was a virtual certainty, in this expert's opinion, and there was nothing any doctor could have done to prevent it.

Maybe, maybe not, was the response of Herskovits's widow. The first expert had testified that Herskovits's chance of surviving five years had gone from 39 percent to 25 percent, a reduction of 14 percentage points in his chance of survival. Nothing in life is guaranteed, and it was true that

Herskovits was very sick, but he had sought out medical attention to get help. He deserved to have that extra 14 percent chance of a longer life; but the doctor, because of his negligence, took that away from him by not making the right diagnosis at the right time.

This tallying of probabilities didn't make sense to the doctor and his attorneys. To succeed in the lawsuit against the doctor, they argued, the plaintiff had to show that it was "more likely than not" that the doctor's actions caused Herskovits's death. Even with the best medical care, the chance of Herskovits dying—according the widow's own expert—was 61 percent. In other words, it was more likely than not that he would have died no matter what the doctor did. The difference between a 61 percent chance of death and a 75 percent chance of death was too thin a reed upon which to base legal liability.

Herskovits had been sick and likely had been dying. The doctor clearly made a mistake, but did the mistake matter? The evidence suggested that the answer was no. The most that medical science could say was that the doctor's mistake hurt Herskovits's chances by a little bit, but there was no way to know whether fortune would have favored him or not. Even if the odds had been slightly more in Herskovits's favor, they were heavily tilted against him, misdiagnosis or no misdiagnosis.

The question for the court was whether the reduction in Herskovits's chance of survival was an injury that the law should recognize, especially since, with or without the reduction, the odds were that Herskovits was going to die. How would you rule?

HOW THE COURT RULED

There was no question that Herskovits's doctor screwed up. His job was to correctly diagnose Herskovits's condition, and he failed miserably. Prescribing cough syrup for cancer is negligence—no two ways about it.

Even so, to win civil cases, plaintiffs must show more than mistakes. They must show that those mistakes caused them harm. The standard of proof plaintiffs must satisfy is known as the "preponderance of the evidence." What this means is that the plaintiff must show that it is more likely than not that the defendant's negligence was the cause of the plaintiff's injury.

What made this case tricky is that it wasn't clear that the doctor's misdiagnosis had harmed Herskovits in any way. According to the plaintiff's own expert, even with a proper diagnosis and the best care possible, it was more likely than not—61 percent was the exact estimate—that Herskovits would not have survived five years.

At the same time, if the plaintiff's expert were to be believed, the doctor's mistake did have an effect. The mistake reduced Herskovits's chance of surviving for five years from 39 percent to 25 percent. That 14 percentage point reduction amounted to decreasing Herskovits's odds of survival by more than a third.

Given that Herskovits was likely to die with or without a correct diagnosis by the first doctor—there was a 61 percent chance that he was going to die even with the best of care—could it truly be said that it was "more likely than not" that the doctor's mistake caused Herskovits's death? The court's answer was yes.

The court's principal reason was pragmatic. In the court's view, the doctor was essentially asking the court to rule that if a patient has less than a 50 percent chance of surviving at the time of a medical procedure, then there could never be any liability for negligence because it was "more likely than not" that the patient was going to die anyway. But if that were the rule, doctors could commit the most egregious and flagrant negligence and never be held responsible, just because the patients were very sick.

No one could ever know what Herskovits's fate would have been had his cancer been detected earlier, as it should have been. But the doctor who had the duty to detect it would not be heard to complain that guesses about Herskovits's future were speculative. It was the doctor's fault that Herskovits never found out whether he would have lived or died with the improved odds that would have come from timely treatment. The doctor's job is not to cure all ills. It is to give patients the best chance at health by correctly diagnosing their conditions and prescribing the best treatments medical science has available.

Proof that the doctor's mistake caused Herskovits's death was, therefore, not required. The increase in the *risk* of harm to Herskovits was injury enough. Whether this increased risk should be considered the cause of Herskovits's death for legal purposes, and what amount of money should be awarded to his wife for the reduction of her husband's marginal chance of survival, were questions best left to the wisdom and judgment of the jury.

So the grieving widow was allowed to press her claim that the reduction of Herskovits's chances cost him his life. If a jury agreed with her, the doctor would have to pay for his mistake, with the exact amount to be determined by the jury. Did the court get it right? You decide.

REFLECTIONS

Talk about probability is so pervasive that sometimes it is easy to lose track of what *probability* means. The meteorologist tells us, for example, that tomorrow there is a 60 percent chance of rain. If it rains, does that mean the probability was correct? If it doesn't rain, does that mean the probability was incorrect? How do you know whether the meteorologist's prediction was right or wrong?

Flipping a fair coin entails an equal probability that the coin will land heads and that it will land tails. In this context, *probability* means something like: if you flipped the coin a thousand times, you would expect to see the coin land heads about five hundred times and tails about five hundred times. Not necessarily exactly half and half, but close. Probability does not tell you whether the coin will land heads or tails on any particular toss. The only way to know what will happen in that case is to toss the coin.

For repeatable events like coin tosses and dice rolls, probability can be understood as the outcomes you would expect to see if the events repeat many times. But life is not a repeatable game. Leslie Herskovits had only one battle with cancer. He didn't have a thousand chances to play out the course of his disease.

The expert's statement that Herskovits had a 39 percent chance of survival with early treatment and a 25 percent chance without it can be understood as saying that if 1,000 people with Herskovits's condition had received early treatment, approximately 390 of them would have lived five years, and 610 of them would have died. And if 1,000 with Herskovits's condition had received the late treatment Herskovits received, approximately 250 of them would have lived five years and 750 of them would have died.

Putting these numbers another way, if Herskovits has a 1,000 lives to live, then in 610 of them he dies whether he gets the early treatment or not. Of these hypothetical 1,000 lives, Herskovits suffers harm from the original doctor's misdiagnosis in only 140 of them (the difference between the 610 deaths he could expect with perfect treatment and the 750 deaths he could expect with the misdiagnosis).

Herskovits, of course, only had one life, and it is impossible to know whether his death was among the 610 that he could have expected given his dire condition, or the 140 deaths that he could have avoided with proper treatment. But maybe this level of certainty is not required.

The law requires that victims of negligence demonstrate that they have been harmed. That demonstration requires not absolute certainty but, in civil cases, only a preponderance of the evidence. In this case, *preponderance of the evidence* simply means that it is more likely than not that the defendant's negligence harmed the victim. It was clear to the court that reducing the chances of survival from bad to worse was a harm that the law could and should recognize. The amount of harm—in other words, the amount of money to be awarded as damages—was a different question. And answering it would be the jury's job.

· · · · ·

Questions

1. The court left it up to the jury to decide how much Herskovits's wife should recover for the decrease in her husband's chance of survival from 39 percent to 25 percent. If you were on the jury, how much would you consider appropriate to award as damages for Herskovits's decreased chance of survival? How would you compute (and justify) that figure?

2. The doctor's expert suggested that the failure to diagnose Herskovits's cancer might have actually extended his life because the misdiagnosis postponed the cancer treatments, which can harm the body as much as the cancer. Of course, the expert's claim cannot be verified with concrete, objective evidence, because there is no way to know for sure how Herskovits would have responded to early treatment, since that early treatment never happened. Nevertheless, suppose, for

the sake of argument, that the probability of the treatment hurting Herskovits was 10 percent and the probability of it helping Herskovits was 90 percent. Should the doctor receive credit for saving Herskovits from the 10 percent risk that early treatment would have harmed him? What if the percentages were reversed and the probability of harm from the early treatment was 90 percent and the probability of benefit was only 10 percent? What if the probability was 50–50?

Read It Yourself

Herskovits v. Group Health, 664 P. 2d 474 (Wash. 1983).

19 Pray at Your Own Risk

The congregants of the Shepard's Fold Church of God gathered together on the evening of February 12, 1974, as they regularly did, for fellowship and prayer. It was a Tuesday night and the birthday of Abraham Lincoln, but neither the pressures of the workweek nor the anniversary of the birth of the Great Emancipator dampened the turnout of the faithful. That night, it was standing room only. The pews were packed, and the aisles were the only places open to latecomers who wanted to join the evening's services.

Reverend Rodney Jeffers was in the pulpit, and he was in rare form. The passion of his sermon whipped up the crowd to new heights of spiritual inspiration. The good reverend could feel the excitement surging all around him. He called for the church doors to be opened. He said something about "running," although exactly what he said was lost in the frenzy of the moment.

Ken Fussell was among the worshippers that night, and when he heard the reverend's call to run, the Holy Spirit grabbed him by the shoulders and dragged him to his feet. He sprinted down the aisle to throw himself into the arms of the good and loving God who called to him. It was not clear what Fussell's plan exactly was, but whatever it was, his short pilgrimage from aisle to altar was cut short when he tripped.

Collided would be a better word, for in the aisle wrapped up in her own prayerful communion with the Holy Spirit was Vonnie Bass, one of the many parishioners who hadn't found a seat and had had to make do with the aisle for her place of worship. As the reverend exhorted the crowd from the pulpit and Ken Fussell leapt to his feet behind her, Bass was standing in the aisle, head bowed in silent prayer. She never saw what hit her, but she found out later. It was Ken Fussell.

When Fussell crashed into Bass, she lost her balance and fell hard, getting severely hurt in the process. The Lord helps those who help themselves, or so the saying goes. So Bass shifted her prayers from church to court and sued Fussell and the Shepard's Fold Church of God for her injuries, Fussell for running into her and the church for allowing its reverend to whip overcrowded worshippers into such a frenzy that injury was sure to ensue.

It was undeniable that Fussell ran into Bass, and that Bass was injured as a result. But Fussell pleaded innocence. At the time of the accident, he was "trotting"—that was Fussell's word—in the aisle under the influence of the Spirit of the Lord. At that moment he had no control over his body. His every action and movement was given over to the Lord's guiding hand. Fussell testified that he had no memory of actually running into Bass, such was the state of his spiritual intoxication.

For his part, Reverend Jeffers argued that he did what he could to prevent the accident. He had recognized that the church was crowded, and more than once he had asked that the aisles be cleared. It was true that he encouraged, as he put it, "open response to the Spirit," and that running or moving "in the Spirit" was a common part of the religious experience at the church. He usually did the running himself, going up and down the aisles to be closer to the congregation; but that night, recognizing that the crowds might be too thick, he had asked that the exterior doors be opened to create more space, and that somebody run for him. By all appearances, Ken Fussell had answered the reverend's call.

Anyway, wasn't Vonnie Bass really at fault here because she was in the aisle? Aisles are for walking and, in the Shepard's Fold Church of God, for running when the spirit moved a worshipper. Shouldn't she have found a seat? And if she hadn't been able find a seat, shouldn't she have found another place to be? If you stand in a freeway, you can't complain if you get hit by a car. She either assumed the risk of getting hit or contributed to the creation of the accident by being at the wrong place at the wrong time. Either way, she shouldn't be able to extract money from Fussell or the church for her own lack of awareness of her surroundings.

Bass took strong exception to this line of argument. She had been going to the Shepard's Fold for twenty-five years and had never seen or heard of anyone ever getting hurt at church. She was praying like everyone else. It was Fussell's job to watch where he was going, and the church's job not to call upon people to run when the aisles were full of people.

What do you think? Did the throes of religious ecstasy excuse Fussell's collision with Bass? Did the church handle the crowded situation in a reasonable way? Did Bass invite her own injury by not taking reasonable care to protect herself in a dangerous situation? How would you rule?

HOW THE COURT RULED

Ken Fussell crashed into Vonnie Bass while in the throes of religious ecstasy. The Holy Spirit, not his own mind, guided his actions. At least, that's what Fussell said. The court was not impressed.

If Fussell were trying to say that he was not responsible for injuring Bass because he was not in control of his body, then he was like a drunk driver claiming the drink made him crash his car. If you blur your judgment with alcohol, you're responsible for the damage you cause, even if you didn't realize you were causing it. Similarly, reasoned the court, if you blur your judgment with religious fervor, you're still responsible for the damage you cause. As the court put it: "A worshiper in church has no more right to run over a fellow worshiper in the aisle than a passerby on the sidewalk." Whether Fussell was in full possession of his wits was irrelevant. He should have been, and so he was negligent when he careened down the aisle of the Shepard's Fold Church and knocked poor Bass off her feet.

Likewise, the church itself had a duty not to create unreasonable risks of injury for its parishioners. Reverend Jeffers could see the church's aisles were crowded with people, and maybe he said a word or two entreating people to clear the way, but even though his requests went unheeded and the danger continued unabated, he preached on, whipping up the crowd and calling on parishioners to run amid the press of people, where the danger of injury ran high. He did not stop the service. He did not clear the aisles. He could easily have done more to protect his parishioners from harm, but he didn't; and so the court found the church, too, responsible for Bass's injuries.

But what of Vonnie Bass's role in this affair? She crowded into the aisle, when clearly that was unsafe. She did not heed Reverend Jeffers's call—weak as it may have been—to clear the aisle. Bass knew that worshippers frequently moved up and down the aisles during the services, the same aisles where she planted herself, bowed her head, and paid no heed to the potential for danger in her surroundings. Did Bass assume the risk or contribute to her own injury?

The court thought not. You can assume a risk only if you know it exists. Bass had been going to the Shepard's Fold Church for twenty-five years without any harm to herself or anyone else that she knew of. Whatever reasonable risks praying in an aisle in church might invite, being run over wasn't one of them.

The root of the accident wasn't that the church allowed movement in the aisles during services, a fact of which Bass was aware. Heedless running in the aisle was the cause. This was, as the court put it, "an unusual and extraordinary hazard, to which [Bass] did not knowingly expose herself." The mere fact that Bass was praying in the aisle did not, therefore, mean that she assumed the risk of getting run over by someone not looking where he was going.

Neither did Bass contribute to her own injury by not paying enough attention. Fussell ran in the crowded aisle heedless of whom or what was in front of him. Bass, in contrast, bowed her head in prayer during a church service. Praying in church is not an unreasonable thing for a person to do, whether in pew or aisle. She had no reason to be on alert for stampeding parishioners. The fault belonged to Fussell, who recklessly ran through a crowd, and to the church that created the hazardous circumstances and encouraged him to do it.

So Bass's courtroom prayers were answered. The church's and Fussell's, not so much. Did the court get it right? You decide.

REFLECTIONS

Negligence, as the name implies, requires some degree of fault, some act of carelessness, incompetence, or neglect. It follows, therefore, that if one person injures another without fault, there is no negligence and, therefore, no liability. How could injury without negligence happen?

Here's one possible scenario: Devon is at a shooting range taking target practice, and Pete walks onto the range while Devon is firing her weapon. If Devon accidentally shoots Pete, there is probably no negligence. Devon didn't do anything wrong. She fired the gun that launched the bullet that caused Pete to be injured, but it was Pete who acted carelessly, by walking into the line of fire. Devon had no reason to expect Pete to be on the firing range, so she is not negligent.

Here's another possible example. After finishing at the shooting range, Devon goes to play softball with some friends. Devon is in the batter's box waiting for the pitch. Pete is playing catcher. The score is tied and this is the last inning; and Devon, being a competitive person, is determined to drive in the winning run. Pete misjudges the length of Devon's bat and sets himself too close to the plate. When the pitch comes in, Devon gives a mighty swing and hits Pete in the head with the bat. Again, Devon is not negligent. She didn't even know Pete was there, and she had no reason to be watching out for him. Since Pete was the catcher, it was his job to stay out of the way of Devon's bat. Again, it was Pete who was careless and neglectful, not Devon.

We could come up with other examples where Devon brutalizes Pete through no fault of her own, but let's stop here to analyze what the shooting range and softball game have in common. In both cases, Devon didn't know where Pete was. If she'd had actual knowledge of his location, she would have been required to take care not to hurt Pete even though Pete was in the wrong place at the wrong time, with the amount of care required depending on the circumstances. In both cases, Devon was engaged in a lawful activity. If Devon were shooting guns or swinging bats in a department store, she might be responsible for anyone she injured while breaking the law, regardless of whether she knew the person was there or not. In both cases, Devon had no reason to take additional precautions against hurting someone. No reasonable person expects someone to walk onto a firing range while live fire is going on. No reasonable person expects a catcher to scoot too close to a batter ready to swing. The fault lies not with the person who caused the injury but with the person who was injured.

Now consider a case where Devon and Pete are both at fault. Devon is going way too fast down a residential street, her mind on an important meeting and not on the road ahead. Pete is hurrying to catch a bus, but he is texting on his phone and not looking where he is going. Pete blindly steps into the street. Devon recklessly runs him down. Who caused the accident?

Devon is negligent for speeding and not paying attention to the road. Pete is negligent for crossing the street while looking down at his phone and not out for oncoming traffic. The negligence of both Devon and Pete contributed to the accident. So who should pay for the injuries?

There are two schools of thought on how to answer that question. According to common law, the ancient rule was: the act of contributing in any way to an accident barred damages of any kind. If Pete has any responsibility for the accident, no matter how small or slight, he gets nothing. This approach is called "pure contributory negligence." The logic is that people should not be able to win compensation for losses that they cause themselves.

The more common rule nowadays is called comparative fault. Under comparative fault, the percentage of responsibility for each person who contributes to an accident is measured, and the injured person can recover up to the other person's proportion of fault. So if Devon is 90 percent responsible for running Pete down because she was going too fast, and Pete is 10 percent responsible because he did not check for cars before crossing the street, Pete can recover 90 percent of the cost of his injuries from Devon. The logic of comparative fault is that each person in the accident pays for his or her share of responsibility. The injurer pays up to her share of the fault. The injured pays by not recovering the cost of his share of the fault.

Comparative fault can yield some odd results, so some jurisdictions employ a variation of the rule. For example, imagine that Pete is 90 percent responsible for the accident. Under a pure comparative fault-regime, Pete could still recover 10 percent from Devon. It can seem unfair that Devon would have to pay Pete anything when Pete is overwhelmingly responsible for the accident, so some jurisdictions have a modified comparative fault rule that prohibits injured parties like Pete from recovering if their own negligence is more than 50 percent responsible for the accident.

Let's return to the case of Vonnie Bass and Ken Fussell. Was their accident anything like the examples described above? Bass was standing in an aisle, which is clearly a path of travel, especially in a church where pastor and parishioners frequently run up and down the aisle to and from the altar. Even though she was in the middle of a path of travel, Bass had her head bowed and was unaware of her surroundings. Fussell did not have actual knowledge that Bass was in his way (he was caught up in religious excitement). And he was engaged in lawful activity, activity that was encouraged by the church's leader. None of these facts points to negligence on Fussell's part, but there is one more question to consider.

Was it reasonable for Fussell to run down the aisle without looking where he was going? Since Fussell lost in court, let's consider, as an exercise, his point of view. First, aisles are for traveling, not for praying. He was traveling in the aisle. She was praying. He was in the right place. She was not. Second, the preacher had called for someone to run. Fussell was answering that call. Bass either didn't hear it or didn't pay attention to it. Either way, she did nothing to move out of the way. Finally, the church was a place where people came to be touched by the Holy Spirit. Bass knew that. That's why she came, too. Yet she didn't pay any attention. Is Bass like Pete in the previous examples?

From Bass's point of view, naturally, the story is very different. The church was overcrowded. That wasn't her fault. If she could have found a seat, she would have taken one. Everyone could see that many people, including Bass, were in the aisle. Everyone, including Fussell, either knew or should have known that the aisles were not free and clear for moving, at least not on that particularly congested night. Running in that crowded space, therefore, was unreasonable and negligent.

The conflict between Bass and Fussell illustrates that the reasonableness of a person's action is nearly always a debatable question that heavily depends on the specific facts and circumstances of a particular case. Because reasonableness depends so heavily on facts, courts almost always leave it to juries to decide whether a particular person acted reasonably. A corollary to this is that predicting whether a jury will find specific conduct to be reasonable is more art than science, often boiling down to guesswork.

. . . . .

Questions

1. In response to Ken Fussell's argument that he was not in control of his own actions because he was possessed by the Holy Spirit, the court ruled that his condition should be treated the same as voluntary intoxication. (If you drink so much that you can't think straight, the law will not permit you to say you didn't know what you were doing.) Is intoxication a fair analogy for religious passion? Why or why not?

2. The court was firm that Vonnie Bass bore no responsibility because all she did was pray in church, which is what everyone who goes to church does. Should the court have given more weight to the fact that Bass voluntarily chose to stand in the aisles where parishioners frequently moved up and down during the services? Would the verdict have been different if Bass had been reading a book? Listening to music with headphones? Lying down in the aisle? Why or why not?

Read It Yourself

Bass v. Aetna Ins. Co., 370 So. 2d 511 (La. 1979).

20 Coin-Flip Wrongdoers

Long after the crisp and clear morning in November 1945 when he set out with a couple of friends named Tice and Simonson to spend a relaxing day hunting, Charles Summers would recall that the line was the most important thing, and that the line had been broken. And that that's when everything had gone wrong. But that was later.

On the day of the hunt, the three friends were focused on quail, their intended quarry. Each man carried a 12-gauge shotgun, locked and loaded. To flush out the shy birds from their hidden dens, the hunters arranged themselves in a straight line and moved together, tramping through brush and bramble, stirring up dirt and rattling the bushes, to scare the birds into frightened flight, where the hunters would be able to see their brown bodies against the clear blue sky and shoot them down. Later, Summers was very clear on this. The line was important. As long as the line held, their prey would always be in front of them and their companions to the side. The line meant a clear field of fire. The line meant safety. The men talked about the line. They agreed on the line. However, on the uneven terrain of quail country, the line did not hold.

As the hunters combed the brush for birds to shoot, they came upon a hill and started to climb. As they ascended, their positions drifted.

Summers got a little ahead, and his friends fell a little behind. Their formation became more of a triangle than a line.

Suddenly, a frantic flutter of feathers rattled the still country air. This was the noise the hunters had been waiting for. They swung their shotguns, searching for the source of the sound. By cruel and careless chance, the cold geometry of the bird's flight took their quarry about ten feet into the air—right above Summers's head.

At most, if Summers had time to think anything at all, he had only a fraction of a second to consider the irony that the all-important line had become a line of fire—with him directly in its deadly path. Surely, his friends would not shoot. Surely, they would see the man below the bird and realize that the spray of shot from their guns would fill the field where their friend stood. Surely, he would be safe. But in that same fraction of a second, the adrenaline rush that the others experienced from the sight of the flushed quail proved stronger and quicker than reflective judgment. Trigger fingers twitched. The sound of two shotguns firing simultaneously rang out across the hillside.

The hunters hit, but not their mark. The spray of shot sailed all around Summers. One shot pellet hit his upper lip. Another tore out his eye. Summers crumpled in a bloody heap. Miraculously, he survived. This was not a case of "he never knew what hit him." Summers knew what hit him—all too well, he knew. What he didn't know was who.

Summers did not appreciate getting shot in the eye and lip—not entirely a surprise—so he sued his buddies Tice and Simonson. He had them for shooting their guns in his direction. They couldn't deny that they had fired, and clearly they shouldn't have discharged their weapons when a person was in their line of fire. That was negligence.

But Summers's lawsuit presented a problem. Negligence isn't a wrong unless the negligent person actually hurts another person or property. If you make a mistake and no one is hurt, the law declares the equivalent of "no harm, no foul." Without proof of damage caused by the negligent act, a lawsuit for negligence cannot succeed.

Summers had no trouble showing damage. He had been hit in the face with shotgun pellets negligently fired in his direction. His trouble was proving *who* had caused the damage. Summers had been hit by exactly two shot pellets, one in the lip and one in the eye. The two pellets could have come from one gun, or each could have come from different ones. There was no way to tell for sure. This presented a dilemma.

In civil lawsuits, a plaintiff has the burden of proving a case by what is known as a preponderance of the evidence. The preponderance-of-the-evidence standard means that, in a civil dispute, the side who wins is the one whose version of events is more likely to be true than not. Although not spelled out in the law, many people use percentages as a convenient shorthand for understanding the preponderance of the evidence as an amount of evidence that establishes a fact with greater than 50 percent probability. In other words, anything better than a coin flip is enough to win.

Summers had most of his case tied up. He was injured through no fault of his own. No matter how enticing the game, you shouldn't shoot in the direction of your hunting partner. Whoever shot him would have to pay for his injuries. But who had fired the shots that injured Summers: Tice or Simonson or both?

You would think that since both Tice and Simonson had fired their guns at Summers, Summers's case would be simple, but the burden of proof complicated things. If Summers sued Tice, Summers would lose because there was an exactly 50 percent chance that Simonson had shot him, which is just under the necessary "more than 50 percent" needed for a preponderance of the evidence. If Summers sued Simonson, Summers would also lose because there was a 50 percent chance that Tice had shot him. Summers could narrow down the culprits to two people, but unfortunately, with two potential wrongdoers, his case against each of them fell just short of crossing the magic 50 percent mark.

Summers protested that this application of the burden of proof wasn't justice. Somebody had shot him, and it was either Tice or Simonson or both. It wasn't his fault that he didn't know which one it was. How was he supposed to know? He had been shot! In the eye!

Tice and Simonson pointed out that what Summers was asking was for the court to lower the standard of proof. A preponderance of the evidence means *more* likely than not. *Equally* likely just wasn't enough. Plaintiffs lose cases every day because they cannot produce enough evidence that a particular defendant caused them a particular harm. Summers happened to be one of them, with a particularly close case, as close to the goal line as one could get, but still short of the end zone. He might deserve sympathy for his injuries, Tice and Simonson said, but he did not deserve special treatment from the law.

Should Summers win his case? And if so, against whom should he win? Tice? Simonson? Or both? Or should Summers be held to the standard of proof and his claim denied? Summers stands on the razor's edge of victory with exactly a 50 percent probability that the person who shot him was one or the other of two equally likely wrongdoers. How would you rule?

HOW THE COURT RULED

If two people act together and injure another person, the collaborators are each independently responsible for paying for the whole injury. (In legal parlance, they are "jointly and severally" liable, meaning that both are responsible for all of the damage caused, and the injured person can recover from either or both.)[1]

In this case, however, Tice and Simonson weren't working together. They each acted independently. When the quail bolted into the air from its cover, Tice didn't know Simonson would shoot and Simonson didn't know Tice would shoot. Each decided to pull his trigger on his own, with no communication or agreement between them. Both Simonson and Tice argued that since they acted independently, Summers could not hold one liable for the wrongdoing of the other.

The court was moved by Summers's predicament. He hadn't done anything wrong. Simonson and Tice were the ones who had fired their weapons in his direction, which they should not have done. While it was certainly possible that only one of them hit Summers, the only reason it wasn't clear who was responsible was because Simonson and Tice had both done the same wrong thing at the same time. To the court, it was unjust for someone who had done something wrong to escape responsibility simply because he was in the company of another wrongdoer.

There may be some injustice in the fact that either Simonson or Tice would be forced to pay damages when his wrongful act didn't actually cause any harm; but the court compared that to the injustice Summers would face if he could not recover anything because it was impossible to prove that the pellets that struck him had come specifically from the gun of one man or the other. If someone had to suffer an unjust loss, it was better that it be a wrongdoer than an innocent person.

The solution, the court decided, was to shift the burden of proof. Summers had proven that either Simonson or Tice shot him. They would both be liable to Summers, unless one could prove that it was the other who had fired the fateful shots. It would be up to them to come up with evidence of innocence or suffer the consequences.

Simonson and Tice might have protested that the court's decision asked them to do the impossible. There is no way either could prove his innocence. To that argument the reply might be that they had urged the court to impose the same impossible task on Summers, the innocent victim. Someone had to lose the game of hot potato with the burden of proof, and in the court's judgment it should be the wrongdoers. If the wrongdoers were being wronged, then they had brought that on themselves by their own wrongdoing.

In effect, the court treated Simonson and Tice as if they had acted in concert, even though they hadn't. If one of the two was truly innocent and could prove it, the court left open a fix: If Simonson or Tice could prove that his shot had done no damage, the innocent shooter could sue the other to recover whatever damages he was forced to pay Summers. But that was something for the two wrongdoers to work out on their own, if they could. In the meantime, they were both on the hook for paying for Summers's damaged eye and lip.

Did the court get this one right? You decide.

REFLECTIONS

The *Summers* case presents the question of what to do when a plaintiff knows he has been the victim of negligence, but he doesn't know who is responsible. In some ways, *Summers* is the easiest version of this dilemma. Summers knew that the responsible person had to be one of two people, possibly both. But what happens if the number of potentially responsible people increases?

For example, consider a case where a patient goes under anesthesia for surgery. While the patient is unconscious, she is injured—say someone drops a scalpel on her leg. Someone in the operating room dropped the scalpel. Everyone in the room denies seeing the scalpel fall. The injured patient, obviously, has no idea who hurt her, and without the testimony of someone in the room, she has no way of proving who dropped the knife.

Plaintiffs can recover only if they can satisfy their burden of proof. In negligence cases, that means the plaintiff must prove by a preponderance of the evidence that the defendant owed him a duty and breached that duty, and that the defendant's breach of duty was the proximate cause of the plaintiff's injuries. But in the case of the dropped scalpel, how can the plaintiff possibly do that when she was unconscious the whole time?

In days gone by, the plaintiff would simply be out of luck; but contemporary courts are more sympathetic, and in these types of cases they apply a modern doctrine with a Latin name: the doctrine of *res ipsa loquitur*. Under the doctrine of *res ipsa loquitur*, the plaintiff's burden of proof will be satisfied, and the defendant will be found liable, if a person is injured in a way that could happen only if someone were negligent, it is clear that the plaintiff could not be at fault, and the negligent act is something that the defendant would normally be charged with avoiding.

So, in the hypothetical surgery, scalpels don't drop themselves, thus the fact that one stabbed the plaintiff is evidence that something negligent happened. The plaintiff clearly was not at fault. She was, after all, unconscious at the time and had totally entrusted her well-being to the surgeon and his team. It is surgeons' responsibility to protect patients under their care. Therefore, it would be appropriate to hold the surgeon responsible for the patient's injured leg.

Both the *Summers* case and the doctrine of *res ipsa loquitur* provided relief to injured people who might otherwise not have been able to meet the ordinary standards of proof. In both cases, the courts were sure that a wrongdoer had injured an innocent party, and in both cases the rule of law was framed to ensure that wrongdoers were held accountable and the innocent individual was provided with some remedy for his or her injury. In these cases and others like them, the law is a flexible instrument that bends to do justice as the judges perceive that justice to be.

.   .   .   .   .

Questions

1. Summers was a sympathetic plaintiff. He had done nothing wrong and had been hit by pellets in the eye and lip. The shooter had to have been one of Summers's two companions, but it was impossible to tell which one because they both fired their guns when they shouldn't have shot at all. Since the hunting companions both wrongfully fired their guns, it may not seem too much of a stretch for the court to put Summers's loss on them both and then let them work out between themselves who did what—if they can. But how far does that principle go? What if Summers had gone hunting with three friends, or four? What if there were a dozen potential shooters, or a hundred? At what point should the risk of making an innocent person pay for an injury he didn't cause outweigh the needs of an injured person to recover?

2. Keeping the hunters in a line was critical to ensuring the hunters' safety. Summers, it seems, got out ahead of his companions, putting himself in his friends' line of fire. Should Summers be held responsible for his own injury because he had not made sure he was always in line with his two hunting partners? Should he be held partly responsible? If he should be held partly responsible, how should responsibility be divided among the men? Should this affect the court's decision to shift the burden of proof regarding the causation of damage from Summers (the injured plaintiff) to Tice and Simonson (the negligent defendants)?

Read It Yourself

Summers v. Tice, 33 Cal. 2d 80 (1948).

21 Growing Your Own

Vernon Bowman, an Indiana farmer, had what he thought was the perfect solution to a frustrating problem. Vernon's crop of choice was soybeans. The trouble with growing soybeans—as with other plants—is that the same nutrients and water that nourish the crops in the fields also feed weeds that crowd out the food, hurt the harvests, and reduce farmers' incomes. The solution is herbicides, chemicals that poison the weeds, and the best herbicide on the market at the time was a product sold under the name Roundup.

Roundup wiped out weeds, but it also had the unfortunate tendency to kill crops too, so it wasn't perfect. Monsanto, the maker of Roundup, had a solution for that. Working in a laboratory, Monsanto's scientists developed a strain of soybean seeds that resisted Roundup. Farmers using Monsanto's "Roundup Ready" seeds could spray the herbicide at will. Weeds would die. Crops would survive. Everyone would win.

Monsanto was a business, and like all businesses, Monsanto liked to make money. It made money selling Roundup, of course. But it also made money selling the Roundup Ready soybean seeds. The trouble with selling seeds, however, is that seeds produce plants that create more seeds. If you're not careful, you could sell one packet of seeds to a farmer and never sell him another, because the farmer could then grow his own.

Monsanto, however, did not grow to be an international, multibillion-dollar conglomerate by letting moneymaking opportunities slip through its fingers. Monsanto would sell its special Roundup Ready seeds only to farmers who agreed to its terms. Farmers could plant the Roundup Ready seeds once, but only once. They could then eat the plants or sell them, but—and this was the critical piece—the farmers could not save any of the soybeans for future planting. If they wanted to plant another crop of Roundup Ready soybeans, the farmers would have to buy the seeds from Monsanto. Again, everyone wins—Monsanto just wins a little more.

Vernon Bowman was a fan of Monsanto's products. He used Roundup, and he used Roundup Ready seeds, but there was one thing that bothered him. Roundup Ready seeds were expensive, and he would have been much happier if he didn't have to pay so much and happier still if he didn't have to pay anything at all.

The trouble was that Monsanto was the only game in town for buying Roundup Ready soybean seeds. Monsanto had a patent on the seeds, which meant that only Monsanto (and the people to whom Monsanto gave its permission) could make, use, or sell the seeds, and Monsanto was not giving permission to anyone to use the seeds unless they agreed to its terms.

But America wouldn't be anything without ingenuity, and Bowman wasn't one to accept a bad hand lying down. He had an idea. An ingenious idea. The kind of idea that giant businesses are built on. He had a loophole.

Bowman went down to the local grain elevator. He knew the place well. This was where he would bring his crops for sale. The elevator company would buy Bowman's and other farmers' soybeans, store the soybeans in its elevator, and then resell them to food distributors and processors. This time, however, Bowman had not come to sell. He had come to buy.

Bowman bought a sack of soybeans that other farmers had sold and brought them back to his farm. Bowman knew that most of his neighbors used Roundup to fight weeds, and he was guessing that most also used Roundup Ready seeds to protect their plants from the weed killer. He planted the purchased soybeans, sprayed his fields with Roundup, and waited for the soybeans to grow.

Some of the plants died. Roundup Ready seeds were expensive, so not everyone used them for every crop. But that wasn't important. What mattered was that some of the plants did not die. They lived. They grew. They produced seeds. And those seeds, Bowman now knew, were Roundup Ready.

American ingenuity had done it again. Bowman had in his hands a crop of Roundup Ready seeds, but this time he had not made any promises to Monsanto to sell the whole crop and not replant any of the seeds. He was free at last. Never again would he have to pay Monsanto an exorbitant ransom for soybean seeds.

The one thing he was not free from, however, was lawyers. Lots of them. It turned out that Monsanto did not much like the idea of an Indiana farmer planting their patented seeds without paying them their due. If word of Bowman's scheme spread—and it inevitably would—Monsanto's Roundup Ready seed business would wither faster than a weed choked by Roundup itself.

So Monsanto did what any big company that sees a major profit center threatened would do. It sued.

Monsanto sued Bowman for patent infringement. Monsanto had a patent on the Roundup Ready seeds, so only Monsanto could make, use, or sell them. Bowman was using Monsanto's seeds. He should be ordered to stop and to pay damages for violating Monsanto's patent rights.

Not so fast, responded Bowman. He wasn't "making" any of Monsanto's seeds. All he was doing was planting soybeans in the ground. The soybeans then did the rest. If anyone was making the seeds, it was nature itself.

Monsanto was overreaching, contended Bowman. Once Monsanto sold the seeds, the buyers had the right to use the seeds, which they did. Those buyers used the seeds to grow soybeans, which is exactly what Monsanto expected them to do. Those buyers then sold the soybeans to a granary, again all in line with Monsanto's expectations. The granary then sold the soybeans to Bowman, completing the cycle. As the legitimate owner of the soybeans, Bowman had a right to use them as he pleased. What Monsanto had not expected was that instead of consuming or selling the soybeans that Bowman legitimately and lawfully bought, he put them back in the ground and let nature do the rest. Maybe Monsanto's lawyers weren't so smart after all.

Bowman got lawyers of his own, and they made the following argument. Under a legal doctrine known as patent exhaustion, a patent holder has the right to sell (or not sell) the patented item once; but once that first sale is made, the patent holder has no right to prevent other people from reselling the item and those later purchasers from using it. The one thing you can't do is use the item to make new copies. Otherwise, the patent is exhausted.

Here, Monsanto had sold Roundup Ready seeds, and Bowman had bought soybeans grown from those seeds, fair and square. Monsanto, argued Bowman, had no right to prevent future sales because of the doctrine of patent exhaustion.

Next time, Monsanto should hire more lawyers, or better ones.

So did Vernon Bowman, Indiana farmer of soybeans, find a loophole that the international conglomerate Monsanto, with its hordes of lawyers, had missed? Or was Bowman's scheme too clever by half, violating Monsanto's exclusive patent right to make the Roundup Ready seeds? How would you rule?

HOW THE COURT RULED

This was a tough case. So tough that it made its way all the way to the U.S. Supreme Court.

What made this case tough was that Vernon Bowman wasn't really "making" seeds. The seeds were making themselves. Grown-up soybeans make seeds. That's just what they do. It was a natural process. Bowman's only involvement was sticking them in the ground. After that, the plants just did their thing.

On the other hand, the seeds weren't planting themselves. Bowman was doing the planting. Bowman chose the time to plant the seeds. He chose the place. He watered the seeds, fertilized them, and yes, protected them from weeds using the best herbicide he could find, Roundup. Bowman knew that many of the seeds he bought from the granary were highly likely to be Roundup Ready. And he knew that Monsanto went out of its way to make sure that everyone who bought its seeds knew that under no circumstances could they plant Roundup Ready seeds that hadn't been purchased directly from Monsanto. This knowledge cast Bowman's scheme in a poor light.

It is true, the court observed, that the doctrine of patent exhaustion meant that Bowman was free to buy the soybeans from the granary. He was free to eat the soybeans that he bought. He was free to resell them to another person. But he was not free to use them to make copies of the patented item, which in this case was the seeds.

Yet that is just what Bowman did. The fact that the new seeds came from living, growing plants and not from a machine didn't make any difference. The way you make new seeds is you grow them from old seeds. The law did not prohibit a specific method of making copies of patented items. It prohibited making copies, period, whatever the method used.

But the seeds are doing the replicating, not me, argued Bowman. Nope, said the court. The seeds don't sprout spontaneously—at least these didn't. They grew because Bowman planted and cared for them. Bowman's soybean harvest was not some beneficent gift from nature. It was the product of his own work—and of his illegal scheme to acquire Roundup Ready seeds without paying the usual fee.

By planting the Roundup Ready seeds, Bowman made new ones, and in doing so, he violated Monsanto's exclusive patent right to make these particular seeds. The little guy loses. The big corporation wins. Monsanto had enough lawyers after all.

So did the court get it right? You decide.

REFLECTIONS

Monsanto's dual inventions of a powerful herbicide like Roundup and useful plants resistant to that herbicide, such as Roundup Ready soybean seeds, were a vast boon to farming. Armed with the company's weed killer and its weed-killer-resistant seeds, farmers reaped harvests that were much more bountiful, and more profitable, than could be achieved using conventional techniques. To run a successful soybean business, farmers needed Monsanto's products, and nothing illustrated that fact better than the lengths to which Vernon Bowman was willing to go to get his hands on Roundup Ready seeds.

Roundup and Roundup Ready seeds, however, did not invent themselves. Monsanto had to invest time and money in the research to develop chemicals that killed weeds while not endangering humans and killing too many crops. Monsanto then had to invest more time and money in the research to develop seeds that were even more resistant to those chemicals. Patents, which guaranteed Monsanto a fixed period of time to make, use, and sell those products, provided the financial incentive to invest in that research. If anyone could freely make copies of Monsanto's inventions, that would be great for the copiers, but it would lead to fewer useful inventions as companies like Monsanto decided not to invest in innovations for which there was no profit.

Bowman's actions were troubling because they undermined Monsanto's ability to recoup its investments in developing Roundup and Roundup Ready seeds. If Bowman's scheme worked for soybeans, it would work for any improvements to seeds for any plants. That would mean that people would not invest in finding those improvements, and without those improvements, there would be less food and everyone would be worse off.

Protecting Monsanto's patent rights, however, came at a cost. The most obvious cost is that farmers had to pay a premium to use Monsanto's herbicide and herbicide-resistant seeds. Those higher costs, presumably, would be passed on to consumers in the form of higher prices. On the other hand, those higher costs would be offset, at least in part, by higher crop yields.

Another cost was limiting Monsanto's incentives to attempt more innovation. Monsanto was making money twice in the soybean market. First, it sold the herbicide that killed the weeds that choked back harvests. Then it sold the seeds for plants that were resistant to the herbicide that Monsanto itself created. Because Monsanto was making money from Roundup Ready seeds, it had no incentive to develop a version of Roundup that didn't kill plants that had not been genetically modified.

The patent system, therefore, represents a tug-of-war between providing enough incentives to inventors to create new inventions and not stifling innovation by preventing other people from building new things based on those inventions. Unlike copyright, patents last twenty years, so Monsanto's exclusive right to Roundup and Roundup Ready seeds wouldn't last forever. Whether the patent system strikes the right balance between protecting inventors and protecting the public is a question that must be continually asked in order to ensure that the system is working for the public good.

.   .   .   .   .

Questions

1. The soybeans Bowman bought from the grain elevator were much cheaper than Monsanto's seeds because they were not certified to be Roundup Ready. Since the doctrine of patent exhaustion allowed Bowman to buy and use the soybeans, could Bowman have avoided infringing on Monsanto's patent rights by growing a crop from the soybeans he purchased from the grain elevator without harvesting and reusing the seeds that crop produced? In other words, could he have gotten one free harvest, or would even that have violated Monsanto's rights?

2. Seeds are products of nature, and generally the products of nature are free to all people to use. Is it fair for Monsanto to patent a seed, even a genetically modified one? What are the pros and cons of allowing patents on genetic modifications of living things?

Read It Yourself

Bowman v. Monsanto Co., 133 S. Ct. 1761 (2013).

22 Your Body, My Body

At only thirty years old, John Moore was too young to be dying, but dying he was—and he was fading fast. As a surveyor on the Alaska pipeline, Moore was used to long days and hard work. The first sign that something was wrong was simple fatigue, surprising for a man of his strength, but easy enough to shrug off, at least at first. But then he started sweating at night and losing his appetite too. That was harder to ignore. Even harder to ignore was the way his stomach had swelled even though he barely picked at his meals. Unexplained bruises began to appear on his arms and legs. Small cuts bled at alarming rates. Moore needed a doctor.

When he had himself checked out, the news was bad, very, very bad. It was not his stomach that was swelling, but his spleen. The spleen? What's a spleen? The spleen is an organ tucked under the ribs just off to the left of the stomach. The spleen filters the body's bloodstream, recycles old red blood cells, and stores white blood cells. Spleens vary in size, but they are usually fist-shaped, purple, and about four inches long.[1] Normally, it is very difficult to feel a person's spleen, but Moore's condition was anything but normal.

Moore had hairy-cell leukemia, a very rare form of cancer of the blood, in which bone marrow produces too many defective white blood cells and these defective cells crowd out the healthy white blood cells needed to fight infection. Eventually, the malignant cells collect in the spleen, causing it to inflate like a balloon. If he were to have any chance, Moore needed serious help, and he needed it fast.

On October 5, 1976, Moore walked into a hospital operated by the University of California, Los Angeles, hoping for a miracle from the hands of the best doctors in the world. There he met Dr. David Golde. Dr. Golde confirmed that Moore had leukemia, and that things did not look good. Hairy-cell leukemia killed 98 percent of the people it afflicted. Chances were that Moore would come out on the wrong end of that lopsided statistic. Although it was a long shot, Dr. Golde recommended that Moore's spleen be removed immediately. Seeing surgery as his only hope, Moore agreed.

There was no time to waste, and so fifteen days later Moore went under the knife. What the doctors found was breathtaking and horrifying: Moore's spleen had ballooned to a massive size. Dr. Golde and his team extracted the gargantuan organ. The spleen, which should have weighed less than a pound, tipped the scales at a monstrous twenty-two pounds. How could such a thing have grown inside Moore's body? And how had Moore remained alive with that monstrosity inside him? After the surgery, Moore and his doctors waited, hoping for the best, but much more likely expecting Moore to die.

Amazingly, Moore did not die. Within days of the surgery, Moore's white blood cell count returned to normal. Those of a religious bent might have declared his recovery a miracle. As a scientist as well as a doctor, Dr. Golde began searching for more earthly explanations for how Moore survived one of the worst cases of hairy cell leukemia he had ever seen. Dr. Golde was determined to figure out how John Moore had beaten the odds.

Before the surgery, Dr. Golde had instructed the surgical staff to preserve Moore's spleen for later study. Hairy-cell leukemia cases were rare, and who knew what secrets would be discovered inside that freakishly oversized spleen if it were properly studied and analyzed. After the surgery was over and Moore was on the road to recovery, he traveled to UCLA several times over the next several years to see Dr. Golde for what Moore thought were routine follow-up visits. Each time Moore came to Los Angeles, Dr. Golde extracted more cells from Moore, including samples of blood, skin, bone marrow, and even his sperm.

Unbeknownst to Moore, these samples were ingredients for an ambitious research program devised by Dr. Golde and his research assistant, Shirley Quan, as the pair searched for the secret to Moore's incredible recovery. Their hope was that, if they could understand what had allowed Moore to survive his cancer, they might discover new treatments that could help save the lives of other leukemia patients.

After years of painstaking study of the cells and tissue extracted from Moore, Dr. Golde and Dr. Quan had a breakthrough. Moore's spleen contained blood cells that produced a unique protein that spurred the growth of white blood cells, which fight infection. This was a fantastic discovery. If the power of these cells could be harnessed, new treatments for leukemia and other diseases might suddenly become possible. Think of the lives that could be saved. And think—granted, a little less high-mindedly—of the money that could be made.

Dr. Golde and Dr. Quan isolated the protein-producing cells, and in 1981 they applied for a patent on the process they used to cultivate the cell line. Three years later, they got the patent, which meant that they had the exclusive right to produce the magic cells that made the miracle proteins thanks to the cells taken from John Moore's body. Dr. Golde dubbed the cell line "Mo" in honor of Moore.

Moore, however, did not feel all that honored. While embedding a few letters from his name in the cell line was fine, nothing says *honor* better than cold, hard cash, and no one had offered him any. Meanwhile, through his university, Dr. Golde had licensed his patented process for cultivating the cell line, earning an initial license fee of hundreds of thousands of dollars; and in the most optimistic projections, the university estimated that the cells could be worth as much as $3 billion. As a sweetener, Dr. Golde also secured a lucrative consulting deal for himself, giving advice on how to develop the cells for future therapies.

The way Moore saw it, Dr. Golde was getting rich, while Moore was getting stiffed. So he sued.

Moore's argument was straightforward. The cells Dr. Golde extracted from his body belonged to Moore because he made them. Moore never gave his permission to have his cells used for medical research. As a result, Moore should be the rightful owner—or at least rightful part owner—of the cell line that Dr. Golde produced from Moore's cells and of the patent that

Dr. Golde obtained on the process for cultivating the cells. Those high-powered cells were the fruit of the tree of Moore's spleen. If money were going to be made from the cells, Moore should get a piece of the action.

In making his argument, Moore invoked the ancient law of conversion. A conversion is when one person takes another person's property without permission. It's like theft, but instead of treating it like a crime, the law of conversion requires the person who took the property to pay the owner the value of the property taken. Moore argued that his cells, because of their unique properties, were worth billions. The cells came from his body. His body belonged to himself. Therefore, so did the cells; and more importantly, so did the profits from the cells.

Dr. Golde and his attorneys responded that, if accepted, Moore's argument would put in jeopardy medical research across the country. Scientists study human cells to develop therapies and cures that benefit all of humanity, but they usually don't know—and often have no way to know—where each individual cell they study came from or whether the original human being from whom the cells originated gave explicit consent to the particular research project. By definition, cell scientists are working with small sacs of protoplasm, and they usually don't have contact with the people to whom an ancestor of the sacs might once have been attached. If someone could show up at any time and assert that a particular cell derives from a cell that, at some point in the past, came from that person's body, scientific study of human cells could grind to a halt, strangled in tangles of lawsuits and competing claims of ownership.

In addition to conversion, Moore made a second argument for why Dr. Golde and his university should compensate him for his cells. The first duty of doctors is to the well-being of their patients. Therefore, if doctors have personal interests in a medical procedure that involves more than taking care of their patients, those doctors have a duty to disclose those interests, so patients can make informed decisions about whether they want the procedure or a second opinion. Dr. Golde had scraped his skin, drawn his blood, and even extracted his sperm. At the time, Moore thought that Dr. Golde was only treating his illness. Only later did Moore find out that he was also a human guinea pig, the subject of a research project that might make his doctor rich but leave him with nothing to show for his trouble.

Dr. Golde replied that Moore had consented to everything that was ever done to him. He was free at any time to refuse, but he never did. The case wasn't about extracting the cells—Moore had agreed to the extractions—and it wasn't about what benefits the doctor might realize. It was about whether the doctor's use of Moore's cells in research harmed Moore in any way, and Dr. Golde emphatically thought not. Once cells have been removed from a patient, using those cells for scientific research could not possibly harm the patient any more than sweeping up hair from the barbershop floor harms the person who came in to get it cut. If there is no possible danger to the patient, there is no reason why doctors should have to tell every patient about every facet of their research programs. If Dr. Golde had not used Moore's cells, they would have wound up in the trash heap, and who would that have served? Not Moore, who would have gained nothing. Not Dr. Golde, who would not have been able to carry out his research and make his discovery. And not the millions of sick people suffering from diseases that might be treated with the therapies that these cells potentially could produce.

So who's right and who's wrong? Did Moore own the cells that Dr. Golde took from his body and the lucrative licensing rights that came with them? Or did Dr. Golde own the cells once they were separated from Moore's body because Moore had no use for them, no way to store them, and no way to make them into anything other than biological waste? And regardless of who owned the cells, did Dr. Golde violate his duties as a physician by not telling Moore, his patient who had entrusted his life to the doctor's care, that he was researching hairy-cell leukemia and was using Moore's cells to do it?

How would you rule?

HOW THE COURT RULED

To prevail in his claim of conversion, John Moore had to demonstrate that he owned the cells that Dr. Golde used in his research. This was harder to do than it might seem.

Without a doubt, Moore's spleen, blood, and other cells belonged to him and him alone while in his body, and no one could take them without his permission. But in this case Moore had given permission to have his spleen and other body parts removed. The surgery that cut out his spleen had saved his life. He had voluntarily allowed the collection of cell tissue and fluid samples at later doctor visits. No one had done anything to Moore or his body that he didn't know about and agree to. At the time of the extractions, Moore had no expectation that his cells would be returned to him. So no one had taken anything from him without his consent. True, Moore hadn't known everything that would happen to his cells after those procedures, but the taking of the cells had been done with his knowledge and consent.

Did Moore own the organs and cells that his doctors removed from his body? The law did not have a ready answer. As courts often do when faced with novel situations, this court searched for an analogy from more established areas of the law. First the court considered the right of publicity. The right of publicity prohibits a business from using your picture in an advertisement without your permission. If the law protects a person against the commercial exploitation of their image, shouldn't the law protect against the commercial exploitation of the person's body itself?

The analogy to the right of publicity, in the court's opinion, missed the mark. A person's name and face are unique to that person. The value of a person's image in an advertisement comes from that uniqueness. Celebrities' images sell products precisely because celebrities are not just like everybody else. They're special. They're recognizable. Their faces and names carry more weight than those of a generic person.

In contrast, scientists study cells, not for their uniqueness, but rather to create molecules that have the same structure in every human being. The whole premise of scientific research on human cells is that the cells represent something that is common to humanity. Unlike in advertising, uniqueness in science is a bug, not a feature. The genetic material taken from Moore that produced the medically valuable molecules was, in its most basic form, no more than the chemical composition of human blood; and at the chemical level, Moore's molecules were special not because they were uniquely associated with *Moore* but rather because they could thrive in any person. It was this generic quality that made them valuable as a potential therapy for other cancer patients. The rationale for the right of publicity's protection of a person's unique identity, therefore, didn't generalize to protection for anonymous, generic, and unidentifiable molecules.

Another analogy the court considered was to the well-established principle that every adult of sound mind has the right to refuse medical treatment. Just as Moore could have refused to allow the doctors to perform the surgery, the analogy went, Moore could also have refused to allow the doctors to use his cells for research. Because the doctors did not tell Moore that his cells might be used for research, the analogy went, Moore never had an opportunity to exercise his right to refuse, and so the cells continued to belong to him because they were taken on false pretenses.

This analogy, too, fell flat with the court. While Moore certainly had the right to refuse the surgery that saved his life or to decline to attend any of the follow-up visits where Dr. Golde extracted more cells from his body, that's not what happened. Moore didn't refuse. On the contrary, Moore consented to the surgery and to the cell extractions. No one tricked Moore about what would happen to the cells and tissue taken from his body. If he ever even thought about it at all, Moore never expected that he would get to keep his extracted spleen or any of his other cells or tissue. What would he have done with them? Where would he have even put them? Moore must have understood that once his spleen and cells were gone, he would never see them again. By allowing his doctors to remove his cells and tissue without any expectation that they would be returned, the closer analogy in the court's view was that of abandoned property. If you throw your things away, you have no cause to complain if someone else picks them up and makes use of them. Moore had discarded his tissue, and so whatever ownership he might have had in the tissue before was discarded, too.

Even if Moore had wanted to keep his spleen as a surgical souvenir, a California law complicated Moore's claim. California required that all human body parts (not attached to a living person) must be buried or incinerated. The only exception was for use in medical procedures or scientific study, and even then, the body parts had to be buried or incinerated when the procedures or study were over. It was true that this law was aimed at protecting public health from rotting body parts and not at whether a person should be paid for use of his cells in medical research. Nevertheless, the existence of this law suggested that a person's right to control severed body parts was drastically limited. Since the law mandated that his spleen and other tissue be destroyed, it was hard to see in what sense Moore continued to own them. He could not have held on to his extracted spleen even if he wanted to. His only options were burial or incineration. The use of the cells for research, therefore, took nothing away from him.

Then there was Dr. Golde's patent. A patent is its own form of property. In Dr. Golde's case, his patent protected the process he used to adapt and grow the cells, which is different from the cells themselves. The cells that were extracted from Moore's body were long gone. What remained—and what possessed all the value—was those cells' progeny, which existed only because of Dr. Golde's patented process. Moore's claim that he owned the cells made from Dr. Golde's patented method, reasoned the court, was inconsistent with Dr. Golde's patent rights. The patent meant that Dr. Golde had an exclusive right to use the patented process. If Moore's ownership of the original cells meant that Dr. Golde couldn't use the patented process to manufacture molecules derived from those cells, then the patent would effectively be nullified. The court didn't think that result made sense.

Finally, the court considered the effects of its decision on other medical researchers. In modern biomedical research, the court observed, biological materials are routinely distributed among different scientists in different laboratories in different universities and research institutions. If the person from whom those biological materials originated could claim to own all of those materials, the court believed that research could grind to a halt under the uncertainty of who owns what. Medical research is difficult enough as it is. The law shouldn't make it harder by creating new forms of property in the materials that scientists need to invent therapies and cures for the rest of us.

Based on all of those considerations—the lack of an analogy to an established form of property, the California law that prohibited Moore from keeping his biologic material, the rights conferred by Dr. Golde's patent, and the effects on scientific research—the court concluded that Moore did not own the cells, and that Dr. Golde could not be liable for conversion.

The court, however, was not entirely unsympathetic to Moore and his legal claims. Patients have the right to refuse medical procedures that they don't want. They also have the right not to have their consent obtained by trickery or deceit.

According to Moore, while Dr. Golde had told him that he was doing scientific research on leukemia, Dr. Golde had also told him that he had no financial interest in the research. Once Dr. Golde applied for a patent on the cell line derived from Moore's cells, Dr. Golde's statement that he had no financial interest in the research became false, and according to the court, Moore had a right to know that.

So while Moore couldn't sue for a cut of the money being made off of his cells, he could sue Dr. Golde for breaching his fiduciary duty as a doctor to tell Moore, as his patient, all the relevant facts before getting his consent to treatment.

For Moore, this compromise was much less than half a loaf. While the cell lines were potentially worth *billions* of dollars, Dr. Golde had not applied for a patent until years after the surgery, so the only injuries Moore could sue for were the pain and suffering of having his blood and other bodily fluids drawn a few times. And even then, he could recover damages only if he could show that he would have refused these follow-up visits with the surgeon who saved his life had he known that the surgeon was using his cells to develop lifesaving cures for the disease that nearly killed him. It was a stretch.

Since Moore had won a point, however minor, his case was returned to the trial courts to determine the damages he was entitled to. Instead of continuing the fight, with little prospect of meaningful reward, "Moore later negotiated what he called a 'token' settlement with UCLA that covered his legal fees based on the fact that he wasn't informed and hadn't agreed to the research."[2]

Moore's case presented thorny legal, ethical, and moral issues that continue to be debated. Pitted against each other were respect for the integrity of a person's body and the need to preserve and promote the scientific research that leads to new medicines to heal the sick and protect the healthy.

Did the court get it right? You decide.

REFLECTIONS

The fundamental building block of legal thinking is the analogy. Answering legal questions often boils down to comparing the current controversy to an earlier one with an established solution and using that solution as a template for resolving the present case. The trick for the advocate is coming up with analogies that will appeal to judges. The challenge for judges is deciding which of all the possible analogies is the most appropriate.

The most common and fertile sources for analogies in legal disputes are precedents. Precedents are earlier legal cases decided by the courts. In deciding a case, courts must state the legal rules underpinning their decisions. These legal rules can then be applied in later cases.

Picking which precedent to apply, however, is not always straightforward. Sometimes, applying precedents feels like forcing the square peg into the round hole. It can be done, but it's tight and not all that pretty.

Applying precedents is especially difficult when courts confront new technologies that bear only rough resemblance to the older technology of the past. The *Moore* case is a good illustration of this problem. In *Moore,* the court struggled to find the appropriate analogy for the extraction and use of human tissue for medical research. Was using human tissue for medical research like the right of publicity that protects people from having their images used in advertising without their consent? Was it like conversion, taking another person's property without their consent? Should human tissue even be considered property at all, since the law required that human medical waste be destroyed?

Especially when new technology is at play, a fair question is whether courts are really competent to decide how to allocate rights and liabilities, or whether those questions are better left to legislatures. When it comes to assessing the trade-offs that different rules might represent, legislatures have certain advantages that courts lack. Legislatures tend to have broader sources of information. Courts are primarily informed by the parties to a lawsuit. In contrast, legislatures can hear testimony from a wide variety of experts and interested parties representing many different points of view. Courts are constrained to apply legal rules derived from precedents or from statutes. Legislatures, as the authors of statutes, are not shackled by past decisions and have the power to devise entirely new systems that balance interests in light of the specific circumstances at play.

After the *Moore* case was decided, the federal government published, in 1991, its policy for the protection of human subjects in research, known as the Common Rule. The Common Rule required that all research on human subjects at institutions that receive federal funds must first be approved by an institutional review board composed of scientists and citizens charged with the responsibility of ensuring that risks to research subjects are minimized and that the research takes place only with the subject's informed consent. Nevertheless, nodding to concerns about impacting scientific progress, which had motivated the court in the *Moore* case, the Common Rule does not require consent for "nonidentifiable" samples, meaning samples that cannot be reasonably traced back to a specific person.

This limitation of the consent requirement, however, may be changing. In January 2016, the U.S. Department of Health and Human Services closed comments on proposed changes to the Common Rule. Under the proposed new rule, "informed consent would generally be required for secondary research with a biospecimen (for example, part of a blood sample that is left over after being drawn for clinical purposes), even if the investigator is not being given information that would enable him or her to identify whose biospecimen it is. Such consent would not need to be obtained for each specific research use of the biospecimen, but rather could be obtained using a 'broad' consent form in which a person would give consent to future unspecified research uses."[3]

Some people believe that the more stringent rules about consent will slow research and burden researchers with paperwork of little value to anyone. Others believe that the proposed rules do not go far enough, and that allowing "broad consent" will mean that anxious patients who put their lives in the hands of their doctors will end up consenting to research that, had they understood it better and been in a less vulnerable moment, they would never have agreed to. The advantage of establishing these requirements via a public rule-making is that both sides of the debate can be heard before a final rule is issued.

When litigants present themselves at the courthouse, however, judges do not have the luxury of a leisurely notice-and-comment period. They have no choice but to resolve their dispute by applying the most closely analogous laws they can identify. For novel and complex problems with meritorious claims on both sides of a question, sometimes legislatures are better equipped to allocate rights and responsibilities. When defining rights and responsibilities, judges must work with the tools they have— precedent and analogy—and do the best they can.

.   .   .   .   .

Questions

1. Should patients like Moore have ownership rights to inventions derived from their tissue? What would those rights look like? For example, should the tissue donor have the right to prevent the research from going forward? What impact would granting those rights have on medical research?

2. If you were an elected representative in a legislature, would you consider establishing a system of rights and responsibilities for cases like John Moore's, where human tissue is used for medical research? What would that system look like? How would your system differ from the rules established by the court in the *Moore* case?

Read It Yourself

Moore v. Regents of University of California, 793 P.2d 479 (Cal. 1990).

23 Imagine No (Copyright) Possessions

Perhaps the most famous song of John Lennon's storied songwriting career came one year after the breakup of the Beatles. On October 11, 1971, Lennon released "Imagine," and the song quickly climbed the pop music charts, hitting number one in the United Kingdom and number three in the United States.

In its list of the "500 Greatest Songs of All Time," *Rolling Stone* magazine ranked "Imagine" third.[1] The music conglomerate BMI recognized "Imagine" as one of the 100 most-performed songs of the twentieth century.[2]

"Imagine" begins with a rolling piano riff before opening up into a series of simple statements that Lennon later described as a "positive prayer." In the song, Lennon challenges listeners to imagine a world without country, religion, or possessions, a world with "nothing to kill or die for," and he calls upon his listeners to join him and other dreamers like himself to build "a brotherhood of man" so "the world will live as one."

Embedded in the mellow melody and sweet harmonies of "Imagine" is an explicit political message, one that John Lennon fully understood. In an interview, Lennon observed that "'Imagine' which says: 'Imagine that there was no more religion, no more country, no more politics,' is virtually the Communist manifesto, even though I'm not particularly a Communist and I do not belong to any movement."[3]

Ben Stein was not nearly as famous as John Lennon or the song "Imagine," but he was a minor celebrity in his own right. A graduate of Yale Law School, Stein worked as a speechwriter for President Richard Nixon, taught at prestigious universities like the University of California, Santa Cruz, and Pepperdine University, and played minor but notable roles in the movies, most famously the monotone pedant whose class is skipped in *Ferris Bueller's Day Off*. For a time, Stein hosted his own television game show called *Win Ben Stein's Money*, and he wrote numerous best-selling books. And Ben Stein did not believe in the theory of evolution.

Not only was Stein a doubter of evolution, but he was also most upset that public schools would teach Darwin's theory but not the religious idea that God created all life on earth—an idea popularly known at the time as the theory of "intelligent design." The basic premise of the intelligent design theory was that only an intelligent designer (i.e., God) could create a world of the complexity that we live in.

Although 97 percent of all scientists believe that Darwin's theory of evolution accurately describes the development of life on earth,[4] Stein felt strongly that the education establishment unfairly excluded intelligent design from standard science curricula. To voice his opposition to the teaching of the theory of evolution, Stein produced a documentary with the provocative title *Expelled: No Intelligence Allowed*. In the documentary, Stein compared schools that declined to teach the theory of intelligent design alongside the theory of evolution to the fascists, Nazis, and communists, who were responsible for the most unspeakable massacres, murders, and genocides of the twentieth century.

In addition to hating the theory of evolution, Ben Stein harbored a particular animosity toward "Imagine," John Lennon's paean to peace and world harmony. "Imagine" represented the worst of liberal pseudo-intellectualism: rejection of religion, disdain for private property, and spurning of national pride in favor of a supremely naive, utopian view of all the world just getting along. Naturally, Stein wanted to include "Imagine" in his movie.

By the time Stein was making his documentary, John Lennon was dead, senselessly murdered by a deranged assassin outside his New York apartment building, and so the rights to the song "Imagine" had passed to Lennon's wife, Yoko Ono. In the same way that Lennon and his song stood for everything Stein opposed, Stein and his movie stood for everything Ono and her late husband scorned: unchecked capitalism, nationalism, and theism. Stein was not likely to get Ono's permission to use Lennon's song in his movie.

So Stein skipped the permission part and just used the song anyway. In the movie, a fifteen-second excerpt from "Imagine" plays over a montage of archival footage: a group of children in a circle, a young girl spinning and dancing, a military parade, and finally a close-up of Joseph Stalin, the former dictator of the Soviet Union and notorious mass murderer of his own people, waving happily. Lennon's lyrics "Nothing to kill or die for / And no religion too" appear on screen as the images fade from one to the other and the music plays.

The song and the sequence of images are sandwiched between two interviews. In the first, a scholar compares religion to a recreational activity like knitting and expresses his wish for a society where science plays a greater role than religion. After the song and the video montage, in the second interview, another scholar argues that without some connection to "transcendental values," human beings are capable of doing terrible things to each other.

Predictably, Yoko Ono sued Stein and his movie producers for using "Imagine" in the movie without permission. Specifically, Ono alleged that Stein had committed copyright infringement. If a work is protected by copyright, the general rule is that only the owner of the copyright—or someone with the owner's permission—is allowed to make copies or publicly perform a copyrighted work. But the law provides a defense to copyright infringement called "fair use."[5] Stein claimed that the fair-use defense protected his use of the song.

The U.S. Constitution authorizes copyright protection "to promote the Progress of Science and Useful Arts."[6] Making sure that authors get paid for the works they create serves that purpose by giving authors a financial incentive to produce more works. At the same time, creative works do not sprout out of thin air. They build upon previous works. Also the public has the right to discuss and comment on creative works. The purpose of fair use is to make sure that copyright protection leaves room for criticism, comment, news reporting, teaching, scholarship, research, and other uses that are in the public's interest. Without fair use, authors could sue critics who used excerpts from their books to write scathing reviews. Teachers could be sued for playing snippets of music to teach students about different chords, styles, and melodies. Fair use allows copying that would otherwise be prohibited when that copying serves some useful societal purpose and doesn't unduly interfere with the creators' ability to market their works.

The Copyright Act sets out four factors to be considered in deciding whether a particular act of copying is a fair use:

a. The purpose and character of the use;

b. The nature of the copyrighted work;

c. The amount and substantiality of the portion used in relation to the copyrighted work as a whole; and

d. The effect of the use upon the potential market for or value of the copyrighted work.

Stein argued that he used Lennon's song only to make the point that utopian thinking leads to dystopian nightmares. Ono contended that Stein was just trying to take advantage of Lennon's fame and his widely cherished song to promote his movie, avoid paying royalties, and make a buck for himself in the process.

The question for the court was whether Stein's use of "Imagine" was copyright infringement or a fair use protected by the law. How would you rule?

HOW THE COURT RULED

Because the copyright statute identifies four factors to be considered in determining whether a particular act of copying is fair or not, the court went through each factor one by one.

Beginning with the purpose and character of the proposed fair use, the court noted that *Expelled* was a commercial film that aimed to make its maker a profit. At the same time, the movie contributed to a broader public debate about what should be taught in schools.

Stein didn't put "Imagine" into the film to promote the documentary to fans of John Lennon's vision of a peaceful world without religion, property, or government. Rather, Stein included the song to criticize it.

Criticism is a classic fair use. The film did not just copy the song but, rather, added something new and thereby altered the song with new expression, meaning, and message. Granted, the new message was not one that Lennon likely would have liked, but that transformation of "Imagine" weighed in favor of finding a fair use.

Turning to the second factor in the fair use analysis, the court observed that "Imagine" was a creative work, a category to which the copyright law gives its highest protection. Works of art, however, tend to mine similar themes, such as love, loss, hope, birth, and death. The challenge for the artist is to find new ways to express these common topics. Stein incorporated "Imagine" rather than coming up with his own song, so the nature of the work weighed against finding a fair use.

Turning to the amount and substantiality of the copying, the court noted that fair use has both a quantitative and a qualitative component. Short quotations and brief excerpts are more likely fair than longer reproductions are. Reproducing the heart of a work is less likely to be fair than offering a taste that might whet recipients' appetite for more.

In *Expelled*, Stein used only fifteen seconds of a three-minute song. Moreover, he took only the part of the song that directly related to Stein's argument. The lines "Nothing to kill or die for / And no religion too" were contrasted with images that suggested that the song's philosophy would lead to lots of killing and lots of dying. Therefore, the amount and substantiality of the copied portions of "Imagine" weighed in favor of fair use.

Finally, there is the effect of the use on the market for the copyrighted work. No one who wanted to buy a copy of the song "Imagine" would be tempted to buy a copy of the movie *Expelled* instead, just to get a fifteen-second excerpt of the song for free. The movie had no conceivable effect on the market for "Imagine."

Putting all of these factors together, the court found that Stein's use of "Imagine" in his documentary was a fair use. Accordingly, Stein did not need to ask for or receive permission to use the song.

Notably, the court's opinion about whether the message Stein wanted to convey in his documentary was better or worse than the message

Lennon attempted to convey in his song played no part in the analysis of whether the use of "Imagine" in the movie *Expelled* was fair use. Fair use provides space to criticize and build upon other people's works. What people build is up to them.

Therefore, Stein won and Ono lost.[7] The song got to stay in Stein's movie, and he didn't have to pay for using it. Was this a victory for freedom of speech or the trashing of an artist's rights? You decide.

REFLECTIONS

The proper scope of fair use is at the center of contemporary debates about who should control popular culture. Groups like the Authors' Guild, the Motion Picture Association of America, and the Recording Industry Association of America have lobbied and litigated for greater intellectual property rights for creators. Groups like the Electronic Frontier Foundation are on the other side of this debate and argue that strong fair use rights allow for the creation of new works that would be impossible if every bit of the culture could only be accessed by acquiring a license and paying a royalty. Mash-ups, fan fiction, song sampling, and innovative technologies like search engines and movie databases might be examples of new works that might never come into being if copyright is overly enforced.

This debate over the proper balance of rights of creators and rights of the public to use creative works is critical, because copyrights last for a very long time. Under current law, creative works are protected by copyright for the lifetime of the author plus another seventy years. That means that a hit song you hear on the radio today, assuming that the artist who created it is young and lives an average life span, will not enter into the public domain and be free for public use until well into the next century. Any use of the song by anyone alive today will have to be either licensed or permitted by fair use.

Although the Copyright Act spells out the four factors for determining fair use, in practice applying those factors can be very difficult, and so it is hard to predict whether a particular use will or will not be considered fair. Is it fair use to display thumbnail versions of images in the results of an online search engine? Courts have said yes, much to the relief of companies like Google.[8] Is it fair use to create a dictionary of characters in the sprawling world of Harry Potter, one of the most successful literary works of all time? One court said no.[9] But at the same time, the court also remarked that dictionaries of literary universes could be fair uses in some cases, just not that one. In fair use cases, outcomes turn on very specific facts, and uncertainty often reigns.

This confusion might seem strange. The law lays out a detailed, four-step test for figuring out when a use is a fair use. Multistep tests are very common in the law, and they provide a sense of certainty; but that sense is mostly an illusion. Rather than dictate outcomes, multistep tests more often set out a methodical system to guide analysis of the problem. Because each step in the test can be given different weight, a judge has wide latitude to conclude that most factors in a case weigh in favor of one side, but still rule in favor of the other side because the other factors should be given more weight. It is in that space of analysis and weighing that lawyers make their arguments, litigants live in limbo, and judges make their judgments.

.   .   .   .   .

Questions

1. In reaching its decision that Stein's use of "Imagine" was a fair use, the court noted that Stein used only 15 seconds from a three-minute song. The implication is that 15 seconds is such a small part of the whole song that using that tiny amount would be very unlikely to affect the market for the song as a whole. That conclusion seems almost certainly correct, but it raises the question of how many seconds of the 180-second song it would take to cross the line. If it is all right to copy 15 seconds, what about 16 or 17 seconds? What about 30 or 90 seconds? How should a court draw the line? Or is it possible that the number of seconds isn't really the determining factor? But if that's the case, why does the court mention it at all?

2. If Stein wanted to release a soundtrack from his movie, should it be considered a fair use to include all or part of "Imagine" on the soundtrack?

Read It Yourself

Lennon v. Premise Media Corp., 556 F. Supp. 2d 310 (SDNY 2008).

24 My Barbie World

The dispute began in Denmark with the improbable dreams of a youthful rock band hoping to make it big. In 1997, Aqua, as the band was called, released their first album *Aquarium*. The songs were a mix of bubblegum pop with catchy tunes and hummable melodies. As unlikely as it might seem, the Danish Europop group found Top 40 success with a cut off of *Aquarium* called "Barbie Girl." This infectious song with its provocative lyrics brought Aqua fame and fortune in Europe and America. It also brought the small Danish band to the attention of a global corporate giant, the storied toymaker Mattel. Mattel was not a fan.

Barbie was one of the most valuable toys in history and was the crown jewel in Mattel's expansive portfolio of products. Barbie had risen from humble origins in the 1950s—when, the court decision states, the doll originally resembled a "German street walker"—to become, after hundreds of redesigns and makeovers, an idealized (many would say overidealized) form of female beauty that, as the court would describe it, symbolized "American girlhood, a public figure who graces the aisles of toy stores throughout the country and beyond."[1] Perhaps more importantly for Mattel, Barbie made Mattel a lot of money.

For the hook of its song "Barbie Girl," Aqua capitalized on the idea that Barbie was a superficial party girl. In a singsong melody, the lyric imagined Barbie singing "I'm a blonde bimbo girl, in a fantasy world." The song sexualized the children's toy, with Barbie asking Ken, her boyfriend, to "dress me up, make it tight, I'm your dolly." The singer coos, "Kiss me here, touch me there, hanky-panky / You can touch, you can play / If you say, 'I'm always yours,' ooh ooh."

Shakespeare, the lyrics might not have been, but they had a point. The chorus underscored Barbie's superficiality, her promiscuous sexuality, and her frivolous focus on parties. "I'm a Barbie girl, in my Barbie world," went the verse. "You can brush my hair, undress me everywhere / Imagination, life is your creation / Come on Barbie, let's go party!"

Needless to say, this depiction of Barbie as ditzy, hypersexualized, fake, and frivolous was not the image that Mattel wanted the public to associate with its doll. While Barbie may have started out as a streetwalker and spent time with cars, pets, boys, and toys, by the 1990s Mattel was working hard to recast its iconic toy into the embodiment of girl power. The company widened Barbie's waist to simulate more realistic proportions. Not just a pretty face with a taste for fashion, Barbie was given careers (and the wardrobe to go with them) in education, medicine, politics, and the military. Barbie was an astronaut, a pilot, an executive, an artist, and many other things as well. What she was not was a bimbo.

Aqua's portrayal of Barbie flew in the face of everything that Mattel was trying to do with its Barbie line of toys. Mattel complained to Aqua and its record distributor, MCA Records. An MCA spokesperson responded that the album contained a disclaimer saying that "Barbie Girl" was "social commentary not created or approved by the makers of the doll." Mattel did not like that response one bit. A Mattel representative shot back: "That's unacceptable. . . . It's akin to a bank robber handing a note of apology to a teller during a heist. It neither diminishes the severity of the crime, nor does it make it legal."[2]

Clearly, Mattel and the band did not agree about how Mattel's Barbie trademark could be used in song. So Mattel sued the Danish rockers, accusing them of infringement of its trademark on Barbie and the associated line of toys.

A trademark "is a word, phrase or symbol that is used to identify a manufacturer or sponsor of a good or the provider of a service." Trademarks help consumers find goods and services from sellers they trust. The most valuable trademarks are from the companies with the best reputations. Trademark law prevents other people from tricking consumers about who is selling a good or service by using marks that are confusingly similar to another person's trademark.

Long before Aqua's band members had strummed their first chords or struck their first synthesizer keys, Mattel had locked up a trademark on Barbie. Barbie was not just a toy but also a brand that represented an array of toys that, Mattel hoped, stood for quality and good, wholesome fun.

Mattel complained that Aqua was using the Barbie name to sell its records. Barbie was right there in the title of Aqua's biggest hit, "Barbie Girl." Aqua was trading on the reputation that Mattel had cultivated over decades of making, selling, and advertising their Barbie products. The law of trademarks existed for precisely the purpose of preventing pirates like Aqua from shanghaiing brands like Barbie for their own commercial purposes.

Aqua responded that "Barbie Girl" was a parody, a deliberate lampooning of the Barbie image. The song wasn't trading on the Barbie brand. It was making fun of it. This wasn't piracy. This was free speech, and it was fully protected by the First Amendment to the U.S. Constitution.

Did Mattel have the right to control the use of its Barbie trademark, one of its most valuable and iconic brands, in Aqua's song? Or did Aqua have the right to take the Barbie name and twist it into a hit song? How would you rule?

HOW THE COURT RULED

As the court put it: "If this [case] were a sci-fi melodrama, it might be called Speech-Zilla meets Trademark Kong." It was free speech versus trademark rights in a knock-down, drag-out battle over a billion-dollar brand.

Mattel's strongest argument was that the public's interest in "Barbie Girl" stemmed from the public's affection for Barbie and the toys, stories, and accessories associated with the doll. If Barbie had not been so famous—fame that the doll acquired only after decades of substantial work and investment on the part of Mattel—no one would have any interest in Aqua's otherwise bland and uninspired song.

Mattel had a point. The corporation's Barbie brand was what made Aqua's "Barbie Girl" song interesting. The very strength of this argument, however, led to Mattel's defeat. For some trademarks, the brands transcend the products they are meant to sell and become an integral part of the public lexicon. Brands like "Cadillac" and "Rolls Royce," for example, have become synonymous with high quality and the high prices people have to pay to buy them. Band-Aids are adhesive bandages sold by Johnson & Johnson. They are also small solutions that cover over but don't cure deep wounds. Sometimes, a trademark is more than just a reference to the maker of a product. Sometimes a mark is an icon.

Barbie was one of those brands that had embedded itself in the public imagination. When a brand becomes a symbol, not just for the product itself, but also for values and ideas in the mind of the public, a trademark owner cannot keep people from using the word to convey that meaning in conversation, writing, or even song.

The fact that the Barbie name was in the title of Aqua's song didn't matter to the court. While trademark law shows little mercy to sellers who slap someone else's mark on their goods, titles—whether for books, movies, or songs—are different. In the court's view, "consumers expect a title to communicate a message about the book or movie, but they do not expect it to identify the publisher or producer."

It was important to the court that "Barbie Girl" was a parody about the Barbie doll itself. The singer proclaims, "I'm a Barbie Girl." She alludes to the doll's materials with the line "Life in plastic, it's fantastic." And then the singer raises an eyebrow at the sexual undertones of the main activity for this doll: changing its clothes and brushing its hair. "You can brush my hair," the singer croons in the chorus, "undress me everywhere." And again later in the song: "I'm a blond bimbo girl, in a fantasy world / Dress me up, make it tight, I'm your dolly."

The song, therefore, is not trying to convince consumers that it is part of the sprawling Barbie franchise. Just the opposite. Barbie—and everything the doll stands for—is the very target of the song's scorn.

A trademark gives its owner protection against competitors selling knockoff products using the same brand. It does not give trademark owners the power to silence critics by forbidding them from making any mention of the product the mark represents. Mattel's trademark claims could not stand.

So Aqua's song could continue to have its moment of pop-music glory on the radio airwaves, and Mattel would have to be satisfied with making its millions of dollars on Barbie sales while some people snickered and smirked at their efforts.

Did the court get this one right? You decide.

REFLECTIONS

Mattel in this case was a victim of its own success. The meaning of Barbie had become so deeply embedded in the culture that it transcended Mattel's brand. Mattel could no more stop Aqua from using the word *Barbie* to communicate this larger, culturally acquired meaning than it could stop the band from using any other words from the dictionary.

Trademark owners must walk a fine line. On the one hand, they want their brands to capture the public imagination, to be on the tips of people's tongues and at the tops of their minds. On the other, if the brand's success divorces the brand from the maker of the product, trademark protections become shaky. Moving stairways are known as escalators. Boiled and dried wheat packaged as pillow-shaped biscuits and sold as cereal is known as shredded wheat. These were once famous brands, but they became so famous that their brand names became synonymous with the products themselves. They became, in the language of trademark law, generic.

A brand becomes generic under the law of trademarks when the public generally comes to understand the product itself by the brand name. A trademark is supposed to inform the public about the *producer* of the product. People buy Apple electronics because they associate the brand with a company that produces high-quality products. If the public associates the mark with the product itself, and not the producer, then the brand is generic, and anyone can use the name, even competitors.

Successful brands, therefore, have to guard against becoming too successful. The online search engine Google dominates Internet searches. Will that dominance mean that *Google* will become synonymous with online searches? If it does, *google* might go the way of shredded wheat and become a generic term—in this case, for searching online. This is something that the owners of the Google trademark very much want to prevent; but they are not in control of the language, and the future of the brand will depend on what people think when they hear the word *google*.

Even when a trademark does not become fully generic, its protection is limited to ensuring that competitors cannot pass their goods off as coming from the owner of the trademark. A new soft-drink maker cannot call its wares "coca-cola cola," even if it manages to exactly replicate Coca-Cola's famously secret recipe. Using the name *coca-cola* would suggest that the drink came from the Coca-Cola Company. On the other hand, artists can write songs about Coca-Cola and comedians can poke fun at the brand, because in those cases no one thinks that the song or the joke is produced by the makers of the fizzy drink.

In this way, trademark law, like other intellectual property such as patents and copyright, strikes a balance. It protects producers from competitors who seek only to capitalize on the trademark owner's hard-earned goodwill, while allowing the public room to speak freely about the brand and its place in the culture.

.   .   .   .   .

Questions

1. Imagine that Aqua's song "Barbie Girl" is licensed by a doll maker that competes with Mattel (let's call this competitor "Bats"), and Bats uses "Barbie Girl" in television commercials that promote Bats's dolls by making fun of Barbie. How should the line between free speech and trademark infringement be drawn in that case? What if the commercial only attacks Barbie dolls and doesn't even mention Bats's competing products?

2. Imagine that large swaths of the public use Google's trademark to refer to online searches—for example, by saying that the best way to get information is to go online and "google" it. If Google is concerned that this usage will dilute and eventually destroy its trademark, what, if anything, should Google do to prevent its mark from becoming generic?

Read It Yourself

Mattel, Inc. v. MCA Records, Inc., 296 F.3d 894 (9th Cir. 2002).

25 A Time for Dying

Gloria Taylor did not know when her life would end, but she had a good idea of how, and the picture wasn't pretty. In 2009, Taylor was diagnosed with amyotrophic lateral sclerosis, more commonly known as ALS, or Lou Gehrig's disease, a fatal neurodegenerative disease that slowly but inexorably weakens the muscles throughout the body. The disease works gradually, but every step is a painful loss of physical autonomy. Bit by bit, as a court would later put it, ALS sufferers "lose the ability to use their hands and feet, the ability to walk, chew, swallow, speak and, eventually, breathe." Taylor would spend her last moments on earth gasping for breath as her lungs ceased to pull in air and she slowly suffocated. Taylor wanted another way.

By 2010, her ALS had rapidly progressed, and Taylor was confined to a wheelchair. Pain was her constant companion. She needed an in-home assistant for the most basic tasks of daily living. She tried to live her life to the fullest that her weakening body would allow, but she knew that the freedom that comes from a healthy body was rapidly slipping away.

Taylor told her family and friends she wanted to find a way to die with dignity. "I don't want to live in a bedridden state, stripped of dignity and independence," she said. That she would die from this terrible disease was a foregone conclusion. Taylor, however, wanted to go out on her own terms, so she went to court and pleaded for the right to choose the time and manner of her passing. This is what she told the court:

> I know that I am dying, but I am far from depressed. I have some down time—that is part and parcel of the experience of knowing that you are terminal. But there is still a lot of good in my life; there are still things, like special times with my granddaughter and family, that bring me extreme joy. I will not waste any of my remaining time being depressed. I intend to get every bit of happiness I can wring from what is left of my life so long as it remains a life of quality; but I do not want to live a life without quality. There will come a point when I will know that enough is enough. I cannot say precisely when that time will be. It is not a question of "when I can't walk" or "when I can't talk." There is no pre-set trigger moment. I just know that, globally, there will be some point in time when I will be able to say— "this is it, this is the point where life is just not worthwhile." When that time comes, I want to be able to call my family together, tell them of my decision, say a dignified good-bye and obtain final closure—for me and for them.

Death may have scared Taylor, but dying from ALS scared her more. "I live in apprehension," she wrote to the court, "that my death will be slow, difficult, unpleasant, painful, undignified and inconsistent with the values and principles I have tried to live by." Taylor understood that her life's end was inevitable, but she pleaded for death on her terms. "What I fear," she explained, "is a death that negates, as opposed to concludes, my life. I do not want to die slowly, piece by piece. I do not want to waste away unconscious in a hospital bed. I do not want to die wracked with pain."

Death at a time and in a manner of her choosing would be a mercy, but the law stood in Taylor's way. The Criminal Code of Canada made it a crime for anyone to aid or abet a person in committing suicide. It was even a crime to "counsel" a person to commit suicide. The code made clear that no person could consent to death being inflicted on them. As a consequence, if you wanted to bring about your own death, you were on your own. The law prohibited help from any quarter.

Taylor knew that, when the time came, she would likely lack the strength to end her life without assistance. So she asked the court to find that the law banning assisted suicide, as applied to the terminally ill, violated her fundamental human rights.

The Canadian Charter of Rights and Freedoms stood above the ordinary laws of the land. The charter guaranteed Taylor and every citizen of Canada "the right to life, liberty and security of the person and the right not to be deprived thereof except in accordance with the principles of fundamental justice."

Taylor argued that these broad principles should guarantee her the right to obtain the help she needed to end her life on her own terms, free from needless suffering, and without burdening her family with the trauma of watching her die in agony.

While only the coldest hearts of stone would not sympathize with Taylor's plight, the law against suicide could not be casually cast aside. The blanket prohibition on helping someone to die served some very important purposes. Without the prohibition, family members might pressure a terminally ill relative to cut short her life for their own benefit, before the relative was ready. It is even possible that fabricated consent might be used to conceal murder. The victim could never expose the fraud. As the saying goes, dead men tell no tales. Safeguards were obviously necessary, and the judgment of the nation's lawmakers was that the only certain safeguard was a complete ban. The court should be cautious before it substituted its judgment for that of the country's elected representatives.

The disabled community also feared any relaxation of the rule against assisted suicide. All too often people take pity on the disabled and despair about the quality of their lives, when the disabled themselves are at peace with their condition and embrace the lives they are living. If the sickly or infirm were legitimate targets for euthanasia, the lives of the disabled might come to be seen as less valuable than those of other human beings. The prohibition placed a burden on Taylor, but eliminating the prohibition, advocates for the disabled argued, would place a burden on the disabled, and that burden was a thumb on the scale in favor of keeping the law intact.

Gloria Taylor stands before the court. She wants the law against assisted suicide overturned. The Charter of Rights and Freedoms contains sweeping, but vague, references to life, liberty, and security. Is that enough to invalidate the law against assisted suicide and give Taylor the freedom to choose when and how to die? How would you rule?

HOW THE COURT RULED

The Supreme Court of Canada began with the observation that prohibiting suicide as the Canadian law did was a valid exercise of power by the government. The government had the authority to pass laws to protect the health and welfare of the country's citizens. The legislature's judgment that assisted suicide endangered health and welfare was a reasonable exercise of that power. The application of the general law to Gloria Taylor's case, however, required special consideration.

Taylor represented a distinct group of people: mentally competent adults suffering from a grievous and incurable disease that inflicts long-lasting and unbearable suffering. The law against suicide worked against this class of people, not for them.

According to the court, the right to life under the Charter of Rights and Freedoms comes into play whenever the law or action by the government "imposes death or an increased risk of death on a person, either directly or indirectly." By prohibiting suicide, and specifically assisted suicide, for the grievously ill like Taylor, the law might speed their deaths by causing some people, as the court put it, "to take their own lives prematurely, for fear that they would be incapable of doing so when they reached the point where suffering was intolerable."

The right to liberty and security under the charter implicated a person's autonomy and quality of life. In the court's view, "an individual's response to a grievous and irremediable medical condition is a matter critical to their dignity and autonomy." By denying people the right to make decisions about their own bodies and medical care, the prohibition on suicide curtailed their liberty. By condemning them "to endure intolerable suffering," the law impinged on their security.

The court observed that the object of the prohibition against suicide was "not, broadly, to preserve life whatever the circumstances, but more specifically to protect vulnerable persons from being induced to commit suicide at a time of weakness." A total ban on assisted suicide helped to achieve this legitimate goal, but its reach went too far. It ensnared people who were acting not out of weakness but out of a clear-eyed calculation that avoiding unbearable suffering was better than putting themselves and their families through torment for a few extra days of life. The law could easily protect the vulnerable by creating safeguards against abuse while allowing the terminally ill like Gloria Taylor to make their own decisions about ending their own lives.

Mindful of the importance of safeguards, the court did not declare a universal right to assisted suicide. Instead, the court invalidated the prohibition on suicide as it was written, but suspended its judgment for twelve months to give the Canadian legislature time to fashion a law that would protect both the vulnerable from undue pressure and the terminally ill from needless and unwanted suffering. Thus, the law would have to change, but alas, not in time for Gloria Taylor. While her case made its slow way through the courts, Taylor passed away before the court's final ruling. In the end, she died of a perforated colon and so was spared the horrific death she had feared and fought in court to avoid.[1]

Gloria Taylor's plea for the right to die with dignity at a time and manner of her own choosing forced the court to strike a delicate balance between accommodating the wishes of the terminally ill and protecting vulnerable people from being pushed into an irrevocable decision to take their own lives. Did the court strike the right balance? You decide.

REFLECTIONS

The United States does not have Canada's Charter of Rights and Freedoms. Rather, its constitutional guarantee of liberty is set forth in the due process clauses of the Fifth and Fourteenth Amendments to U.S. Constitution. The Fifth Amendment reads, "No person shall . . . be deprived of life, liberty, or property, without due process of law." The Fourteenth Amendment reads, "Nor shall any State deprive any person of life, liberty, or property without due process of law."

These American constitutional guarantees of liberty bear a close resemblance to the Charter of Rights and Freedoms' guarantee of "the right to life, liberty and security of the person and the right not to be deprived thereof except in accordance with the principles of fundamental justice." It is possible to imagine that if confronted with the same question, the U.S. Supreme Court would come to the same conclusion as the Supreme Court of Canada. It's possible, but wrong.

In *Washington v. Glucksberg,* a unanimous U.S. Supreme Court concluded that the U.S. Constitution does not guarantee a person a right to
assistance with suicide. "We begin, as we do in all due process cases," wrote
the U.S. Supreme Court, "by examining our Nation's history, legal tradi-
tions, and practices." The American court was impressed to find that "in
almost every State—indeed, in almost every western democracy—it is a
crime to assist a suicide." This tradition extended far into the past. In the
thirteenth century, Henry de Bracton observed that slaying oneself was a
felony. In the seventeenth century, Sir William Blackstone called suicide
"self-murder" and ranked it among "the highest crimes."

In the American colonies, the lawmakers of Providence Plantations
called "self-murder" "unnatural" and decided that the property of those
who slayed themselves would be forfeited to the king. The same rule
applied in colonial Virginia.

Over time, forfeiture of property as a penalty for suicide was gradually
abolished, because it came to be seen as unfair to punish the family for a
crime committed by a relative. But the prohibitions on assisted suicide
largely remained in place through the end of the twentieth century and
into the twenty-first.

In its decision, the U.S. Supreme Court acknowledged that the "liberty"
protected by the due process clause encompasses "more than fair process"
and "more than the absence of physical restraint." The court had interpreted
the clause as guaranteeing such things as the right to marry, to have children,
to direct the education and upbringing of one's children, to have marital privacy, to use contraception, to maintain bodily integrity, to seek abortion, to
have consensual sex acts between adults, and to have a same-sex marriage.
In each case, these liberty interests were, in the court's view, "deeply rooted
in the Nation's history and tradition." Not so with assisted suicide.

In light of the consistent and widespread bans throughout the nation's
history, the court concluded, assisted suicide did not meet the high thresh-
old for protection as a fundamental liberty guaranteed by the due process
clause. Instead, whether to allow or prohibit assisted suicide was a question that should be resolved through the democratic process. On the con-
troversial question of a right to assistance in ending one's own life, the
courts in the United States would take their direction from the people's
elected representatives, rather than deciding the questions themselves.

Of all the stages of life—birth, adolescence, first love, marriage, children, and grandchildren—death and dying are the hardest to contemplate. In life, we fight to live, grow, and thrive at every turn, but there comes a point when the fight is over. So it has always been and likely always will be. While the end of life may be the most personal of experiences, the law plays a role even here. What role that should be and where that role should be decided are equally important questions. The question of who should decide arises anytime fundamental rights are at play; and as these cases illustrate, the resolution of that question may not be easy.

.   .   .   .   .

Questions

1. The U.S. Supreme Court and the Canadian Supreme Court approached the question of assisted suicide from very different perspectives. The Canadian high court focused on the individual, her health, her suffering, her personal autonomy, and her ability to control her own body. The U.S. Supreme Court focused on history and tradition. Is one approach better than the other? Does the best approach depend on the question asked?

2. In *Glucksberg*, the U.S. Supreme Court claimed that individual rights were guaranteed by the due process clause only when those rights were "deeply rooted in the Nation's history and tradition." Looking at the list of rights identified by the Supreme Court described above, are you convinced that all of them are, in fact, deeply rooted in the nation's history? If history alone is not by itself the decisive factor, what criteria should the Supreme Court use when considering whether something should be considered a fundamental right protected by the Constitution and the due process clause?

3. By deciding that Canada's Charter of Rights and Freedoms guaranteed the right to die to the terminally ill, the Canadian Supreme Court made it impossible for democratically elected majorities to reach the opposite conclusion. Did the Canadian court go too far and short-circuit the democratic process, or is this an issue that should be put outside the realm of political debate? What criteria might a court use to determine when to declare a fundamental right and when to allow the lawmakers elected by the people to decide what should or should not be a right?

4. The Canadian Supreme Court stayed its decision (temporarily prevented it from going into effect) for one year to give the Canadian Parliament an opportunity to rework the ban on assisting with suicide, to accommodate the wishes of terminally ill people like Gloria Taylor. If you were a lawmaker, what safeguards

would you require before allowing a person to help another person bring about her own death?

5. The Canadian Supreme Court concluded that prohibiting suicide for the terminally ill violated the right to liberty and security because it limited people's right to make decisions about how to treat their own bodies and what medical care they would receive, leaving them to suffer. How far does this logic go? For example, limiting access to prescription drugs also restricts people's right to make decisions about how to treat their bodies and what medical care they might receive. Should prescription drug laws be invalid under the Charter of Rights and Freedoms? If not, why not? What about restricting the practice of medicine to licensed physicians? Does that limit the right to make decisions about one's own body by restricting the sources of medical care? At what point should a person's interest in determining her own medical care yield to the state's interest in regulating the practice of medicine and the distribution of drugs? Is this right to determine one's own medical treatment limited only to people suffering from a "grievous and irremediable medical condition" like Gloria Taylor? Why or why not?

Read It Yourself

Carter v. Canada (Attorney General), 2015 SCC 5.
Washington v. Glucksberg, 521 U.S. 702 (1997).

26 The Voice of God

Christmas had all the makings of misery for Stephen. In May, his wife had left him. She packed her things and moved from their Alaska home to Seattle to live with her mother. Stephen still had his children, which was a blessing, but the children had left to spend Christmas with their mother, and that made him very nervous. Would they come back? What did they think about their parents' split? Did they blame him? This would be the first Christmas Stephen had spent alone in more than a decade. He had a lot of time to think, to brood, to meditate on life, the universe, and everything.

No one would have criticized Stephen for succumbing to despair, but succumb he did not. His children returned home, and shortly after Christmas, Stephen suddenly "got [his] relationship back" with Jesus. According to Stephen, Jesus began speaking to him—directly, as in one-to-one, back-and-forth conversation. And there was good news. Jesus told him that all of his sins were forgiven and he should get on a path to repent-ance. Jesus told him to go to church, and he specifically recommended that he talk to his neighbor who lived across the street. Naturally, Stephen heeded Jesus's call—who wouldn't when the Almighty gave a direct sug-gestion? Stephen talked to and prayed with his neighbor, who attended a Pentecostal church. The neighbor put Stephen in touch with his pastor.

For the first time in his life, Stephen began to spend a significant amount of time in prayer.

One night after his revelation, Stephen went to the room where his twelve-year-old daughter was sleeping. He shook her awake. It was the middle of the night, but Stephen didn't care. He had something important to tell her. Jesus had spoken to him, and now he needed to pass that message on to her. Stephen talked to his daughter about going to church and how she should join him on a path of repentance. Religion had never been a big topic in the family, and her father's ardent proselytizing in the middle of the night made the daughter nervous. As the daughter later reported to her grandfather, who later relayed the story to Stephen's treating psychiatrists, Stephen's newfound religious fervor was "creeping her out."

It didn't help that this was not Stephen's first encounter with voices inside his head. Six years earlier, Stephen had also heard voices. Those voices filled him with dread and terror. Eventually, he was gripped with "total fear," and he asked some people to take him to a hospital. At the hospital, the voices didn't go away. They grew louder and more insistent. Stephen tried to resist, but the voices commanded him to jump off a two-story ledge. Stephen listened, Stephen obeyed, and Stephen jumped. As a result of the fall, he broke his ankle, gashed his head, sustained a concussion, and had to use a wheelchair while he recovered from his injuries. Stephen was diagnosed with bipolar disorder, and his doctors put him on antipsychotic medication, which he took for a year or two before stopping. Based on his psychiatric illness, Stephen applied for and started receiving disability benefits from Social Security.

Stephen's father and twelve-year-old daughter were worried that history was repeating itself. In January, after the holidays were over, Stephen's family went to court to ask that Stephen be committed to a psychiatric institution where he could get the help he needed for his mental health, and where Stephen would be safe from hurting himself—or anyone else.

The laws of Alaska allowed a court to confine a person against his will for medical treatment if the court found clear and convincing evidence that the person was mentally ill and either was likely to cause harm to himself or others or was "gravely disabled."

The court conducted a hearing to decide whether Stephen should be committed. At the hearing, a psychiatrist testified against Stephen. The psychiatrist was the medical director for psychiatric services for the local hospital. In the psychiatrist's opinion, the voice of Jesus that Stephen claimed to be hearing was very similar to the voices Stephen had heard six years earlier that led him to jump off a ledge. According to the psychiatrist, Stephen's belief that Jesus was speaking directly to him was delusional. "A delusion," explained the psychiatrist, "is a belief that is arrived at by other than rational means which is not subject to change by the normal means of logic and persuasion."

The good doctor could understand believing in Jesus if a person grew up in a religious household, where religion was part of his culture and history. But to start hearing the voice of God out of the blue? That was crazy.

But there was more. Stephen had said that ever since Jesus began talking to him, he was feeling happier than he had ever felt before in his life. The psychiatrist pointed out that someone in Stephen's situation shouldn't be that happy. Stephen's wife had left him. It was possible that he could lose his children. His father thought he was crazy, and his daughter was freaked out by his behavior. And Stephen was facing the possibility of an involuntary commitment by order of a court. A man in Stephen's situation, the psychiatrist reasoned, should be considerably more sober.

Given Stephen's past history with mental illness, the psychiatrist concluded that Stephen continued to suffer from bipolar disorder and was currently in the manic phase. The psychiatrist pointed out that Stephen was on state disability because of his mental illness. The psychiatrist was particularly concerned that Stephen had refused medication to treat his condition.

In the psychiatrist's opinion, Stephen ran a very high risk that the voices in his head would shift from benign to pernicious, which could lead to a repeat of the suicide attempt of six years before, or worse. There were, after all, young children in Stephen's house.

For his part, Stephen claimed that things were different this time. The voices that had led him to his suicide attempt had made him fearful and depressed. The voice he heard now made him feel content and at peace. Jesus had forgiven his sins, and he was optimistic about his future.

Yes, he was on disability, but that didn't mean that he couldn't take care of himself or his family or that he was a threat to anyone.

As for refusing to take the antipsychotic drugs his doctors wanted him to take, Stephen stated that the reason he was opposed to medication was because the drugs made him feel "somehow not like himself, not in touch with [his] feelings," and because he believed the medicine would interfere with his ability to hear Jesus's voice. He was willing to go to therapy, but drugs were not an option. Even so, Stephen stated that "if the court ordered him to take medication, he would not harm people and would take an injection."

With this evidence, the court had to decide. Was Stephen gravely disabled, to the point where he should be confined against his will in a hospital for medical treatment? Or was he just a person who, after wandering in the wilderness, had found comfort and joy in religion? Should he be remanded to the custody of psychiatrists, or should he be returned to his home to be with his daughters? How would you rule?

HOW THE COURT RULED

The court began by discounting the statement by Stephen's daughter that her father's behavior was "creeping her out." The daughter's statement had been relayed to the psychiatrist through Stephen's father. The court viewed this as hearsay upon hearsay and not entitled to any significant evidentiary weight.

Next, the court contrasted Stephen's current experience with the voices he had heard six years earlier and which had led him to jump off a ledge. Back then, Stephen was fearful and distressed. Now, according to Stephen's testimony, he was calm, at peace, and optimistic about the future.

The court acknowledged that Stephen had been twice diagnosed as suffering from mental illness, first in 2004 after his failed suicide attempt, and again in 2010 by the psychiatrist who testified in the case. But the court reasoned that mental illness alone does not justify the significant deprivation of a person's liberty that comes from involuntary confinement.

For the same reason, the court was not concerned that Stephen was on state disability because of his mental illness. A person can be mentally ill and still be able to take care of himself. In fact, Stephen had done just that for many years.

For the court, it was significant that Stephen had not categorically refused all medical treatment. Stephen was willing to talk to a psychiatrist. He had only refused to take the drugs the doctors believed he needed. Stephen's preference for one form of treatment (therapy) over another (medication) was not a blanket refusal to get any help at all and, therefore, not evidence of a disability so grave that involuntary commitment was warranted.

Most importantly for the court, Stephen appeared to be functioning on his own before and during the hearing. He was capable of rational conversation and was feeding and taking care of himself and his children.

The court was especially troubled by the suggestion that Stephen's sudden and unexplained religious conversion might be construed as evidence of mental illness. The psychiatrist had testified that he considered Stephen's religious views to be delusional because they came out of the blue rather than from his culture and upbringing. Getting religion, the court believed, should not itself be evidence of insanity. Stephen's conversations with Jesus brought him a sense of peace and happiness. They didn't make him dangerous or gravely disabled.

Therefore, the court concluded that Stephen did not meet the law's requirements for involuntary commitment. He was not gravely disabled, nor was he a threat to himself or others. So Stephen left the courthouse a free man, much to the dismay of his father, who feared for his son's life and the lives of his grandchildren. Did the court get this one right or wrong? You decide.

REFLECTIONS

Religion is a tricky thing. Take, for example, the case of the Pastafarians. Formally known as the Church of the Flying Spaghetti Monster, Pastafarians claim to believe that "an invisible and undetectable Flying Spaghetti Monster created the universe 'after drinking heavily.'"[1] The Pastafarian afterlife is filled with beer volcanoes and strippers. Some might argue that Pastafarianism is a joke, a parody of religion, not a real religion with real beliefs that deserve to be taken seriously. The challenge that Pastafarianism poses, however, is: How can you tell? What is a real religion?

The First Amendment to the U.S. Constitution guarantees every person the right to "free exercise" of his or her religion and simultaneously forbids the government from "establishing" any religious orthodoxy. Among other things, these two restrictions limit the government's power to define what is and is not a religion. Religion does not depend on belief in a "Supreme Being." Nor must a person be part of an established church. Beliefs may be "religious" if they emanate from deeply and sincerely held ethical and moral beliefs that impose a duty of conscience and occupy an important place in a person's life.[2] But that can mean many things to many people.

Religious beliefs are highly personal, idiosyncratic, and, by their nature, defined by faith and not necessarily empirical evidence. Religious beliefs, therefore, cannot be judged based on their objective truth or falsity. On the contrary, the First Amendment's guarantee forbids courts from ruling on the truth of religious belief systems. As the Supreme Court put it: "Courts are not arbiters of scriptural interpretation."[3] Religious beliefs "need not be acceptable, logical, consistent, or comprehensible to others."[4] Beliefs can be religious even if they are "new, uncommon, not part of a formal church or sect, only subscribed to by a small number of people, or . . . seem illogical or unreasonable to other people."[5] What that means is that the law's protection for religious beliefs is not limited by the size of the group or the reasonableness of the belief. All religious beliefs must be treated equally.

It is often impossible to say whether a person's claimed beliefs are "religious" or simply personal preferences. Rather than inquire into the truth of religious beliefs, courts often focus on whether the professed beliefs are truly sincerely held. Judging the sincerity of a person's personal beliefs is not an easy thing to do when what a person believes is entirely inside that person's mind.

Courts are likely to be especially suspicious about whether a religious belief is sincerely held if the belief lines up neatly with a person's personal interests. New beliefs are more suspect than established ones. Acts inconsistent with professed beliefs suggest insincerity. Professed beliefs that are invoked only when convenient, and set aside when not, cast doubt on those beliefs.

Consider the case of the First Church of Cannabis, a new religion stating that the consumption of marijuana is a sacred sacrament.[6] In many states, possession and use of marijuana is illegal. Do those laws intrude upon the rights of adherents to the First Church of Cannabis to practice the free exercise of their religion? Or is this religion simply a transparent and cynical cover for potheads to get high?

For the most part, modern courts have not been sympathetic to claims for exemptions from general laws on religious grounds. In the early 1990s, the Supreme Court ruled that the Constitution's guarantee of free exercise of religion does not block generally applicable laws merely because a person believes their religion requires them to do what the law prohibits.[7]

Many people, however, did not like the Supreme Court's narrow view of the protections of the free exercise clause. So a few years later, Congress passed the Religious Freedom Restoration Act (commonly referred to by the acronym RFRA).[8] The act prohibited the federal government from imposing substantial burdens on a person's exercise of religion, "even if the burden results from a rule of general applicability." Under RFRA, to limit activity that is part of a religious practice, the government must show that it has a "compelling interest," and that the restriction is "the least restrictive means of furthering that compelling interest." That is a high standard.

Consider the case of a religious group that believes it must use a hallucinogenic tea in its ceremonies. The tea is banned by the federal government. Ignoring the law, some members of the group bring the tea over the border anyway, get stopped by a customs agent, and are indicted for illegal importation of a controlled substance. The members defend themselves, arguing that the prohibition on importation of this particular hallucinogenic drug substantially burdens their religion. Without the special tea, they cannot connect to a higher being. According to the group's members, the ban on this drug did not serve a compelling government interest, and therefore, they should be exempted from the law that applies to everyone else who does not hold this group's beliefs about the sacredness of the tea.

The government responds that the ban does serve compelling government interests. The ban protects the health of anyone who would use the drug, including members of this religion, and it prevents the group from diverting the drug to nonbelievers for fun and profit.

How would you rule? Under the Constitution, the group would lose, because the ban on the tea is a general law. RFRA, however, changed the equation: when a similar case came to the Supreme Court, the group won, because, applying RFRA, the government could not prove that using the tea as a sacrament would really injure the group's members, or that the government would be unable to prevent the drug from getting out to the wider population through means other than a complete ban.[9] RFRA, therefore, creates a special exemption for religious acts, at least in some cases. So the First Church of Cannabis might be all right after all, at least under federal law as it stands today.

But let's turn back to Stephen. He wasn't seeking an exemption from the law because of his religion. The question in his case was whether his professed religious experiences proved that he had lost his mind. Stephen claimed that Jesus was talking to him directly and giving him instructions, which he was bound by sacred duty to follow. These beliefs were new. They changed his behavior. They made his friends and family nervous. They seemed disturbingly similar to a psychotic episode that had led Stephen to jump off a ledge half a decade before. Were these beliefs the product of a new round of psychotic delusions, or were they evidence of a genuine religious experience like that shared by millions of people?

The sincerity of Stephen's beliefs was hard to question. While certainly new and out of the blue, his beliefs conferred no personal or financial benefit. On the contrary, the beliefs had driven a wedge between him and his father and his oldest daughter.

From the perspective of judging Stephen's sanity, more important than his sincerity was the direction his beliefs were pushing him. The court concluded that Stephen was heading in a good direction. The voice in his head was soothing and calm, producing a feeling of peace and contentment that Stephen had not felt before. A man at peace was unlikely to be a danger to himself or to others.

The risk, of course, was that the voice could change and lead Stephen to violence or self-destruction. But the court was not assessing Stephen's possible future mental health. The healthiest person can become sick, and no doubt Stephen could fall back into the bad place he had been when he jumped off the ledge outside his hospital room's window. If his mental condition changed, then a different result in a future commitment case might be warranted. But unless and until that happened, Stephen was entitled to the same right as everyone else to believe what he wanted to believe and live his life accordingly.

.   .   .   .   .

Questions

1. Many people hold religious beliefs, but the relatives of most do not seek to have them involuntarily committed. How much weight should be given to the concerns of a person's friends and family? What elements of Stephen's claim to be hearing the voice of Jesus raised questions about his mental stability? What elements of Stephen's beliefs are common among religious believers?

2. The psychiatrist testified that a delusion is "a belief that is arrived at by other than rational means which is not subject to change by the normal means of logic and persuasion." Do you think this is a good definition of *delusion*? How would this definition be applied to common religious beliefs? Is there a reliable way to distinguish between religious beliefs that are reasonable and those that are delusional?

3. The court discounted the daughter's reported statement that her father's conduct was "creeping her out," because the daughter did not personally testify at Stephen's hearing; rather, her statement was made to her grandfather, who conveyed it to the doctor, who repeated it in court. What if the daughter's comment had not been introduced as hearsay? In other words, if the daughter had testified at the hearing and said that she was "creeped out" by her father's actions, would that have changed the outcome of the case? How should the daughter's concerns about what she perceived to be her father's strange behavior be weighed against Stephen's freedom to have religious beliefs and practices that are unique and personal to himself?

4. What do you think about the Religious Freedom Restoration Act? Is it an appropriate accommodation of religious beliefs, or is it an unfair exemption from the law that is highly susceptible to abuse?

Read It Yourself

In re Stephen O., 314 P. 3d 1185 (Alaska 2013).

27 Judging Jenna

Jenna was a young teenage girl with an adventurous side, and her mother, Sherry, didn't like it. Sherry liked Jenna's best friend, Kelsey, even less. Kelsey was a bad influence on Jenna, at least that was the opinion of Jenna's mom. And like every mother, Sherry wanted to protect her daughter from bad influences.

Perhaps giving up her chance at a mother-of-the-year award for respecting her daughter's privacy, Sherry was snooping through Jenna's cell phone and found, to her horror, text messages that she considered to be "inappropriate" and "sexually explicit." From the messages, Sherry learned that Jenna and Kelsey had "gone out" for a while in eighth grade when they were "going through a phase." Sherry was devastated. Reading those text messages was like having all of her worst nightmares come alive.

Making matters worse, the text message chain included Kelsey's mother. Jenna's mom could not have been more horrified. How could a good parent have read those text messages and done nothing to stop them? The messages seemed to suggest that Kelsey was already having sex—at only fourteen! Inconceivably, to Sherry, Kelsey's mother had gone so far as to buy a vibrator for Kelsey. Maybe that was fine for Kelsey (not really), but it most certainly was not fine for Jenna.

If Kelsey's parent condoned—and even participated in!—these explicit conversations and did nothing to stop the sexual adventures of her own fourteen-year old girl, what kind of trouble was Kelsey capable of getting Jenna into? Jenna's mom didn't want to find out.

Sherry told Jenna in no uncertain terms that she was not to spend time with Kelsey. Period. No discussion. End of story. To seal the deal, Sherry also called Kelsey's mother to tell her that Jenna was forbidden to see Kelsey and that she should keep Kelsey away from Jenna.

Kelsey's mom was not a child to be bossed around. She was a grown woman and fully capable of making her own decisions about how to raise her own daughter. Sherry was being totally unreasonable and blowing things out of all proportion. Teenage girls talk about things, including boys and, yes, even sex. That's a good thing, not something to be feared. You can't fight puberty. Girls will want to explore their bodies, their feelings, and their relationships. The best that parents can do is not turn their backs on what is going on with their kids. Kelsey's mom was bound and determined to support her daughter through the transformations of her teenage years.

Kelsey's mom didn't like the idea of her daughter losing a dear friend; so ignoring Sherry's decree, she secretly sent a text message to Jenna, telling Jenna not to tell her mom about their private conversations. The girls were fourteen, for goodness sake. They were old enough to decide for themselves who their real friends were.

For her part, Sherry did what she could to steer Jenna away from Kelsey, and her efforts must have been working, because one day Kelsey and her mother showed up to talk to Jenna at a church where Jenna was volunteering. For Kelsey's mom, this was all perfectly innocent and natural.

Sherry didn't see things the same way. Sherry had told Kelsey's mom to stay away from Jenna, and she hadn't. Sherry had had enough. She called the police, and then she went to court. On April 9, 2013, Jenna's mom asked the court to issue a protective order commanding Kelsey and her mother to keep away from Jenna. The legal basis for her request was that Kelsey and her mother had committed the crime of stalking.

State law provided a couple of definitions of stalking. One definition defined stalking as "the willful, malicious, and repeated following or harassment of a person by an adult, emancipated minor, or minor thirteen (13) years of age or older, in a manner that would cause a reasonable person to feel frightened, intimidated, threatened, harassed, or molested and actually causes the person being followed or harassed to feel terrorized, frightened, intimidated, threatened, harassed, or molested."

Another definition of stalking was the following:

Stalking also means a course of conduct composed of a series of two or more separate acts over a period of time, however short, evidencing a continuity of purpose or unconsented contact with a person that is initiated or continued without the consent of the individual or in disregard of the expressed desire of the individual that the contact be avoided or discontinued. Unconsented contact or course of conduct includes, but is not limited to:

a. following or appearing within the sight of that individual,

b. approaching or confronting that individual in a public place or on private property,

c. appearing at the workplace or residence of that individual,

d. entering into or remaining on property owned, leased, or occupied by that individual,

e. contacting that individual by telephone,

f. sending mail or electronic communications to that individual, or

g. placing an object on, or delivering an object to, property owned, leased or occupied by that individual.

According to Sherry, Kelsey and her mother had stalked Jenna by sending text messages that Jenna's mother had expressly disapproved, and by visiting Jenna when Jenna's mother had expressly forbidden it. Jenna's mother felt frightened, intimidated, threatened, harassed, and molested for and on behalf of her daughter. Just think what these people with their loose morals might do to her daughter! The text message and the visit at the church satisfied the law's requirement of "two or more separate acts" of unconsented contact. This stalking had to stop.

For Kelsey's mom, the request for a protective order made no sense. All she was trying to do was make it possible for two fourteen-year-old girls to decide for themselves whether they wanted to be friends. She wasn't hurting anyone. At most, she was trying to keep alive the friendship of two teenage girls who had been best buddies. Whatever you might call that, *stalking* wasn't it.

Kelsey's mom pointed out that Jenna herself had testified that she didn't feel intimidated, threatened, frightened, or harassed by Kelsey or her mom. If Jenna wasn't bothered by the contacts, how could she be the victim of stalking?

Jenna's mom saw things differently. She had told Kelsey's mom that she and Kelsey should stay away from Jenna, but they had ignored her—twice. First, Kelsey's mom sent Jenna a text message, and even worse that message was an attempt to undermine Sherry's parental authority over her daughter by suggesting to Jenna that she should ignore her mother and keep her friendship with Kelsey secret from her. Then, Kelsey and her mother physically went to Jenna while Jenna was volunteering at a church.

For Sherry, that was enough—more than enough—to qualify as stalking. All she was asking the court to do was to support a mother's right to choose the people her young teenage daughter spends time with. She was the parent. Jenna was the child. A parent's job is nothing if it isn't to keep her children out of trouble, and that's just what she was doing. She just needed a little help from the court because Kelsey and her mother wouldn't respect her decision.

The two mothers have made their cases. Should the courts intervene if a teenager starts running with a crowd that the parents don't like? How should Jenna's desires figure into the equation, if at all? Does Kelsey's opinion matter? The daughters wait for the court to decide the future of their friendship. Should a mother's preferences take precedence over her daughter's? How would you rule?

HOW THE COURT RULED

The stalking statute required the victim to feel fearful, intimidated, threatened, or harassed. When the victim was a minor, who had to have those feelings? Was it Jenna, as the person who was the object of the alleged stalking? Or was it Jenna's mother, as the parent?

Jenna was fourteen. For the court, this fact was decisive. A fourteen-year-old girl doesn't have the right to decide how she is going to live her life. Her parents do.

Jenna's mother told Kelsey's mother in no uncertain terms that she didn't want Jenna to have anything to do with Kelsey or her family. Kelsey's mother completely disregarded Jenna's mother's parental authority. Kelsey's mother sent a text message to Jenna against her mother's wishes. She even surprised Jenna (and Jenna's mother) by taking Kelsey to Jenna's church, where Jenna was working as a volunteer, a place no one expected them to be.

While fourteen-year-old Jenna might not have considered any of this threatening or harassing—and maybe she even welcomed it—Jenna's mother perceived a threat to her daughter. The law does not require, the court believed, parents to stand idly by while their children are in danger.

Kelsey's mother felt that if Jenna thought it was all right to be friends with Kelsey, then it was all right for Jenna and Kelsey to be friends. The court, however, put no weight on what Jenna did or didn't want. Jenna was a minor, and minors don't have the power to give consent against their parents' wishes, at least where it comes to friends. As the court put it: "As the parent and sole custodian of her minor child, [Jenna's mother] had the right to decide with whom her daughter associated and who could contact her daughter."

In other words, the only consent that mattered was Jenna's mother's. Because Jenna's mother withdrew her consent to allow Kelsey to contact Jenna, and because Kelsey and her mom disregarded that decision more than once, the court concluded that they had violated the laws against stalking, and therefore, that an order commanding Kelsey and her mother to stay away from Jenna was appropriate.

In its decision, the court struck a blow in favor of the rights of parents and against the autonomy of teenagers. Did the court get it right? You decide.

REFLECTIONS

Parenting is hard. The law charges parents with the legal obligation to raise, safeguard, supervise, and care for their children. They must ensure that their children attend school. They must ensure that they are adequately fed, clothed, and sheltered. If children fall sick, parents must respond. Parents may be legally responsible for the torts and even certain crimes their children commit. To discharge these duties imposed by law, parents must exercise substantial control over their children's lives. This isn't always easy. Ask any teenager—or the parent of one.

Parents have rights in addition to responsibilities. Children may be fond of telling their parents that it is a free country, but they usually misunderstand where that freedom lies. The Supreme Court has held that "the liberty interest of parents in the care, custody, and control of their children—is perhaps the oldest of the fundamental liberty interests recognized by this Court."[1] The Constitution itself, therefore, entitles parents (and legal guardians) to direct the upbringing and education of their children. It is a free country. It's just that the freedom, in general, belongs to the parents.

When dealing with divorcing parents who disagree, courts may put their views of what's in the best interest of the children ahead of the opinions of either parent. But that is an exception to the rule that courts generally defer to parents because "the law's concept of the family rests on a presumption that parents possess what a child lacks in maturity, experience, and capacity for judgment required for making life's difficult decisions."[2]

This does not mean that children have no rights. The obligations that the law imposes on parents are for the benefit of children. If parents fail to live up to those obligations, the courts can declare them to be unfit; and in the most extreme cases, the parents' rights to raise their children can be terminated by the state. It is also possible that states can confer additional rights on minors that limit the parents' authority. For example, according to the Guttmacher Institute, twenty-six states allow minors to access contraceptive services without their parents' consent, and twenty more allow it in some circumstances. In contrast, only two states allow minors to consent to abortions. The others require either prior notification of the parents or the consent of at least one parent.[3]

Children also have certain rights against the outside world. Children have the right to engage in free speech, although the power of schools to regulate student speech is far greater than the government's power over the adult population.[4] Children have the right to enjoy literature, arts, and entertainment, provided their parents do not object.[5] Naturally, children have the right not to be victims of crime.

Despite these rights, children must generally yield to the will of their parents. Restraining orders—especially under an antistalking law—may be an unusual way for parents to control their children's friendships. But in a contest of wills between parent and child, the courts are, as a general matter, much more likely to support a parent than the child, for good or for ill.

·   ·   ·   ·   ·

Questions

1. The court emphasized that Jenna is a minor, and that, therefore, her parent gets to decide who may or may not contact her. Should this power to prevent others' contact with a child apply only to contact by a child's friends, or should it apply in other contexts? What if Jenna wants medical treatment or advice? Should her mother be able to prevent her from going to the doctor even if Jenna wants to? When should a parent get to make decisions for a teenage child, and when should the child be able to make decisions for himself or herself?

2. The reason Jenna's mother objected to Jenna's friendship with Kelsey appears to have been that she feared Kelsey was a bad influence on Jenna. Kelsey, it seems, was sexually active, with her mother's approval, and Jenna's mother seemed to be afraid that Kelsey's actions would encourage her daughter to do the same thing. If a parent tries to shield a teenage child from a "bad influence," does it matter whether the influence is truly "bad"; and if so, who should decide what's "bad" and what's not? For example, should a religious parent be able to get a restraining order preventing nonreligious children from communicating with his child? Should a nonreligious parent be able to get a restraining order preventing a teenager from going to church? At what point, if at all, does a parent's attempt to control a teenage child violate the First Amendment rights of the child? What about the rights of people who might want to talk to the child?

3. Jenna was fourteen. Would the case have been different if she had been seventeen? What if she were ten? Does it matter how mature Jenna is, or should age be a bright line?

Read It Yourself

Muscato v. Moore, 2014, OK Civ. App. 93.

28 Three Generations

As America and the world recovered from the shocking bloodbath of the first World War, the State of Virginia grew concerned about the gene pool of its population. Virginia recognized that there was little it could do about the mentally disabled already living in its state, but the State wanted a way prevent their mental illness from spreading from one generation to the next. So, on March 20, 1924, Virginia declared an emergency and enacted the Eugenical Sterilization Act, a law that allowed the state to sterilize people with mental disabilities against their will. The state justified the law as a public safety measure. "Mental defectives," as the law at the time called those suffering from mental illness, were a "menace" because their offspring tended to suffer from the same mental defects and thereby became a burden to society as a whole. Against this perceived threat to society, the harm to the sterilized individual was relatively minor, because, according to Virginia, sterilization posed no "serious pain or substantial danger to life."

Carrie Buck was eighteen years old when she came into the care of the State Colony for Epileptics and Feeble Minded shortly after Virginia's sterilization law went into effect. Buck's mother, too, had found herself in the same mental hospital, and Buck herself had a baby that the state feared would share Buck's and Buck's mother's mental infirmities.

The superintendent of State Colony saw Buck as the personification of the threat to society that Virginia's sterilization law was meant to guard against. At only eighteen, Buck had already started procreating; and the superintendent feared that if left unchecked, Buck might flood the population of Virginia with carbon copies of her defective genes, and that each of her children, when grown, would inevitably become wards of the state and burdens to the good citizens of Virginia. The superintendent was determined not to let that happen.

As required by the law, the superintendent filed with the board of directors of State Colony the paperwork necessary to sterilize Buck. Notice of the petition was duly sent to Buck, and a guardian was appointed to protect her interests. The superintendent presented evidence of Buck's illness to the board. After due deliberation, the board gave the superintendent the green light to cut Buck's fallopian tubes. Buck's guardian appealed to the county circuit court and, losing there, appealed to the state supreme court of appeals, which also rejected Buck's pleas. Finally, Buck's case came to the U.S. Supreme Court.

Buck's lawyers argued that the sterilization law violated her constitutional rights to due process and to equal protection of the laws guaranteed by the Fourteenth Amendment to the U.S. Constitution. Sterilization, they said, could never be justified. The mentally ill had just as much right to have children as anyone else in the state of Virginia. Procreation was a basic human right, and Virginia had no right to carve out of Buck's body, against her will, her capacity to have children.

In his defense, the superintendent pointed to the finding of the board and the lower courts that Buck was "the probable potential parent of socially inadequate offspring, likewise afflicted, that she may be sexually sterilized without detriment to her general health and that her welfare and that of society will be promoted by her sterilization." In other words, Buck's children were likely to be bad for society; and not only would sterilization not really harm Buck, but on the contrary, it would also be good for her, freeing her from worries about raising children she was ill-equipped to care for. As a bonus, the people of Virginia would have fewer mouths to feed on the public dole.

Carrie Buck was a ward of the state. So was the one child she already had. The Virginia courts had found it likely that Buck's future children, if she had any, would also become dependents of the state. According to the doctors in the asylum, Buck was "feeble minded," and they believed that her mental infirmities would likely be passed from parent to child. Were these reasons enough to justify the state in taking by force and against her will Buck's ability to have children? The people of the state of Virginia thought so. Buck's guardian appealed to the courts to make them stop. How would you rule?

HOW THE COURT RULED

Justice Oliver Wendell Holmes Jr. wrote the decision for the Supreme Court. At the outset he noted that it was the considered judgment of the elected representatives of the state of Virginia that sterilization of the mentally infirm was in the best interests of the state and its citizens, including the person to be sterilized, who then would not be burdened by children he or she wasn't capable of caring for. To overturn this legislative judgment would require significant proofs, and the court didn't see them. On the contrary, as the superintendent had pointed out, the lower courts had found that Carrie Buck could be sterilized "without detriment to her general health" and "her welfare and that of society would be promoted by her sterilization."

Buck had not been denied the equal protection of the laws. Virginia's sterilization law reasonably distinguished been the mentally healthy and the mentally ill. Treating the mentally ill differently was not unequal. By necessity, to protect the health and welfare of its citizens, the states must have the power to separate the sick from the healthy and treat them differently according to their conditions.

The court acknowledged that the loss of the ability to bear children was a real burden on Buck, but saw it as an acceptable, individual sacrifice for the collective good. According to Justice Holmes, the needs of the state often demand individual sacrifice, including sacrifices much greater than the right to reproduce. Here is how Justice Holmes put it:

> We have seen more than once that the public welfare may call upon the best citizens for their lives. It would be strange if it could not call upon those who already sap the strength of the State for these lesser sacrifices, often not felt

to be such by those concerned, to prevent our being swamped with incompetence. It is better for all the world, if instead of waiting to execute degenerate offspring for crime, or to let them starve for their imbecility, society can prevent those who are manifestly unfit from continuing their kind. The principle that sustains compulsory vaccination is broad enough to cover cutting the Fallopian tubes.

Buck's due process claims met an equally icy reception. In the court's view, Buck had received a fair trial. Her case had been reviewed by an impartial board. It had been reviewed again by a court and yet again by another court. By the time Buck's case arrived at the Supreme Court's door, the facts were clear enough, and numerous, independent, reasonable reviewers had concluded that her sterilization was lawful and appropriate. Carrie Buck was a threat to society. Justice Holmes put it in the bluntest of terms: "Three generations of imbeciles are enough."

The sterilization was approved. The state of Virginia could cut Carrie Buck's fallopian tubes and prevent her from ever having another child, whether she liked it or not. Did the court get this one right? You decide.

REFLECTIONS

In the annals of the Supreme Court, the case of Carrie Buck lives in infamy. After the court's endorsement of Buck's forced sterilization, many states throughout the nation followed Virginia's lead and enacted their own mandatory sterilization laws. Over the next half century, Virginia would go on to sterilize more than eight thousand people.

While the sterilization laws were couched in terms of promoting the welfare of the individual as well as of the state, the true motives behind Virginia's version can be inferred from another law Virginia enacted the same day: the Racial Integrity Act. The Racial Integrity Act made it "unlawful for any white person in [Virginia] to marry any [person] save a white person." This racist law would remain in force for nearly a half century, until the Supreme Court finally struck it down as unconstitutional in *Loving v. Virginia,* a case where the high court recognized that the right to marry was a fundamental right protected by the Constitution that could not be curtailed based on the race of the couple.[1]

In the early part of the twentieth century, many people, with Virginia leading the charge, fretted over maintaining racial purity, which at the time principally meant preventing elite Anglo-Saxon whites from mixing with poorer whites and racial minorities. The fig leaf used to justify this racist objective was eugenics, a pseudoscientific philosophy that was popular in the day.

While today eugenics is discredited and roundly repudiated, at the time the philosophy had many adherents, who cited as its foundation the truly revolutionary insights of Charles Darwin, the nineteenth-century English naturalist and geologist and one of the most influential thinkers and scientists in history. Along with Alfred Russel Wallace, Darwin introduced the world to the theory that the multiplicity of life-forms on earth comes not from divine creation but from evolution of the species. The driving force of evolution, and Darwin's key insight, was natural selection. Every living creature differs to some degree from all others; and equipped with their natural endowments, for good or for ill, all compete to survive and to reproduce. Those with the traits best suited for survival tend to reproduce the most; and over time, these favored traits come to dominate the species, while the traits of their less well adapted brothers and sisters tend to fade away. In *On the Origin of Species*, Darwin's magisterial introduction to the theory of evolution, Darwin described natural selection this way:

> It may be said that natural selection is daily and hourly scrutinizing, throughout the world, every variation, even the slightest; rejecting that which is bad, preserving and adding up all that is good; silently and insensibly working, whenever and wherever opportunity offers, at the improvement of each organic being in relation to its organic and inorganic conditions of life. We see nothing of these slow changes in progress, until the hand of time has marked the long lapse of ages, and then so imperfect is our view into long past geological ages, that we see only that the forms of life are now different from what they formerly were.

In the closing passage from *On the Origin of Species*, Darwin waxed lyrical about the beauty and power of evolution and natural selection decisively shaping through gradual, barely perceptible change all living things on our small planet: "Thus, from the war of nature, from famine and death, the most exalted object which we are capable of conceiving, namely, the production of the higher animals, directly follows. There is grandeur in this view of life, with its several powers, having been originally breathed into a few forms or into one; and that, whilst this planet has gone cycling on according to the fixed law of gravity, from so simple a beginning endless forms most beautiful and most wonderful have been, and are being, evolved."

The idea that evolution slowly improves each species by weeding out the weak and rewarding the strong with ever greater numbers of offspring, until the weak are extinguished and only the strong, the fit, remain, captured the imagination of many late-nineteenth- and early-twentieth-century intellectuals who thought to apply the lessons of natural selection to the improvement of the species of most interest to humans: human beings themselves.

These intellectuals, later known as social Darwinists, espoused the philosophy that governments should not aid the poor, the weak, or the sick because their ailments were evidence of their lack of fitness, and supporting them and their offspring would lead to their continuing to procreate, thereby weakening the human race. Nature should take its course, argued the social Darwinists, and the most frail and vulnerable members of society should be allowed to fall by the wayside while the strong, the rich, and the healthy populate the world.

This idea of social Darwinism—that curtailing the offspring of the sick and feeble strengthens society overall—was very much in vogue among the upper classes when Virginia enacted its sterilization law and the Supreme Court later approved it. In social Darwinism, the upper classes found a comforting justification for their high stations and affluent lifestyles and for their disdain and disregard of the needy and poor.

The *Buck* case illustrates how every act of judgment is necessarily a product of its time and the philosophy, morals, and experience of the human being who sits as the judge. In ruling on Carrie Buck's case, Justice Holmes might have benefited from recalling his own admonition in his dissent in *United States v. Abrams* that "time has upset many fighting faiths." If he had, he might have questioned whether the philosophy that purported to justify the irrevocable step of taking away Buck's ability to have children might not endure, and whether the rights of the individual against the demands of the state deserved more protection from the Constitution and the courts.

Instead, Justice Holmes and the Supreme Court deferred to the judgment of the elected representatives of the state of Virginia. Because of this deference, the court put the burden on Carrie Buck to demonstrate that the state's concerns about the quality of the gene pool in the state were unfounded, instead of requiring the state to prove that sterilizing Carrie would meaningfully improve the welfare of the state. Faced with the philosophy of the moment, it is not clear what Carrie could have said or done to convince the court that her body should not be sacrificed for the illusion of stamping out mental illness.

It is worth noting that social Darwinism developed without the imprimatur of Charles Darwin himself, and it seems that the founder of Darwinism would likely have disapproved of the social Darwinists' most radical proposals to abandon the poor and the sick. In *The Descent of Man*, Darwin's sequel to *On the Origin of Species*, Darwin noted that natural selection itself had created the feelings of sympathy that lead people to care for one another: "The following proposition seems to me in a high degree probable—namely, that any animal whatever, endowed with well-marked social instincts, the parental and filial affections being here included, would inevitably acquire a moral sense or conscience, as soon as its intellectual powers had become as well, or nearly as well developed, as in man."

Darwin suggested that uprooting this natural sympathy would likely degrade the noblest part of human nature and create great evil in the pursuit of imaginary benefits: "The aid which we feel impelled to give to the helpless is mainly an incidental result of the instinct of sympathy, which was originally acquired as part of the social instincts, but subsequently rendered, in the manner previously indicated, more tender and more widely diffused. Nor could we check our sympathy, even at the urging of hard reason, without deterioration in the noblest part of our nature. . . . If we were intentionally to neglect the weak and helpless, it could only be for a contingent benefit, with an overwhelming present evil."

For human beings, who depend on the help of others from the moment of our births to the end of our days, one of evolution's greatest achievements was the cultivation of compassion and caring for our fellow travelers in this world. By turning their backs on their brothers and sisters, the social Darwinists sought to rip out "the noblest part of our nature," the essential traits of sympathy, kindness, and generosity that allowed for the cooperation and collaboration that serve as the foundation of society and the social order. In a sense, the social Darwinists proved Darwin right, but not necessarily in the way they imagined. Their determination to neglect the weak and helpless, and to condemn those they considered unfit and unworthy, traded illusory benefits for "an overwhelming present evil": the loss of humanity's humanity. While the social Darwinists touted their embrace of natural selection, there was nothing natural about their decisions to rid the world of people they thought inferior. How many people could have been spared needless suffering if the proponents of this callous philosophy had considered its source more carefully?

In 1974, Virginia repealed its sterilization law. On January 28, 1983, Carrie Buck passed away and was buried next to her only child, Vivian, who had died decades earlier at the age of eight. In 2002, the governor of Virginia apologized to Buck on behalf of the state. A marker now stands in Buck's hometown memorializing the state's failed experiment with eugenics and the woman who fought an unjust law and lost—until the judgment of history reversed the judgment of the courts.

•   •   •   •   •

Questions

1. The opinion of Justice Holmes in Carrie Buck's case hinges on the court's deference to the judgment of the representatives of the people of the state of Virginia who were duly elected to the state legislature and charged with making laws to safeguard the people's health and welfare. The legislature thought sterilization was best for the people, and the court would not disturb that judgment without the strongest of proofs, which Justice Holmes concluded were lacking in Carrie's case. Was Justice Holmes's deference to the legislature the right approach? Is it right in general and wrong in this case? When is it appropriate for courts to defer to legislative judgments? When should courts intervene and declare that a legislative enactment has gone too far and violated a fundamental right?

2. Justice Holmes compared Virginia's sterilization law to laws that mandate vaccinations. Because mandatory vaccination laws are constitutional, Holmes reasoned, mandatory sterilization (with appropriate safeguards) is also constitutional. How apt is this analogy? Are there differences between vaccinations and sterilizations that might justify treating them differently, or was Holmes correct

that the two should be treated the same? What about quarantines? Should quarantines be constitutional, or should they be considered violations of individual rights? When is it appropriate for the state to wield power over the bodies of its citizens, and when is it inappropriate?

3. Justice Holmes also compared compelled sterilization with compelled service in the military. If the state can force its citizens to fight and die in war for the good of the state, Holmes asked, why shouldn't the state have the power to compel its citizens to make the much smaller sacrifice of surrendering the ability to have children for the same good of the state? Is the analogy to military service a good one? Was Justice Holmes correct that military drafts and compelled sterilizations should be treated the same? Could the analogy be turned around and used to call the legitimacy of the draft into question? In other words, how persuasive would the argument be if put the following way: compelling a person to be sterilized violates his fundamental rights; therefore, the greater demand that a draft imposes on a person to fight and possibly die against his will even more seriously violates fundamental rights?

Read It Yourself

Buck v. Bell, 274 U.S. 200 (1927).

29 A Good Walk Spoiled

The game of golf is a good walk spoiled, an anonymous wag once quipped.[1] But what makes golf "golf" and not something else? And who decides what is golf and what is not? In one case, it fell to the U.S. Supreme Court to ponder that imponderable question.

Casey Martin was a golf phenom. Before he turned fifteen, he won seventeen Golf Association junior events in Oregon. As a senior in high school, he won the state championship. In college, he played golf for Stanford University and was part of the team that won the 1994 national championship. After graduating, he turned pro, and Martin more than held his own against the best of the best, finishing in the top ten in six tournaments over two years.

What made Casey Martin's golf prowess even more amazing was that he was a very sick man. The Supreme Court would later describe his condition this way: "Since birth he has been afflicted with Klippel-Trenaunay-Weber Syndrome, a degenerative circulatory disorder that obstructs the flow of blood from his right leg back to his heart. The disease is progressive; it causes severe pain and has atrophied his right leg."

By the time Martin was finishing his college career, his condition had worsened to the point where walking caused him pain, fatigue, and anxiety. If he walked too much, he could start bleeding spontaneously and possibly develop life-threatening blood clots. His leg might break and have to be amputated. Walking a golf course became nearly impossible, but Martin loved the game and did not want to give it up.

In college, Martin managed to stay in the game by getting waivers from the National Collegiate Athletic Association for rules that required players to walk and carry their own clubs. As a pro, Martin succeeded in tournaments that allowed players to ride courses in golf carts. But then he hit a wall.

The Professional Golfers' Association of America ran the top golfing tournaments in the country. PGA Tour tournaments were where the best of the best competed, and where the top prize money went to the winners. Martin knew in his heart that he could compete at that elite level, and he desperately wanted his shot at the big time.

Getting on the PGA Tour was not easy. To qualify for the tour, three paths were available. You could win three tournaments in another series, called the Nike Tour, or be among the top fifteen money winners. Alternatively, you could qualify by getting a high enough score in an open preliminary round usually held a week before a PGA Tour tournament. Or you could go to Q-School.

Q-School (short for "qualifying school") was less a school and more an extended tryout. In a typical year, over a thousand PGA Tour hopefuls would compete through three stages to win a coveted spot at the big dance. In the first stage, aspiring pros had to play four 18-hole rounds of golf at different locations. This eliminated about half of the crowd. The second stage was another 72 holes of golf. Fewer than two hundred hopefuls would make it through. For those few remaining, the third and final stage entailed playing 108 more holes. Of these last competitors, maybe thirty would make it onto the PGA Tour. Martin was determined to be one of those lucky few.

But there was a catch. A book with the highly unimaginative title of *The Rules of Golf,* published jointly by the United States Golf Association and the Royal and Ancient Golf Club of Scotland, spelled out—what else?—the rules of golf; but for the PGA Tour, special additional rules applied. These rules were called the "Conditions of Competition and Local Rules," a set of rules affectionately or not-so-affectionately known as the "hard card."

While *The Rules of Golf* made no mention of how a player was to get around the golf course, the hard card required that all players walk. No carts. No help. No exceptions.

For the first two stages of Q-School, players could compete using golf carts, but for the third and final qualifying stage, the hard-card rules applied. No carts were allowed at PGA Tour tournaments, so no carts were allowed at the final qualifying competition.

The hard card's prohibition on golf carts made it impossible for Casey Martin to break into the PGA Tour. He had demonstrated that he could hit a ball into a distant cup with the best players in the world, but he couldn't do it if he had to walk a course measuring approximately five miles, as eighteen holes of golf required. But Martin was a tenacious competitor, and he had not gotten as far as he had by giving up easily.

Martin turned to the Americans with Disabilities Act, a law passed in 1990 that prohibited discrimination against the disabled. Because he was afflicted with Klippel-Trenaunay-Weber Syndrome, Martin qualified for protection under the law. To ensure that disabled people have equal access to public events, the ADA requires event organizers to make reasonable changes to rules to allow disabled people to participate, or, in the words of the ADA, "to make reasonable modifications in policies, practices, or procedures, when such modifications are necessary to afford such goods, services, facilities, privileges, advantages, or accommodations to individuals with disabilities, unless the entity can demonstrate that making such modifications would fundamentally alter the nature of such goods, services, facilities, privileges, advantages, or accommodations."

Martin asked for what he thought was a "reasonable modification": to use a cart to get around the golf course. The PGA Tour disagreed. The PGA Tour thought that the no-carts rule was a very important part of its tournaments. Famous golfers like Jack Nicklaus and Arnold Palmer testified that walking the course introduced an element of fatigue that tested the players' endurance, and that this endurance challenge was as much a part of the game as swinging a club and putting a ball in a cup. Letting Martin play in PGA Tour tournaments with a cart would, as the PGA Tour saw it, "fundamentally alter the nature" of the game they were playing, something the ADA expressly stated was not required.

Martin countered that if the purpose of the no-carts rule was to test players' ability to handle fatigue, he already had that covered. Even using a cart, he would have to walk around the course to get to his ball and to scout the terrain. With his disease, the fatigue from that exertion was much greater than anything his healthy opponents would experience.

Anyway, the game of golf is not who can walk the course the best. It is who can put a ball into a faraway cup with the fewest swings of a club. You could tell that walking was not essential to the game of golf, because the hard card's no-carts rule applied only to PGA Tour events. It was not part of the canonical *Rules of Golf.* It did not apply to amateur events or to other tournaments. It did not even apply to the first two stages of Q-School. No reasonable person would consider walking the course a "fundamental" part of the game of golf.

And so the arguments were teed up. On the one hand, Martin, a gifted golfer, argued that golf was only hitting balls into holes, and therefore, that carts were a perfectly acceptable accommodation to allow a disabled person like himself to play the game. On the other hand, the PGA Tour that organized the most prestigious (and most lucrative) golf tournaments in the United States argued that their special hard-card rules reasonably required the most rigorous standards to test the athletic abilities of the most accomplished players at the highest levels.

Is walking a fundamental part of the game of golf as played on the PGA Tour, or is the walking requirement a rule that can and should be bent so that an otherwise qualified and capable disabled person could have a chance to compete? How would you rule?

HOW THE COURT RULED

The purpose of the Americans with Disabilities Act, observed the court, was to combat the ways society had tended to isolate and segregate individuals with disabilities. Exclusion of the disabled could take many forms. Outright discrimination—we won't serve people in wheelchairs—was one. But another was the more insidious discrimination of arbitrary rules or barriers that disabled people couldn't overcome. A paradigmatic example of this type of discrimination might be a steep stairwell with no elevator or ramp. Anyone healthy enough to clear the obstacles is welcome. Those too disabled to overcome them have to keep out. It was this less overt, but equally exclusionary, discrimination that the ADA meant to end by requiring reasonable modifications in policies, practices, or procedures.

There was no question that if Casey Martin were ever going to compete in the PGA Tour, the rule in the hard card prohibiting players from using carts to get around the golf course would have to be changed, at least for him. He was ready and able to swing clubs and hit balls into cups, but the disease that afflicted him made it impossible from him to walk eighteen holes.

Although it was clear that Martin was disabled and needed a modification of the PGA Tour's rules to play, the ADA puts a limit on changes that must be made to accommodate the disabled. If letting Martin use a golf cart would "fundamentally alter the nature" of the game of golf, then he was not entitled to the change in the rules.

What does it mean to "fundamentally alter the nature" of a game? This is where things got tricky. If some hypothetical other Martin wanted to run in a marathon, but asked to drive the course in a cart because he wasn't able to use his legs to run it, he would be disappointed. Most people would quickly agree that running is a "fundamental" part of a marathon. If you're not running on your feet, you're not doing a marathon.

If this hypothetical Martin said, "Fine, I'll run on my feet, but I just can't run a long time, so please make an exception to the distance rule so I have to run only 10 miles instead of the full 26.2," he too would go away disappointed. Changing the distance of the marathon for one runner would give him an advantage over the other runners, so the competition itself would be fundamentally altered.

Would Casey Martin riding from hole to hole in a golf cart be a fundamental change to the game of golf? Would riding in a golf cart give Martin an unfair competitive advantage over the other players?

The Supreme Court thought not. The game of golf, in the opinion of the court, was all about hitting a ball into a distant cup in as few shots as possible. It was not about how you got around the course.

Weighing heavily in the court's conclusion was the canonical *Rules of Golf.* The *Rules* did not prohibit riding in a golf cart. Millions of amateur players used carts to play the game. Other professional tournaments allowed golf carts, and even the PGA Tour itself allowed carts for the first two stages of its qualifying tournament, Q-School. Over the years, golf had changed many of its rules—multiple golf clubs, golf bags, caddies, carts that were pulled by hand: all were introduced at one time or another—but the one thing about golf that never changed was hitting a ball into holes. Therefore, that unchanging piece of the game defined its fundamental nature, and Martin riding in a cart would not alter that fundamental element.

But what about giving Martin an unfair advantage? The other players would have to deal with the fatigue that came from walking, while Martin could rest and relax as an electric cart zipped him from fairway to fairway. To this argument, the court shrugged. The fatigue of walking a golf course, in the court's view, was just not that big a deal. Players walk golf courses over a five-hour stretch and have plenty of chances to rest. They just don't get all that tired.

Anyway, the court pointed out that many professional players preferred to walk. In tournaments that allowed players to use carts, the majority of them walked anyway. They could stay warmer when it was chilly, and they could develop a better sense of the course. If walking really were an obstacle inherent in the game, competitors would avoid the obstacle if they had the choice. The fact that they didn't demonstrated that walking the course wasn't much of an obstacle, so whether Martin walked or not didn't matter all that much.

At most, the court concluded, walking is a peripheral part of golf. It is certainly not fundamental. At least in Martin's case, whatever fatigue walking was supposed to inject into the game would be more than sufficiently supplied by the debilitating effects of his disease. At the end of the course, cart-riding Martin would undoubtedly be at least as tired as his walking competition. Martin's request to use a cart, therefore, was a reasonable modification that did not alter the fundamental nature of the PGA Tour's tournaments.

So the PGA Tour had to make an exception to its rules, and Martin got to use a cart. Did the court get it right? You decide.

REFLECTIONS

A dictionary definition of *discrimination* is "the practice of unfairly treating a person or group of people differently from other people or groups of people."[2] The key part is treating people "differently." America is the land of opportunity, and this means that all people, no matter their color, creed, or gender, should have an equal chance to succeed in the public square. The essence of the antidiscrimination laws, therefore, is the requirement that people not be treated unequally because of their protected characteristics, like their race, sex, or sexual orientation. Disability discrimination, however, is different.

For the disabled, treatment exactly equal to that of their healthy peers often means being shut out from opportunity. For the disabled to compete on a level playing field, rules often have to bend. A good example would be the collegiate sprinter who happens to be deaf. The sprinter may have the speed to outrun her competition; but because of a hearing disability, she can't hear the shot of the starting gun used to signal to the runners that the race has begun. Telling her to listen for the sound of the gun like all the other runners effectively means that she will start every race half-a-stride behind. Equal treatment is, for her, unequal.

Therefore, the laws prohibiting discrimination against the disabled require "reasonable accommodations" for qualified disabled people. This requirement that rules be changed makes disability cases particularly difficult to deal with. It is not sufficient to respond to a claim of discrimination that everyone else is treated the same.

All reasonable accommodations must be granted unless they impose an undue burden or fundamentally alter the activity. The answers to the three questions prompted by this statement—is an accommodation reasonable, is the burden it imposes (for all accommodations impose *some* burden) undue, and does the accommodation result in a fundamental alteration?—largely depend on the specifics of a person's disability, the accommodation requested, and the nature of the activity. When rights depend on fact-specific situations, it can be difficult to predict the outcome, and disputes are sure to follow. Ask Casey Martin and the PGA Tour.

Sometimes, the law can't do better than setting out a general principle and hoping the courts, exercising good judgment, will correctly sort out just from unjust applications. In disability cases, sometimes accommodations will be simple and straightforward. For example, for the deaf sprinter, races don't have to start with a sound. They could start with a flash of light that all the racers could see. No one gets a head start, but the hearing impaired sprinter isn't left behind. In other cases, it is harder to tell. Casey Martin's might be an example. Extra time allowed on high-stakes standardized tests like the ones required to get into law or medical school is also sometimes questioned by those who have to take the test in the standard time.

Since its enactment in 1990, the Americans with Disabilities Act has opened doors to work, school, and public accommodations for millions of disabled people who had been effectively shut out by arbitrary and unnec-essary barriers like buildings without elevators and stairs without ramps. At the same time, there will always be some people who suspect that disa-bled people—by requiring differential treatment in response to their dif-ferent health conditions—are getting an unfair leg up. Because of the imprecision of the law's requirements, disputes are inevitable, and wise and thoughtful judging is critical.

· · · · ·

Questions

1. How does one tell if a particular rule of a particular game is fundamental or peripheral? Is there a general principle that can be articulated, or is it just what-ever judges think?

2. The court's ruling talks about the game of golf as if golf is, and can only be, one thing. For example, the court compares the PGA Tour's rules with how golf was played hundreds of years ago in medieval Scotland, when the game was first invented. Does this make sense? Is it possible to think of golf as a family of games that share common elements, but which also have individual variations, each of which has fundamental rules that define it and distinguish it from the other variations? For example, could there be two kinds of golf: walking golf and riding golf? Would any of the court's analysis have to change if the court had considered PGA Tour golf to be its own unique variation of the game (just as seven-card stud is a variation of poker)?

3. Justice Antonin Scalia dissented from the court's ruling in Martin's case. He skewered the court for meddling with a question that he thought the court had no business (and none of the expertise necessary for) answering. He wrote,

> We Justices must confront what is indeed an awesome responsibility. It has been rendered the solemn duty of the Supreme Court of the United States . . . to decide What Is Golf. I am sure that the Framers of the Constitution, aware of the 1457

edict of King James II of Scotland prohibiting golf because it interfered with the practice of archery, fully expected that sooner or later the paths of golf and government, the law and the links, would once again cross, and that the judges of this august Court would some day have to wrestle with that age-old jurispruden- tial question, for which their years of study in the law have so well prepared them: Is someone riding around a golf course from shot to shot really a golfer? Either out of humility or out of self-respect (one or the other) the Court should decline to answer this incredibly difficult and incredibly silly question.

What do you think of Justice Scalia's argument? Should the courts have stayed out of this "silly question"?

Read It Yourself

PGA Tour, Inc. v. Martin, 532 U.S. 661 (2001).

30 That's My Mother You're Talking About!

Hustler magazine achieved fame and fortune by publishing unapologetically graphic photographs of naked women. Despite *Hustler*'s popularity in certain circles, not all people were pleased with the pictures the magazine purveyed. While some might shrug that *Hustler*'s fare was not for them and move on, others took to public forums to fulminate against *Hustler* and argue that the magazine's very existence was a sign that America was scraping new lows of decadence and degradation.

In the early 1980s, Reverend Jerry Falwell was one of *Hustler*'s most visible and vocal critics. Reverend Falwell worried about the magazine's effects on its readers. He especially fretted over the evils that might ensue if *Hustler*'s images of unclad females reached the vulnerable, immature eyes of children. He took it upon himself to turn public opinion against the magazine.

Mark Twain once sagely advised, "Never pick a fight with people who buy ink by the barrel." Reverend Falwell soon found out what Twain was talking about.

In the November 1983 issue, *Hustler* readers turning to the page just behind the cover found Reverend Falwell's picture smiling back at them. Reverend Falwell's photo was part of a fake ad for Campari liqueur, which at the time was famous for an ad campaign where, under the provocative tagline "You'll never forget your first time," celebrities recounted the first time they had sex. Reverend Falwell's first time, as portrayed in the parody, was a doozy.

The ad was in the form of a fake interview with Reverend Falwell. When asked where he first did the deed, he fictionally replied that his first time was in an outhouse. And who was his first partner? None other than his mother. As the fake Falwell said in the fake interview: "I never really expected to make it with Mom, but then after she showed all the other guys in town such a good time, I figured, 'What the hell.'"

When the fake interviewer expressed fake surprise that fake Falwell's fake first time was with his mother, the fake Falwell was quoted as replying that it wasn't all that strange, because "looks don't mean that much to me in a woman."

According to the interview, at the time Reverend Falwell and his mother were drunk on—what else?—Campari liqueur. The ad concluded with Reverend Falwell giving Campari his highest endorsement by saying, "I always get sloshed before I go out to the pulpit. You don't think I could say all that [expletive] sober, do you?"

The famous showman and circus owner P. T. Barnum once remarked that there is no such thing as bad publicity and when it came to the press, "I don't care what you say about me, just spell my name right." Needless to say, Reverend Falwell did not share that sentiment about the depiction of him and his mother in *Hustler*.

Reverend Falwell decided to take action. He filed a lawsuit. He alleged that *Hustler* had defamed him—smeared his good name and damaged his reputation—by knowingly publishing false information about him and his beloved mother. He also sued for intentional infliction of emotional distress, a tort that punishes outrageous conduct that's undertaken with the purpose of causing severe emotional suffering in another person.

The jury ruled against Reverend Falwell on his defamation claim. It was their opinion that the fake ad could not "reasonably be understood as describing actual facts about [Reverend Falwell] or actual events in which [he] participated." In other words, *Hustler* hadn't injured Reverend Falwell's reputation, because no reasonable person would think that the ad was really information, as opposed to a made-up joke.

On the other hand, the jury agreed with Falwell that the ad was outrageous and would cause any reasonable person extreme emotional distress. So the jury awarded Reverend Falwell one hundred thousand dollars in damages for his emotional distress, as well as punitive damages against *Hustler* and its publisher. *Hustler* had no intention of paying Reverend Falwell a dime, and it appealed the verdict to the U.S. Supreme Court.

The big question for the Supreme Court was whether and how the First Amendment's guarantee of freedom of speech affected Reverend Falwell's case against *Hustler*. In 1964, in the landmark case of *New York Times v. Sullivan*,[1] the Supreme Court announced that the First Amendment limited the ability of public officials to sue their critics for defamation. Defamation requires a false statement of fact, meaning that mere opinion cannot be defamation; but for public officials, it was not enough to show that public criticism was false as a matter of provable fact. The false statement also had to be made with "actual malice," which meant that the statement was made either while knowing it was false or with a reckless disregard of whether it was false or not. This rule was later extended to public figures, like Reverend Falwell. The question in the Falwell case was whether the First Amendment offered *Hustler* any protection for its fake ad about Reverend Falwell on the claim for intentional infliction of emotional distress.

While criticism comes with the territory for those who live in the public eye, Reverend Falwell felt that *Hustler* had crossed a line. What it had published was entirely fabricated, so it easily satisfied the *Sullivan* case's requirement that the statement in question must be an intentional falsehood. What's more, the fake ad demeaned him and his mother. It had nothing to do with the issues that Reverend Falwell promoted. It was a caustic, personal attack. It was outrageous. Any decent person would agree, and the jury in his case did in fact agree. In short, *Hustler*'s outrageous claims about him and his mother were a paradigmatic example of why the intentional infliction of emotional distress is treated as a wrongful act in virtually every state in the country.

Hustler thought Falwell should get thicker skin. The ad was a joke. The fact that the joke stung was just proof that the lampoon had hit its mark. Public figures like Falwell should get used to ridicule or retire from public life. As the saying goes, if you can't stand the heat, get out of the kitchen.

Did *Hustler* go too far, or was Reverend Falwell too sensitive? The jury had sided with Reverend Falwell, but the question for the court was how the freedom of speech protected by the First Amendment should factor into the equation. How would you rule?

HOW THE COURT RULED

The law, observed the court, does not hold the intentional infliction of emotional distress in high regard. Every state has made the intentional infliction of emotional distress a civil wrong and authorized victims of this conduct to sue the perpetrators for the damage they cause.

Likewise, false statements of fact are not particularly valuable contributors in the grand scheme of public discourse: false statements "interfere with the truth-seeking function of the marketplace of ideas, and they cause damage to an individual's reputation that cannot easily be repaired by counter speech, however persuasive or effective."

Even so, in a country that values robust and free debate, people will make mistakes in the heat of public discourse, and so false statements are inevitable. Attempting to stamp out all false statements through lawsuits and the liability that comes with them could effectively silence all discussion, because no one is always perfectly free from error. To preserve the breathing space that free debate requires, the court had previously decided that, for public officials, lawsuits about false statements are permissible only if the person making the statement did so "with knowledge that it was false or with reckless disregard of whether it was false or not."

In *Hustler's* case, the fake interview with Reverend Falwell, in which he supposedly confessed to sleeping with his mother in an outhouse, was false, clearly, and *Hustler* knew that it was false, so *Hustler's* knowledge of the falsity of its fake ad was not in doubt. Moreover, the tort of intentional infliction of emotional distress punished the intent to cause injury, and that's what made it distinctive even from defamation claims; and in this case, the facts easily supported the jury's conclusion that at least one of *Hustler's* objectives in publishing its mock interview was to hurt Reverend Falwell's feelings.

Yet in the rough-and-tumble world of public affairs, the court noted, many things are said and done with less than the purest of motives. If every speaker who criticized another could be hauled into court based on the allegation that his or her *motives* were impure, the courts would be choked with disputants, and many a mailer, newsletter, newspaper, and radio or television show would have to close down.[2] The goal of the most biting commentary is often to injure the object of its disdain. Citizens criticize public officials to drive them from office and defeat their agendas. They criticize public figures to hound their ideas out of the public sphere and alienate their supporters. The First Amendment, therefore, cannot permit a speaker to be sued solely for the intention of inflicting injury on a public figure. If it did, only those who never engaged in public dialogue about public affairs would be safe from lawsuits.

The court pointed out that satire and caricature, especially in the form of political cartoons, have always been part of America's political discourse. By definition, satire and caricature use deliberate distortions and calculated exaggerations to make their point. "The art of the cartoonist," wrote the court, "is often not reasoned or evenhanded, but slashing and one-sided," and that's what makes cartoon and caricature so powerful.

In Reverend Falwell's eyes, *Hustler*'s fake ad was so outrageous that it was outside the bounds of traditional political cartoons, and the court agreed that the ad was in poor taste. If there were a standard that would protect incisive political cartoons while excluding *Hustler*'s vulgar parody, the court would have been ready to adopt it. But the court could not think up a rule that clearly distinguished good satire that stings from bad satire that stings. What's outrageous and hurtful to one person is funny and biting to another. The difference is personal opinion. If juries could impose damages anytime someone wrote something a jury didn't like, then anyone with an unpopular opinion could be crushed by lawsuits. That's a risk that the First Amendment could not permit.

Oscar Wilde once quipped, "The only thing worse than being talked about is not being talked about." Between the parody and the Supreme Court's subsequent decision, Reverend Falwell achieved a sort of immortality—in the eyes of the law, at least—that would almost certainly have eluded him if he had not become entangled in this messy dispute with *Hustler*. The court ruled that *Hustler*'s fake ad was a parody of a public figure and so was fully protected by the First Amendment no matter how outrageously its pointed mockery stung, no doubt much to the relief of late-night comedians everywhere. The tort of intentional infliction of emotional distress could not be used to impose liability on speakers simply because a jury decided that a joke was in poor taste. The judgment Falwell had won from the jury was reversed. *Hustler* never paid a dime.

Did the court get it right? You decide.

REFLECTIONS

Courts must draw distinctions. That is the essence of judging. The permissible must be sorted from the impermissible, the lawful from the unlawful. But sometimes lines cannot be drawn finely enough to reliably distinguish between valuable behavior that the law should protect and destructive conduct the law has no interest in promoting. The *Hustler* case illustrates one of those times.

Society as a whole would be unlikely to miss overly much the magazine's fake advertisement with its false claims about Reverend Falwell's first sexual experience. It did not increase the store of human knowledge. It did not offer insight into public affairs. At most, it provided a reason for giggles and smirks to *Hustler*'s readers, and this slight benefit came at the expense of Reverend Falwell's feelings. If the parody had never been published, the country, in all likelihood, would have been able to carry on just fine.

On the other hand, the lampooning of public figures has the power to shape public opinion on affairs of national interest. One well-placed barb might carry more weight than a tome of turgid argument. How could a court frame a rule that protects the incisive political satire that can change the course of the country from puerile jokes whose loftiest aspirations are sidelong snickers? The difference between the two is almost always in the eye of the beholder.

The line that the Reverend Falwell asked the court to draw ultimately was impossible. If artists and pundits and commentators were exposed to lawsuits anytime a judge felt that their efforts were less than earthshaking, the pressure to self-censor could easily overwhelm the desire to participate in the national conversation about public affairs. Because of the importance of robust speech, and because of the presumption in favor of freedom embodied in the First Amendment, the court chose a rule that protected hurtful, spiteful, juvenile jokes, so as not to endanger earnest participants in public debates.

Because Reverend Falwell's lawsuit demanded a decision, a line had to be drawn, and the court drew it. But because of the difficulty in making distinctions in the area of speech about public figures, the court eschewed nuanced differentiations between legitimate and illegitimate criticism. As the Supreme Court noted in a different case, one person's vulgarity is often another's lyric.[3] The blanket of protection offered by the freedom of speech spreads wide, allowing the bad so as not to smother the good.

.   .   .   .   .

Questions

1. Reverend Falwell was a public figure because he had inserted himself into national debates through television, radio, and print. In so doing, as the Supreme Court ruled, he had to accept that he would become the object of satire, some of which would be decidedly unpleasant and distasteful. But what about Reverend Falwell's mother? Could she have sued *Hustler* for intentional infliction of emotional distress, or would her claim have failed because, without referring to her, *Hustler* could not make the joke it did about her famous son?

2. Imagine that a reputable news outlet heard about the story about Reverend Falwell and his mother and, not realizing that the story was a made-up joke, the news outlet republished the story as fact. If that happened, should Reverend Falwell be able to sue *Hustler* on the theory that once the story had made its way into a reputable publication, his reputation was damaged because people might believe the story was really true? Should he be able to sue the news outlet? Should such lawsuits be precluded by the First Amendment?

Read It Yourself

Hustler Magazine v. Falwell, 485 U.S. 46 (1988).

31 Funeral Crashers

It is hard to imagine a loss more painful than that of a parent losing a child. For a parent going through that grief, you would think that sympathy and compassion are universal. But you would be wrong.

Fred Phelps was a preacher on a mission to spread the word of God to anyone who cared to listen—and to the great many more who did not. According to Phelps, God hated America and was out to punish it. America's great sin, Phelps preached, was its tolerance of homosexuality, and the principal target of God's wrath was the United States military.

To the surprise of no one, Phelps had trouble gaining a significant audience for his idiosyncratic views of God's will. His ministry, known as the Westboro Baptist Church, had a minuscule following and few prospects for significant growth. Phelps needed something dramatic, something spectacular, something that couldn't be ignored by the ignorant masses and the unhallowed media, something that would grab the public's attention and generate publicity for his message. Since God hated America and God hated America's military, Fred Phelps decided to take his message of hate to what he saw as the military's most vulnerable spot: the funerals of fallen American soldiers.

Matthew Snyder was a lance corporal in the U.S. Marine Corps. He fought honorably in the United States' war in Iraq and was killed in the line of duty. His father wanted to give his son a decent burial in their hometown of Westminster, Maryland. The local newspapers picked up the story of the local fallen hero. So did Fred Phelps.

Phelps gathered six of his followers (two daughters and four grandchildren), packed their things, and headed to Westminster. He and his holy army picketed and carried signs at the Maryland State House, the U.S. Naval Academy, and finally, as a twisted capstone, Matthew Snyder's funeral. Phelps and his followers stayed on public land next to public streets and waved signs with not-so-charming slogans such as "God Hates the USA/Thank God for 9/11," "America is Doomed," "Don't Pray for the USA," "Thank God for IEDs,"[1] "Thank God for Dead Soldiers," "God Hates Fags," and the simple summary of all of the above "God Hates You."

Phelps and his pack staked out a spot about a thousand feet from the church where Matthew Snyder's funeral was held. They sang hymns and shouted Bible verses to whoever would listen, mainly news crews more than happy to publicize the Phelpses' vitriol to boost ratings by stoking the public's sense of righteous outrage.

Matthew's father, Albert, and the other members of Matthew's funeral procession passed within two hundred to three hundred feet of the Phelpses' demonstration as they made their way to the church where the funeral would be held. Albert couldn't see the slogans on the signs as he passed, but later that night their ugly words hit him with full force as he watched them repeated on television by a local news broadcast.

Seeing Phelps and his family celebrate the death of his beloved son, and watching them claim that God himself had struck his son down as punishment for America's sins, set Albert Snyder's blood to boiling. What Phelps had done was outrageous, so Snyder took Phelps, his daughters, and the whole Westboro Baptist Church to court.

Snyder sued the Phelpses and the church for intentional infliction of emotional distress. Under the laws of Maryland, intentional infliction of emotional distress occurs when a person "intentionally or recklessly engage[s] in extreme and outrageous conduct that cause[s] the plaintiff to suffer severe emotional distress." Albert Snyder could think of few things more extreme and outrageous than celebrating the death of a man's son at the boy's funeral.

At trial, Snyder testified how the Phelpses' attempt to defile the memory of his son ripped him apart emotionally. Now whenever he thought of his lost son, Snyder could not get out of his head the vile image of Fred Phelps and his pack of followers picketing his son's funeral. The anger at the thought would shake him to his core, and he would wind up crying and throwing up. Psychologists came to testify on Albert Snyder's behalf. Albert, they said, was severely depressed, and the depression was destroying his health.

Fred Phelps and his family objected to the whole lawsuit. The First Amendment guaranteed them freedom of speech, and that included the right to say whatever they wanted about God, America, slain soldiers, and even Albert's dead son, Matthew. Freedom of speech wasn't limited to saying nice things that everyone agreed with or bowing to conventional decorum. It was about protecting the free flow of ideas, even if that meant a little rough-and-tumble in the process.

A jury ruled for Snyder and against Phelps and the church. The jury found that Phelps and his church were liable for intentional infliction of emotional distress and awarded Snyder $2.9 million for his pain and suffering and an additional $8 million in punitive damages to punish the Phelps clan for their outrageous conduct. The judge reduced the punitive damage award to $2.1 million, so when the dust settled, Fred Phelps owed the Snyder family a cool $5 million.

Phelps did not take the verdict like a lamb lying meekly down with a lion. He appealed his case all the way to the U.S. Supreme Court.

So who prevails? Does the law vindicate a father's grief, or does it protect Phelps's invective, no matter how vile and hateful it may be? Should Phelps have stayed away from Matthew Snyder's funeral, or did he have the freedom to spew his vitriol from any street corner he liked, even one deliberately chosen to provoke maximum anger and offense? It's common decency versus free speech. How would you rule?

HOW THE COURT RULED

No one could deny that what Fred Phelps did—picketing the funeral of a fallen soldier and celebrating his death in the face of his stricken family— was deeply offensive and mean-spirited.

On the other hand, as offensive as the manner, timing, and location of his expression may have been, the topics that Phelps addressed—the (perceived) moral decline of the country, permitting homosexuals to serve in the military, and God's divine judgment for the country's sins—were certainly of public importance. These were topics debated routinely across the country from kitchen tables to water coolers, from local diners to the halls of the United States Congress.

True, Phelps's signs undoubtedly generated more disgust and revulsion than interest or engagement, but they addressed the moral conduct of the country. In his own twisted way, Phelps was expressing his concern for the future of the country by openly worrying that the decisions of its leaders were leading its people down a path that, if followed to its logical conclusion, would end in the country's destruction. The fact that many, most, or even every single person who saw Phelps's signs might disagree with his message did not change the fact that Phelps was engaging in political debate about issues of paramount public concern.

It was completely understandable that Albert Snyder and his family saw Phelps's actions as a personal attack against their family, and it was undeniable that Phelps took unseemly pleasure in their son's death. Phelps capitalized on Matthew Snyder's funeral to seize a platform and gain attention for his views, and that decision made Phelps's words especially hurtful to the Snyder family and added to their already immeasurable grief.

Yet Phelps and his family did not burst into Matthew Snyder's funeral itself. They stood on public ground adjacent to a public street that was merely near the funeral. Americans by proud tradition have taken time and again to the public streets to express their views, and those streets do not become off-limits merely because certain passersby might take particular offense at the views expressed.

In this case, the Phelps family had a right to be where they were. The First Amendment did not allow them to be silenced merely because others disagreed with their words. It is undeniable, the court believed, that if the Phelpses had stood in the exact same place, but with signs that read "God Bless America" or "God Loves You," no jury would have fined them.

Under the First Amendment, ruled the court, "speech cannot be restricted simply because it is upsetting or arouses contempt." The same protection that wraps in freedom any words that are wise and uplifting also casts its cloak around words that are misguided or hurtful. The jury found that Phelps and his family were guilty of "outrageous" conduct, and no doubt they were, but the First Amendment does not permit a standard as vague and malleable as "outrageousness" to determine what can or cannot be said in a public debate about issues of public concern. If it were otherwise, speech could be limited to content and speakers that jurors liked, and dissenting voices could be silenced.

The risk of censorship by juries was, for the court, unacceptable. The court firmly believed that "in public debate [we] must tolerate insulting, and even outrageous, speech in order to provide adequate 'breathing space' to the freedoms protected by the First Amendment." Writing for the majority of the court, Chief Justice John Roberts eloquently distilled the core belief behind the freedom of speech: to maintain the potency of public dialogue, all speakers, even those who intend to injure, wound, and offend, must find protection under the First Amendment: "Speech is powerful. It can stir people to action, move them to tears of both joy and sorrow and—as it did here—inflict great pain. On the facts before us, we cannot react to that pain by punishing the speaker. As a nation, we have chosen a different course—to protect even hurtful speech on public issues to ensure that we do not stifle public debate."

So Albert Snyder left with the court's sympathies but nothing else. Fred Phelps walked away with a victory and the stamp of approval of the highest court in the land to carry on with his ministry preaching his gospel of intolerance. That was, the court concluded, the price of freedom of speech.

Did the court get it right? You decide.

REFLECTIONS

Not everyone, of course, agreed with the Supreme Court's decision in *Snyder*. Justice Samuel Alito would have upheld the jury's verdict against Fred Phelps and his clan. In Justice Alito's view: "Our profound national commitment to free and open debate is not a license for the vicious verbal assault that occurred in this case. . . . [Phelps's church may not] intentionally inflict severe emotional injury on a private person at a time of intense emotional sensitivity by launching vicious verbal attacks that make no contribution to public debate." The divide between Justice Roberts's uncompromising defense of speech in all its forms, and Justice Alito's willingness to draw more nuanced distinctions, at least in extreme cases, illustrates that the meaning and scope of the phrase "freedom of speech" can be highly contested—as it has been since the time those words became part of the U.S. Constitution in 1791. The evolution of the understanding of this lofty but vague phrase is a reflection of America and its changing values.

Given the centrality of the First Amendment and the freedom of speech in modern America, it may come as a surprise that it was not until the twentieth century that the U.S. Supreme Court first considered a case concerning whether a federal law violated the First Amendment, and that, when it did, free speech lost.

In 1917, gripped by fear of Germans because of World War I, and shaken by the threat of Bolsheviks who might export their revolutionary ideology to American shores, the United States enacted the Espionage Act of 1917, which, among other things, made it a crime to undermine the war effort. Hundreds of prosecutions followed, and in 1919 a series of four cases made their way to the Supreme Court. In each case, the convicted person claimed the protection of the First Amendment. In each case, the Supreme Court let the convictions stand.

In *Schenck v. United States*, Charles Schenck was convicted for attempting to obstruct the draft by handing out leaflets urging draftees not to show up for duty. In *Frohwerk v. United States*, Frohwerk was convicted for fomenting disloyalty, mutiny, and refusal of duty in the military and naval forces of the United States by publishing articles in German that argued that it was a great and monumental mistake for the United States to side with France and fight against Germany. In *Debs v. United States*, Eugene Debs, a national leader of organized labor who had garnered more than a million votes in an unsuccessful run for president of the United States, was convicted for obstructing the draft by giving a speech. In it, he sympathized with fellow socialists who had been imprisoned for obstructing the draft and said that prudence prevented him from saying all he thought about the war, which the court found to be enough of an intimation of opposition to the war to support the conviction. Finally, in *Abrams v. United States*, five

Russian-born immigrants, three of them self-avowed "rebels," "revolution-ists," and "anarchists," were convicted for "disloyal, scurrilous and abusive language about the form of Government of the United States" for distribut-ing pamphlets that called President Woodrow Wilson, among other things, a coward and a shameful hypocrite.

Perhaps startlingly to modern sensibilities nursed on decades of pro-tection for speech far more offensive and antagonistic than what landed these defendants in jail, the Supreme Court rejected the free speech claims of all of the convicted speakers. In the minds of the Supreme Court jus-tices of the day, the freedom of speech, evidently, did not include speaking out against the government.

And yet at this nadir of the protection of speech was planted a seed of the more robust protections for speech that would arise later in the twen-tieth century and in the twenty-first century. While the Supreme Court allowed all of the convictions to stand, the court, for the first time, admit-ted the possibility that government could violate the First Amendment by punishing speech. The seminal event that would turn the tide in future cases was the dissent of Justice Oliver Wendell Holmes Jr., who, after vot-ing to affirm the convictions in *Schenck, Frohwerk,* and *Debs,* changed his mind in the *Abrams* case and penned a startling and eloquent defense of freedom of speech as the ultimate tool for finding truth in a confusing and chaotic world. Because of the power and lasting impact of Justice Holmes's dissent, it is worth quoting the key passage in full:

> Persecution for the expression of opinions seems to me perfectly logical. If you have no doubt of your premises or your power and want a certain result with all your heart you naturally express your wishes in law and sweep away all opposition. To allow opposition by speech seems to indicate that you think the speech impotent, as when a man says that he has squared the cir-cle, or that you do not care whole-heartedly for the result, or that you doubt either your power or your premises. But when men have realized that time has upset many fighting faiths, they may come to believe even more than they believe the very foundations of their own conduct that the ultimate good desired is better reached by free trade in ideas—that the best test of truth is the power of the thought to get itself accepted in the competition of the market, and that truth is the only ground upon which their wishes safely can be carried out. That at any rate is the theory of our Constitution. It is an experiment, as all life is an experiment. Every year if not every day we have

to wager our salvation upon some prophecy based upon imperfect knowledge. While that experiment is part of our system I think that we should be eternally vigilant against attempts to check the expression of opinions that we loathe and believe to be fraught with death, unless they so imminently threaten immediate interference with the lawful and pressing purposes of the law that an immediate check is required to save the country. . . . Only the emergency that makes it immediately dangerous to leave the correction of evil counsels to time warrants making any exception to the sweeping command, "Congress shall make no law . . . abridging the freedom of speech." Of course I am speaking only of expressions of opinion and exhortations, which were all that were uttered here, but I regret that I cannot put into more impressive words my belief that in their conviction upon this indictment the defendants were deprived of their rights under the Constitution of the United States.

Justice Holmes's stirring dissent in *Abrams* framed the way the First Amendment's protections would one day come to be understood. His metaphor of thoughts and opinions competing in the marketplace of ideas is still invoked to explain and justify why the protection of speech—even speech with which we violently disagree—is vital to sorting truth from falsehoods.

The *Snyder* case is the descendant and inheritor of the spark struck by Justice Holmes in his dissent in *Abrams*. Today, the modern Supreme Court has generally embraced the freedom of speech in its strongest form, admitting limitations only in narrowly circumscribed classes of cases. For example, the government may ban obscenity, defamation, fraud, incitement to imminent illegal action, and speech integral to criminal conduct, but outside of these well-defined and limited cases, the government's power over the people's speech is much more limited. Fred Phelps can spout his poison, as we've seen. Nazis can march through Jewish neighborhoods.[2] People can sell and possess movies of kittens being crushed under stilettos for the sexual gratification of their audiences, notwithstanding the laws that ban acts of animal cruelty.[3] Under this contemporary view, the First Amendment does not permit the government to weigh on an ad hoc basis whether speech is worth protecting. The First Amendment reflects the judgment that, outside the boundaries of the narrow exceptions handed down by history, speech must be broadly protected lest those who are powerful abuse their authority in order to suppress those whose views and ideas they find inconvenient, unpleasant, or challenging to their positions.

A country's commitment to freedom of speech, it has been argued, can best be measured by the quantity of hateful, hurtful, and obnoxious speech that its laws will protect. By that measure, the fact that Fred Phelps was allowed to purvey his noxious stew of hate shows that the freedom of speech in America is alive and well.

·   ·   ·   ·   ·

Questions

1. An important fact in the court's decision was that Fred Phelps was protesting the direction that the country had taken. Would the outcome have been different if the Phelps clan's signs had been only about Matthew Snyder (for example, if the signs had read "God Hates Matthew Snyder") without making any reference to larger political issues like the military and the war in Iraq?

2. Another important fact for the court was that the Phelps family had stood on public land, where they had a right to be. Would it be permissible under the First Amendment for Maryland to pass a law that banned picketing within half a mile of a funeral? What about two miles? What about ten? How would this case have been different if the Phelps family had broken such a law?

3. Has the modern Supreme Court struck the right balance for the freedom of speech? In the past the court gave the government and the people's elected representatives more leeway in deciding what speech was permissible and what was not. In many European countries, speech that is deemed especially offensive and hurtful has been banned. Should the government have more power to decide what the people can and cannot say? What would be the benefits of giving government that power? What would be the dangers?

Read It Yourself

Snyder v. Phelps, 131 S. Ct. 1207 (2011).

32 Bench Memo

A tall tale tells the story of a judge who was fed up with court being delayed by people coming late. One day, when everyone for that day's trial was assembled, the judge stomped up the steps to his high bench, black robes billowing darkly behind him. Taking his seat, he glared angrily at everyone around him. The constant late-starting had to stop. Court began promptly at 9 A.M.—no exceptions.

From his towering position above everyone in the courtroom, the judge wagged an admonishing finger at the lawyers and said, "If you're not here at 9 A.M. sharp, I will hold you in contempt." He then turned to the parties who were sitting nervously next to their legal counsel and gave them the same warning. "If you're not here at 9 A.M. sharp, I will hold you in contempt." Next, he swiveled in his high-backed leather chair to face the jurors in the jury box. "If you're not here at 9 A.M. sharp, I will hold you in contempt."

A hush fell over the courtroom. The judge's instructions hung heavily in the air, but one timid hand went up from one of the jurors, who bravely said in a soft voice, "I have a question."

"What is it?" demanded the judge, ready to get on with the business of the day.

"What happens if *you* are not here at 9 A.M.?" the juror asked.

The judge responded without missing a beat. "If I'm not here, it's not 9 A.M."

Yes, it's good to be the judge. At least sometimes. Other times, being the judge is the hardest thing in the world. The lives of real people are put into the hands of judges who will decide their fates, with wisdom and grace if all goes well, but sometimes with just a guess and a hope for the best.

John Marshall, the most influential chief justice of the U.S. Supreme Court, famously wrote that "it is emphatically the province and duty of the judicial department to say what the law is."[1] What does it mean to say what the law is? The law lays down general rules that may seem clear enough in the abstract, but which very often, upon close examination, can become maddeningly opaque. That's where judges and judging come in. As Chief Justice Marshall explained, "Those who apply the rule to particular cases must, of necessity, expound and interpret that rule."[2]

Expound and interpret. Many of the cases we've seen in these pages challenged the judges who decided them to define the meanings of words. By their nature, words are frequently susceptible to multiple meanings, not all of them equally intuitive. A contract that says "no refunds" can sometimes allow for refunds. Some body parts are more private than others. Sometimes a fruit can be a vegetable.

The courts may weigh in on whether walking is part of golf and whether throwing a ball at a batter's head is part of baseball. But at other times they will hold back, such as when a court declined to say whether a rock concert was so bad as to be the equivalent of no concert at all. Some questions have no answers.

No matter the difficulty, however, courts are required to act. When a dispute hits the courthouse steps, there must be a winner and a loser. Deciding not to decide is still a decision, at least for the parties to a lawsuit. One person walks out the courtroom doors with what he or she wants. The other doesn't.

If you have worked your way through the cases, controversies, and questions in this book, you have experienced firsthand the kind of considerations courts must ponder before making a decision and will have armed yourself with tools to make informed decisions of your own.

The law is perpetually in a state of flux. It is contested every day in courtrooms throughout the country and debated in the halls of Congress and state legislatures. But it is not solely the province of the high and mighty. The law is a river that is fed from many streams. As the public's views of justice evolve, the law's river floods one day and dries up the next, cutting well-worn ruts through the hardest rock and then shifting suddenly if storms send the waters tumbling down new paths. Each twist and turn is shaped by the acts of legislators, the arguments of litigants, and of course, the rulings of judges, but also by the thoughts, beliefs, and attitudes of the people. Including you. You too can be part of the law's evolution.

You can and should have your own opinion about right and wrong. You can and should shape the course of the law. You can and should decide for yourself whether the law and the courts are wise and just or foolish and unfair. At times, they can be both.

Your work in these pages is done, but there is more to do. My ardent hope is that you will use the ideas described in this book to bring your most critical thinking to the most difficult problems you encounter, that you will listen, consider, analyze, and reflect, and then, when your reasons and thoughts are clear, that you will decide for yourself what is right and what is wrong and participate in the public square as a full-throated advocate for a more perfect understanding of justice.

This court stands in recess. When it commences next is up to you. It won't start without you. If you're not here, it's not 9 A.M. So begin when you're ready—when you're ready to rule.

Notes

INTRODUCTION

1. See, for example, Restatement (Second) of Torts § 941 comment c.

1. A DUTY TO DIE

1. Jean-Francois Bonnefon, Azim Shariff, and Iyad Rahwan, "The Social Dilemma of Autonomous Vehicles," *Science*, June 24, 2016, no. 352: 1573–1576.

2. BRINGING A GUN TO A FISTFIGHT

1. See Daniel W. Park, *The Legal Mind* (San Diego, CA: LexPrep, 2013), pp. 41–49.
2. Raymond S. Nickerson, "Confirmation Bias: A Ubiquitous Phenomenon in Many Guises," *Review of General Psychology* 2, no. 2 (1998): 175–220.

3. DON'T LIE TO ME

1. *Lynum v. Illinois*, 372 U.S. 528 (1963).
2. *Salinas v. Texas*, 133 S. Ct. 2174 (2013).

3. *New York v. Quarles,* 467 U.S. 649 (1984).

4. 18 U.S.C. § 1001 is a good example.

5. For a discussion by the U.S. Supreme Court, see *United States v. Scheffer,* 523 U.S. 303, 309–12 (1998).

4. SHOW ME YOURS

1. *United States v. Miller,* 425 U.S. 435 (1976).

2. *Smith v. Maryland,* 422 U.S. 735 (1979).

3. *Katz v. United States,* 389 U.S. 347 (1967).

4. *United States v. Jacobsen,* 466 U.S. 109 (1984).

5. Sir Edward Coke, *The Third Part of the Institutes of the Laws of England: Concerning High Treason, and Other Pleas of the Crown, and Criminal Causes* (London: Printed by M. Flesher, for W. Lee, and D. Pakeman, 1644).

6. Sir William Blackstone, John Fletcher Hargrave, et al., *Commentaries on the Laws of England: In Four Books; with an Analysis of the Work,* vol. 4 (New York: Harper and Brothers, 1854).

7. Quoted in *Miller v. United States,* 357 U.S. 301, 307 (1958).

8. Leonard W. Levy, "Origins of the Fourth Amendment," *Political Science Quarterly* 114, no. 1 (Spring 1999), www.jstor.org/stable/2657992.

9. *Maryland v. King,* 133 S. Ct. 1958 (2013).

10. *United States v. Jones,* 132 S. Ct. 945 (2012).

11. *Kyllo v. United States,* 533 U.S. 27 (2001).

12. *Riley v. California,* 134 S. Ct. 2473, 2484 (2014).

13. Ibid.

5. DEAD DOGS DON'T BARK

1. *Graham v. Connor,* 490 U.S. 386, 396 (1989).

2. *Tennessee v. Garner,* 471 U.S. 1 (1985).

6. WHEN IS FRUIT A VEGETABLE?

1. This is what the U.S. Supreme Court held in *King v. Burwell,* 135 S. Ct. 2480 (2015), when it rejected a challenge to the Affordable Care Act, the law that established Obamacare.

8. IS A BURRITO A SANDWICH?

1. *Frigaliment Importing Co. v. B.N.S. Int'l Sales Corp.,* 190 F.Supp. 116 (SDNY 1960).

2. *Michigan Journal of Race and Law* 14 (Fall 2008): 1.

9. HAUNTED CONTRACTS

1. Sean Alfano, "Poll: Majority Believe in Ghosts," CBS News, October 29, 2005, www.cbsnews.com/news/poll-majority-believe-in-ghosts/.

10. THAT JET WON'T FLY

1. See Apple's Licensed Application End User License Agreement, retrieved on August 29, 2015, from www.apple.com/legal/internet-services/itunes /appstore/dev/stdeula/.

2. See Chris Hoffman, "10 Ridiculous EULA Clauses That You May Have Already Agreed To," MakeUseOf, April 23, 2012, www.makeuseof.com /tag/10-ridiculous-eula-clauses-agreed/.

11. WHAT HAVE YOU DONE FOR ME LATELY?

1. According to the U.S. Bureau of Labor Statistics, fifteen dollars in 1925, adjusted for inflation, would be just over four hundred dollars in 2014. See www .bls.gov/data/inflation_calculator.htm.

2. John Roberts quoted in "My Job Is to Call Balls and Strikes and Not to Pitch or Bat," CNN, September 12, 2005, www.cnn.com/2005/POLITICS/09/12 /roberts.statement/index.html.

12. THE DANCER WHO DIDN'T DANCE

1. In 2014 dollars, one thousand dollars represents about eighty-one hundred dollars. See Bureau of Labor Statistics, www.bls.gov/data/inflation_ calculator.htm.

2. In 2014 dollars, twenty-five thousand dollars was equivalent to just a little less than two hundred thousand dollars. See Bureau of Labor Statistics, www .bls.gov/data/inflation_calculator.htm.

3. This definition was quoted by the court from a legal treatise called the Restatement of Contracts. That and the other Restatements of the Law are widely used summaries of legal principles.

4. (1863) EWHC QB J1.

5. (1903) 2 K.B.740.

14. AND THE BAND PLAYED ON

1. Scott Stapp, *Sinner's Creed* (Carol Stream, IL: Tyndale House, 2012), p. 175.

2. Letter reproduced in "Creed Issue 'Apology' over Chicago Gig: 'It's Only Rock and Roll,'" Blabbermouth.net, January 10, 2003, www.blabbermouth.net /news/creed-issue-apology-over-chicago-gig-it-s-only-rock-and-roll/.

15. DON'T DO ME LIKE THAT

1. *Tort* is the legal term for a wrongful act that leads to liability in civil courts, usually in the form of money damages.

16. THE FIVE-YEAR-OLD DEFENDANT

1. 2016 Utah LEXIS 36.

20. COIN-FLIP WRONGDOERS

1. With joint and several liability, all the defendants are liable for the whole injury, but this does not mean that the plaintiff can recover the whole injury from each of them. The plaintiff can recover only once. The plaintiff can pick and choose which defendant(s) to recover from, but only up to the total amount of his or her injury. The unlucky defendant(s) chosen by the plaintiff to pay the debt is, however, not necessarily left holding the whole bag. He or she has the right to recover from the other defendant(s) a proportional share of the damages paid to the plaintiff.

22. YOUR BODY, MY BODY

1. See "Digestive Disorders Health Center," WebMD, accessed April 28, 2016, www.webmd.com/digestive-disorders/picture-of-the-spleen.

2. Dennis McLellan. "John Moore, 56; Sued to Share Profits from His Cells," *Los Angeles Times,* October 13, 2001, http://articles.latimes.com/2001/oct/13 /local/me-56770 (lat.ms/WJ6zdn).

3. U.S. Department of Health and Human Services, "Notice of Proposed Rulemaking Summary," last visited January 8, 2016, www.hhs.gov/ohrp/human-subjects/regulations/nprm2015summary.html.

23. IMAGINE NO (COPYRIGHT) POSSESSIONS

1. "500 Greatest Songs of All Time," *Rolling Stone,* last visited January 8, 2016, www.rollingstone.com/music/lists/the-500-greatest-songs-of-all-time-20110407/john-lennon-imagine-20110516.

2. "BMI Announces Top 100 Songs of the Century," BMI, December 19, 1999, www.bmi.com/news/entry/19991214_bmi_announces_top_100_songs_of_the_century.

3. John Blaney, *Lennon and McCartney: Together Alone*, 1st ed. (London: Jawbone Press, 2007), p. 52.

4. Pew Research Center, "Public Praises Science; Scientists Fault Public, Media," July 9, 2009, www.people-press.org/2009/07/09/section-5-evolution-climate-change-and-other-issues/ (http://bit.ly/1o2n5dJ). In contrast to the near-uniform endorsement of the theory of evolution by scientists, nearly four in ten Americans agree with Stein and believe that God created the earth and the people upon it. See Gallup, "Four in 10 Americans Believe in Strict Creationism," December 17, 2010, www.gallup.com/poll/145286/Four-Americans-Believe-Strict-Creationism.aspx (bit.ly/1taeEoC).

5. 17 U.S.C. § 107.

6. U.S. Const., Art. I, Sec. 8.

7. David Kravets, "Ben Stein Wins Right to Use Lennon's 'Imagine,'" *Wired*, June 2, 2008, www.wired.com/2008/06/ono-loses-bid-t/.

8. *Perfect 10, Inc. v. Amazon. com, Inc.*, 508 F. 3d 1146 (9th Cir. 2007).

9. *Warner Bros. Entertainment, Inc. v. RDR Books*, 575 F. Supp. 2d 513 (SDNY 2008).

24. MY BARBIE WORLD

1. For its description of the early versions of Barbie as a "German street-walker," the court cited M. G. Lord, *Forever Barbie: The Unauthorized Biography of a Real Doll* (New York: William Morrow, 1994), 32.

2. *Mattel, Inc. v. MCA Records, Inc.*, 296 F. 3d 894, 908.

25. A TIME FOR DYING

1. "Assisted-Suicide Crusader Gloria Taylor Dies in B.C.," *CBC News*, October 5, 2012, www.cbc.ca/news/canada/british-columbia/assisted-suicide-crusader-gloria-taylor-dies-in-b-c-1.1164650.

26. THE VOICE OF GOD

1. Wikipedia, "Flying Spaghetti Monster," accessed August 17, 2015, https://en.wikipedia.org/wiki/Flying_Spaghetti_Monster.

2. See, e.g., *Welsh v. United States*, 398 U.S. 333, 340 (1970) (plur. opn.).

3. *Thomas v. Review Board*, 450 U.S. 707, 716 (1981).

4. Ibid., 714.

5. U.S. Equal Employment Opportunity Commission, *EEOC Compliance Manual,* Directives Transmittal no. 915.003, July 22, 2008, www.eeoc.gov/policy/docs/religion.html.

6. Matt Ferner, "Indiana's Marijuana Church Sues State, Claims Pot Prohibition Infringes on Its Religious Beliefs," *Huffington Post,* July 10, 2015, www.huffingtonpost.com/entry/indianas-marijuana-church-sues-the-state-claims-pot-prohibition-infringes-on-its-religious-beliefs_559ff718e4b096729156024d.

7. *Employment Division v. Smith,* 494 U.S. 872 (1990).

8. 42 U.S.C. § 2000bb et seq.

9. *Gonzales v. O Centro Espirita Beneficente Uniao Do Vegetal et al.,* 546 U.S. 418 (2006).

27. JUDGING JENNA

1. *Troxel v. Granville,* 530 U.S. 57, 65 (2000).

2. *Parham v. J.R.,* 442 U.S. 584, 602 (1979).

3. Guttmacher Institute, "State Policies in Brief: An Overview of Minors' Consent Law," August 1, 2015, www.guttmacher.org/statecenter/spibs/spib_OMCL.pdf.

4. *Tinker v. Des Moines Independent Community School District,* 393 U.S. 503 (1969).

5. *Brown v. Entertainment Merchants Association,* 131 S. Ct. 2729 (2011).

28. THREE GENERATIONS

1. *Loving v. Virginia,* 388 U.S. 1 (1967).

29. A GOOD WALK SPOILED

1. This is frequently attributed to Mark Twain, but it's not clear that he ever said it at all. See "Golf Is a Good Walk Spoiled," Quote Investigator, May 28, 2010, http://quoteinvestigator.com/2010/05/28/golf-good-walk/.

2. *Merriam-Webster,* s.v., "discrimination," accessed August 21, 2015, www.merriam-webster.com/dictionary/discrimination.

30. THAT'S MY MOTHER YOU'RE TALKING ABOUT!

1. *New York Times v. Sullivan,* 376 U.S. 254 (1964).

2. This case took place in the era before the Internet, blogs, and social media, but the same could be said for these more recently developed forms of mass communication—probably even more so.

3. *Cohen v. California*, 403 U.S. 15, 25 (1971).

31. FUNERAL CRASHERS

1. *IED* is an acronym for "improvised explosive device." IEDs were frequently used by enemy insurgents in the United States' war in Iraq to ambush and kill American service members.

2. *National Socialist Party of America v. Village of Skokie*, 432 U.S. 43 (1977).

3. *United States v. Stevens*, 559 U.S. 460 (2010).

32. BENCH MEMO

1. *Marbury v. Madison*, 5 U.S. (1 Cranch) 137; 2 L. Ed. 60 (1803).

2. Ibid.

Index